Collateral Damage

Petraeus / Power / Politics
and the Abuse of Privacy
[The Untold Story]

Jill Kelley

First Printing: 2016
ISBN: 978-0-9974065-1-1

Kelley Publishing, LLC

Dedication

This book is dedicated to every law-abiding citizen who honors the First and Fourth Amendments to the Constitution of the United States. The price of our rights and liberties truly is eternal vigilance. We must stand strong, together, to ensure that the voices of the innocent will be heard. If we can make a dent in the government's disrespect for the rights of innocent Americans, then speaking up publicly is important and worth it.

Sincere thanks to my family, and those who stood by me during the turmoil, including:

My loving husband, who has always believed me and believed in me.

My children, for giving me the strength to stand up to the bullies by correcting the lies about their mom.

My parents, who have been my role models for character and conviction. They raised me to be strong, tenacious and willing to fight for our freedom and democracy. Throughout this life-changing experience, my parents gave me their unconditional support to become a tireless advocate for the protections of electronic communications and internet data security.

Friends who also endured unjust pain as a result of this scandal, including: General John and Kathy Allen; General David and Holly Petraeus; General James Mattis; Admiral Bob and Jane Harward; Admiral Bill and Georgeann McRaven; and Agent Fred and Sara Humphries.

Contents

Acknowledgments

I would like to thank my team of experts:

Alan J. Kaufman, attorney and project counselor. Alan is the former SVP and General Counsel of Penguin. Alan currently sits on the Advisory Boards of The Beacon Press and The Artist Book Foundation; he was also elected to the Board of Directors of The Palm Beach County Film and Television Commission.

F. Robert Stein, vetting attorney. Bob was former Vice President and General Counsel to Warner Publishing. He is currently Of Counsel at Pryor Cashman LLP.

Julie Lipkin, copy editor. Julie's vast editing experience includes newspapers and books.

Bruno Bowden, technology adviser. Bruno was one of the creators of Google Earth. He is currently an angel investor for technology startups.

Lura Lee, assistant writer. Lura was the former policy correspondence writer for President Bill Clinton. Her experience includes technical writing, and historical writing.

Foreward

Americans should be able to seek help from law enforcement without having their private lives turned to tabloid fodder. Jill Kelley's story is both a warning and a call to action; reading it will make you question the judgment of high officials and recognize the need for stronger privacy protections. If Jill Kelley brings the same formidable spirit to her new role as a privacy advocate that she brought to her work as a CENTCOM ambassador, perhaps we will finally achieve some long overdue reforms.

Ben Wizner
American Civil Liberties Union
Director, Speech, Privacy & Technology Project

Introduction

There was a time, less than two years ago, when my name was known only among diplomatic circles, our military coalition, and the intelligence community.

Since then I have become unwittingly embroiled in an international scandal that turned my life upside down and led to the downfall of two of our nation's most iconic military and intelligence leaders. It's the story of a jealous lover turned stalker. It's the story of a government that flagrantly abused the constitutional limits on citizen privacy. Through no fault of my own, my career was destroyed, my reputation ruined, and my integrity questioned. I became a pariah. The story was maliciously spun by powerful figures and government entities bigger than I. The only way to vindicate myself is to share the real truth by way of a book.

I hope that by telling my side of the story, I can repair my name and begin to build a new career path. I know I can never go back to the day that Paula Broadwell decided to stalk my family, or the time that she and General David Petraeus had a regrettable affair. Their actions, and the subsequent bad actions of several political characters involved, created a cascade that was so damaging to my family, and the leaders of this country, that it is hardly fathomable.

I can make sense of it only with the benefit of hindsight. Things that weren't important in the moment become immensely meaningful in retrospect: seating arrangements, side comments, email handles. There are so many unsettling conversations, convenient coincidences and "so-called" accidents of fate in this story.

But before I get into the chronology of the story, I feel I need to clear the air on a few key topics.

I have never had an affair. I have never cheated on my husband with any man outside of my marriage vows. Never happened. N-O-T-H-I-N-G. Furthermore, I believe that I never acted inappropriately. I am happily married. I was faithful then and I continue to remain faithful.

My unfettered relationships with the generals and other leaders holding important positions did not come about through my physical attributes. In fact, I find this idea to be quite chauvinistic.

The truth is, I simply have a gift for creating personal connections and bridging dialogue. I grew up with hardworking immigrant parents who had some global contacts, and I earned many more of my own along the way. I enjoy talking to people, as I'm gregarious and warm. I have a gift for facilitation and I used it for good. Furthermore, I believe in serving my country, and I used my extroverted personality and people skills to do so. Much of the work I did was officially unpaid, hence the term "honorary." Unfortunately, the masterminds of the (still unfolding) political farce used me as a pawn. By creating a bogus scandal, they tried to belittle the role that I actually played. This was all in an effort to cast aspersions away from the bad actors and their true crimes. It worked.

Ambassadorial facilitation is a legitimate role, with historic roots, and is completely current and necessary. The world of war and politics would not work without certain connected people facilitating and hosting events where the real business is done. There are many honorable men and women in political circles who are professional and semiprofessional facilitators. Sometimes they get temporary official titles, like "special envoy" and "honorary ambassador"; sometimes they are just more names on a guest list, with no official title. Most facilitators are unpaid, but these people are movers and shakers. It's all perfectly legal. I never got paid or took a bribe. I did what I did because I liked doing it, and had the capabilities to do it.

Maybe I need to put that in the past tense. I don't know. I never doubted that part of myself before this drama. But now I seem to find myself having to explain myself at every level. Specifically, I have to explain what some people might think of as naiveté; people have questioned my motivations, friendships, and understanding of how the events connect. This constant questioning continues into the present: people are suspicious of me and want to figure me out. In fact, at the time of this writing, another recent batch of Hillary Clinton emails also appeared that even her people were trying to figure me out.

Maybe, in 2016, we're all supposed to be jaded and cynical about powerful men's behavior. Should career women expect this type of behavior? No one thought General David Petraeus was the type of person who would have an affair. Maybe reading this today you can't believe it. All I can say is that I thought — we all thought — Petraeus was not the type of man to engage in an affair. We just didn't hold that as a possibility. That's probably why things went as out of control as they did.

In retrospect, my view is that Paula's actions were similar to that of a stereotypical movie trope of a crazy mistress. I feel as though her participation in the affair was a setback for hardworking, professional women. But that's all retrospective understanding. Hindsight really is 20/20.

In the moment we didn't even think about that possibility. Petraeus was *obviously* incapable of an affair ... *obviously* too well-respected by both Democrats and Republicans to be the target of a political sting. So, it logically followed, we *obviously* thought that this person stalking, terrorizing, and threatening to puppeteer us — and by "us" I mean General John Allen, General James Mattis, General Petraeus, other foreign ambassadors, and me — must be an international terrorist.

For a long time, I assumed my stalker was a man. No one even entertained the idea that it might be a woman. My original labeling of the person as a "stalker" indicated the gender I assumed. The very word "stalker" conjures images of a male perpetrator. Over time, as the emails escalated in frequency and intensity, we definitely thought it was a foreign or rogue agent. A male terrorist. Perhaps a Yemeni spy or double agent with Petraeus or our government as the target of the actions. Who would have believed it was a jealous mistress?

I was in contact with the CIA director and top generals during wartime! We were getting real-time threats taunting us and telling us where we were to sit, how to act. This person (or people, or state-sponsored organization) knew about itineraries of the director of the CIA, the head of the war, the Central Command leadership, ambassadors to our foreign allies, etc. All of these itineraries were supposed to be top secret. The CIA director's emails were being accessed. He was compromised. There was a mole, or a spy, or something. Something was very wrong. We were being swallowed up by an ocean of confusion.

I think about the absurdity of it all, with the gift of hindsight. We weren't in a spy novel. We were caught up in a spin cycle of infidelity, intrigue, and politics, which took on epic proportions.

My story is about personal relationships, professional communications, and private emails. My narrative reveals all the ways personal relationships can be used and abused. Sometimes personal relationships were used constructively; sometimes they were abused out of vengeance, or out of some megalomaniacal sense of self-importance.

This story embodies every American's greatest fears on how our personal communications could be used for personal agendas or political motivations now that we live in a world with intrusive surveillance and a government that collects our private emails. Although I am proud of what I did for my government, I am not proud of how the government treated me. Although I am a proud daughter of immigrants living the American Dream, I am not proud that I am now an "example" of breaches to the constitutional protections that challenge the very roots of the American Dream.

I embrace the chance to tell my story. I hope it will bring awareness of this national epidemic and prevent such a life-changing tragedy from ever happening to another family again — especially at a time when our government continues to improperly collect private information on everyone.

You know the story of General David Petraeus' rise to glory, fall from grace and the affair that brought him down. Now you can learn the real story, the untold story, the collateral damage.

Chapter 1: Compromised

The world never expected such an unscripted resignation. I certainly wasn't prepared for the shocking email I received immediately after he resigned. This is the unknown story behind the resignation of CIA Director David Petraeus.

> On Nov 9, 2012, at 4:35 PM, "Petraeus, David H Former COMISAF" <david.h.petraeus@afghan.swa.army.mil> wrote:
>
> Well, I guess she can't compromise me then....
>
>
> From: Jill and Scott Kelley shared email
> To: Petraeus, David H Former COMISAF
> <david.h.petraeus@afghan.swa.army.mil>;
> Subject: Re: RE: RE: RE: RE: RE:
> Sent: Fri, Nov 9, 2012 10:30:00 PM
>
> No..... she doesn't have the Director "compromised" now!

Before we get to that email, let's go back. November 9, 2012, began as an ordinary Friday in Tampa. I was at lunch planning my week ahead for a couple of upcoming ambassadorial receptions in Washington, D.C., when my phone played the familiar tone announcing the arrival of a new email. I took a moment to glance at the screen. The text was from the chief of staff at the British Embassy. I was anticipating the message that his embassy wanted to host General Allen and me in the same week, but the subject heading drew my attention:

> From: Gideon Bresler (Restricted)
> Sent: 09 November 2012 14:57
> To: Jill and Scott Kelley shared account
> Subject: !
>
> Jill
>
> Just watching the news!
>
> G

Chief of Staff to the Ambassador
British Embassy, Washington
Tel: (202) 588-XXXX
FTN: 8430-XXXX

That unnerving email was followed by a daunting one, minutes later. Mistakes from the original emails are preserved and redactions are signified by "...."

Begin forwarded message:
From: Gideon Bresler (Restricted)
Subject: FW: !
Date: November 9, 2012 at 3:03:26 PM EST
To: Jill and Scott Kelley shared email

.... terrible for the nation and the world that he's gone.

Call me when things calm down.

Gideon

My face turned white. My stomach dropped. David resigned? Today? What was going on? I knew something else must have happened — something terrible to make him decide to resign today. It wasn't as if he suddenly had an epiphany and decided today was the day to tell the world he had done a terrible thing. There was more, and I had to find out what.

My mother and daughters were at the table with me. I turned to my mother and asked her if she'd stay with my daughters at lunch, and then I gave them a wavering smile. "Sorry. Something's come up and Mommy needs to leave."

I drove back to the house as quickly as I could. In my head I was replaying the countless confessions and admissions told to me over the course of the investigation of the previous months, with what I learned was going on behind the scenes at the FBI, the Department of Defense and the White House.

Driving home, I wasn't seeing the road; I was seeing countless flashbacks of trying to warn David about the shocking secret meetings that various whistleblowers had informed me of — all of which were later verified. But David never heard them; he would go out of his way to change the subject.

When I finally pulled up in my driveway, I took out my cellphone. Wiping my tears, I sent an email to David:

From: Jill and Scott Kelley shared email
Sent: Friday, November 09, 2012 4:03 PM
To: Petraeus, David H Former COMISAF
Subject: Re: RE:

.
I'm so sorry David. I'm in tears!

I wanted to tell you what I knew from the many private sources...
[But] you didn't want to hear it -it was killing me!

I tried protecting you over and over, and wanted you to know what I knew, and the meetings that were going on around you, and your fate. I tried, David. I tried....

I will always support you and stand behind you, and protect you -as you know I have.
My thoughts and prayers are with you, David.
I'm sorry....

He wrote back a heart-wrenching response, but, again, did *not* ask me what I knew.

On Nov 9, 2012, at 4:08 PM, "Petraeus, David H Former COMISAF"
<david.h.petraeus@afghan.swa.army.mil> wrote:

I screwed up terribly, Jill, and needed to try to do the honorable thing after having done the dishonorable thing... Thx for your thoughts and prayers. We'll get through this, but it will be hard.
....

I was dealing not only with his loss, but the fact that it was preventable. And now I wanted him to finally hear it! Despite his being flooded with calls and emails from famous leaders, reporters, and former colleagues from all around the world trying to get their head around his sudden resignation, I demanded he call me:

> **From: Jill and Scott Kelley shared email**
> **Sent: Friday, November 09, 2012 4:08 PM**
> **To: Petraeus, David H Former COMISAF**
> **Subject: Re: RE: RE:**
>
> **Can you call me**
> **You need to know something**

As I waited for his response, I went inside and turned on the TV. Several channels were reporting the news: David Petraeus, director of the CIA, had resigned after admitting to an extramarital affair. It came as a complete shock to me. The reporters didn't say who he'd had the affair with, but I knew the answer: Paula Broadwell, a major in the Army Reserve who had spent months with him in Afghanistan. She had taken on the role as his biographer, and had just published the now aptly titled "All In: The Education of General David Petraeus".

Broadwell, I had only recently learned, was the stalker who had terrorized us all through emails. A dozen disjointed puzzle pieces clicked into place in my head as bewildering aspects of my friend's recent behavior snapped together. Everyone else just knew Broadwell as someone who idolized David Petraeus. When she appeared on The Daily Show to tout her book, Jon Stewart joked, "Is he awesome, or incredibly awesome?" She made a career of traveling the country, accepting speaking engagements on her favorite topic — David Petraeus.

But for David to admit the affair meant that things had spun way out of control. Obviously he'd been outed, or was about to be. All I could think of was the familiar quote: "Hell hath no fury like a woman scorned."

> **From: Jill and Scott Kelley shared email**
> **Sent: Friday, November 09, 2012 4:11 PM**
> **To: Petraeus, David H Former COMISAF**
> **Subject: Re: RE: RE: RE:**
>
> **No it's VERY important!!!!!**
> **You need to call me**

My phone rang, and I snatched it up. "I'm sorry, Jill." David spoke in a grief-stricken voice. "I'm sorry."

Even though I knew I shouldn't kick a man who was down, I couldn't control my anger. "How could you resign?" I practically yelled into the receiver. "And how dare you have an affair? I asked you if you were having an affair with the person stalking me and you lied! Why would you not tell your best friend the truth about what was going on? I know almost everything about you, for God's sake! How could you leave that detail out?"

"I'm sorry," David repeated, his voice subdued and defeated. "But I didn't tell Holly, either."

Holly. My stomach dropped. Poor Holly. Like most military wives, her life had been one of frequent moves and sacrifices, and yet I had never heard a word of complaint. She loved David and was completely loyal to him. Their move to Washington with David's appointment to the CIA had been a happy event for Holly, who was enjoying civilian life. Now this.

I closed my eyes and tightened my grip on the phone. "I think you owe me an explanation," I said, leveling my voice. "Start at the beginning."

There was a moment of silence, and then he drew a deep breath. "Last month the FBI interviewed me and I came clean. I told them the whole story and thought it was over. But Paula wouldn't stop trying to threaten me to go public and tell the whole world about the affair. And after she said it again today, I decided to beat her to the punch and tell the world myself through my resignation."

His next admission startled me. David told me that Paula Broadwell resented how close David and I were, and even ordered him to stop talking to me. I thought that was bizarre. My friendship with David and Holly was not a threat in any way. Our relationship was one of mutual respect, caring, and a common devotion to America. There had never been anything nefarious about it. Our families spent holidays together. My kids adored the Petraeuses. It was all on the up-and-up.

He recounted a version of his FBI interview. Later, I learned from reporters that he had minimized and avoided telling me the extent to which he had tried to protect Broadwell so that she wouldn't go to jail. Instead, he focused on an explanation of her actions: jealousy and obsession.

"Now I have nothing left to lose," David said wearily. "She can't compromise me anymore."

In that phone conversation, I told him about the puzzle pieces that were finally fitting together. It had just become clear to me that government officials had used this FBI investigation as an opportunity to snoop into important people's private emails for their own political agendas. A small cadre of powerful people enabled an obsessed person to put our country's national security at risk. I told him about the senior-level meetings held around him because it was known that he was "compromised." The result? There was effectively no central intelligence from approximately June 28, 2012, to November 9, 2012.

After Director Petraeus' historic resignation, Petraeus immediately called me to explain his shocking resignation and details about the abusive FBI investigation and his interview. He filled me in with the holes of the story that were unknown to me. And I did the same for him. Shortly after the call Petraeus and I exchanged a flurry of emails...one of them being:

> **From: Jill and Scott Kelley shared email**
> **Sent: Friday, November 09, 2012 4:31 PM**
> **To: Petraeus, David H Former COMISAF**
> **Subject: Re: RE: RE: RE: RE:**
>
> **Forgot to mention, another thing I wanted to tell you but you wouldn't.....**
> **CENTCOM [Central Command], SOCOM [Special Operations Command] etc all knew Paula Broadwell stalking them and me.**
>
> **The FBI told them, and they started questioning if our country's intelligence was being compromised ....**
> **Paula actually mentioned in a surveillance that she had you "compromised" ....**
>
> **Her name is already in the news as the mistress.**

Petraeus then wrote the most unsettling email on the topic:

On Nov 9, 2012, at 4:35 PM, "Petraeus, David H Former COMISAF" <david.h.petraeus@afghan.swa.army.mil> wrote:

Well, I guess she can't compromise me then, ….

Bottom line: I did something terrible and dishonorable….

Still in shock and complete dismay about our phone call, I wrote back that evening:

From: Jill and Scott Kelley shared email
To: Petraeus, David H Former COMISAF
<david.h.petraeus@afghan.swa.army.mil>;
Subject: Re: RE: RE: RE: RE: RE:
Sent: Fri, Nov 9, 2012 10:30:00 PM

No..... she doesn't have the Director "compromised" now!

David, I'm proud that you were pre-emptive and went forward .....since the FBI and the Commanders all took Paula's emails seriously when she said she would "Go to the Media, and make National Headlines, and tell the spouses and embarrass the leadership of our country"
They agencies took this a credible threat, and didn't want to take any chances, since Paula was causing all sorts of collateral damage - because she couldn't control her insanity.

You know I didn't want her arrested in efforts to protect you....
With that said, I'm glad you came forward. It was the most honorable thing to do.

I already received a hundred emails, phone calls, and text messages from all your Military Commanders, Ambassadors, and WH people asking me about you.

My anger started to dissipate. Yes, David had made a mistake, but I hurt for him. What a terrible position he'd been living in for the past six months, since everyone (she, and now government officials) were holding his affair over his head. He was like a hostage who shoots himself to escape the torment! My feeling as we ended the call was one of sadness, but also relief. Both Scott and I felt protective of David, and that evening Scott had a heartfelt email exchange with David, which will give you a sense of how we all felt:

From: Scott Kelley personal email
Sent: Friday, November 09, 2012 6:31 PM
To: Holly Petraeus; Petraeus, David H Former COMISAF
Subject: You are in our thoughts and prayers

Holly and David-
Please realize our thoughts and prayers are with you throughout these difficult times.
We remain steadfast in our friendship and support. You are family to us-Let us know if we can help in any way.

Love,
Scott

Scott T. Kelley, MD FACS

At this point, David was remorseful:

On Nov 9, 2012, at 6:47 PM, "Petraeus, David H Former COMISAF" <david.h.petraeus@afghan.swa.army.mil> wrote:

Thx, Scott. I screwed up royally and, having done the dishonorable thing, I needed to try to do the honorable thing. Deeply appreciate the kind words/support. ....(And a hug for my BFF, pls.)

Scott was sympathetic:

From: Scott Kelley personal email
Sent: Friday, November 09, 2012 9:18 PM
To: Petraeus, David H Former COMISAF
Subject: Re: You are in our thoughts and prayers

Don't be too hard on yourself, there will be plenty of enemies out there to do that for you.

You are a good person with a good heart. Your family is all that matters right now... This too, will pass.

History should and will remember your contributions, sacrifice and leadership in the end.

Again, we are here if you need anything- we're here as always, as family.

STK

"All men make mistakes, but a good man yields when he knows his course is wrong, and repairs the evil. The only crime is pride."
— Sophocles, Antigone

Scott T. Kelley, MD FACS

Chapter 2: My Upbringing and Sense of Duty

To understand the story, you have to understand my history. As this book is autobiographical, I feel I need to give you a sense of who I am so you can understand my roots, connections, and my interests in politics. Understanding my history will form a backdrop to help explain why I responded to this situation as I did.

I was born in Lebanon on June 3, 1975, at the beginning of a vicious civil war that would set our nation on fire. My twin sister Natalie and I entered the world as our parents and older siblings watched the ominous clouds of smoke rising above Beirut, the once-magical city that our family had long called home.

Before the war my family's life had been a happy and comfortable one in Beirut, a city known as the Paris of the Middle East. My parents owned a beautiful waterfront residence, and my father was an admired classical pianist and a scholar of Arabic and Middle Eastern history. My parents were devout Catholics. In fact, my father was raised in an Italian seminary, and when he was young he had studied to be a priest. Then, on a church trip to the beach, he met my mother. They fell in love — and it was the true love of soul mates. Today they are as much in love as if they'd just married. They became, for me, the ideal of what a marriage should be, models of honor and respect and dedication and loyalty.

The Church was always at the center of our family's universe. And a big part of that devotion was a commitment to learning and doing good. I recall the central message my father taught me. He often said: "I'll tell you who you are if you show me who your friends are." By that he meant we should surround ourselves with people of honor and integrity.

In a different time, my parents would have enjoyed a life of complete happiness and security in Lebanon, but in 1975, with Beirut burning, they decided we had to leave. When Natalie and I were three months old, my father left to set up a life for us in the United States. We followed him nine months later. When we came to America we had nothing. My mother had fled with just the clothes on her back, a baby on each arm, and five-year-old Caroline and three-year-old

David in tow. As quiet and demure as she is, I've realized, as I've gotten older, that my mother showed herself to be an incredibly strong woman when she made that journey on her own. Both of my parents had that undeniable immigrant courage — risking everything and leaving their home and families behind to give their children a better life. I have often wondered if I could have been that courageous.

I was the fortunate recipient of two particular virtues from my parents — a love for people and an affinity for the world. I am the person I am thanks to my remarkable parents.

And because my parents sacrificed everything to bring us to America, Dad never let us forget how privileged we were and how much we owed. "You came to this country," he would say. "Now you don't take, you give." We were always pressed to think about what we could give back.

That ethos defined our family life in our adopted home as we set about reclaiming what we lost by building new lives for ourselves in America. Honor and loyalty were important values. We were told, "Honor is not what you do when someone's looking; it is what you do when they are not looking. You are given trust as a gift. When you betray the person, you lose the gift." I thought of this many, many times over the years, always being guided by these basic principles in life.

Work ethic was also an ongoing discussion in our family; our parents reinforced their most important message: Become a doctor. My mother instilled that work ethic early on in our life when she had us work in her restaurants. "You see how late the hours are in a restaurant?" Mom would say. "This is why you should work hard, study hard, be a doctor." Becoming a doctor was considered the gold standard of success.

I was a fiercely competitive young woman, and I was definitely the more outgoing twin. And since I was more ambitious than Natalie, people would occasionally dub me the "evil twin." The term would make me smirk and reply, "No — dominant, not evil!" But I have to admit I was an unstoppable force, a whirlwind, a force of nature. To me the worst thing in the world was to be indifferent or apathetic. I always cared, sometimes too much. I was not content with being mediocre.

I noticed that some of my wealthy classmates didn't seem very motivated. I admit I was a little judgmental about that. How can you have the American Dream handed to you and not take advantage of it? I was constantly hearing about the "land of opportunity," and I was determined to seize my opportunities.

Maybe it was my parents' constant pushing, which combined with my will and constant drive, but I accepted the challenge of becoming a doctor. I was so sure of my calling that when I got to high school, I asked the principal to allow me to take extra science classes instead of the required business classes.

I was a self-professed "nerd" in high school. I often skipped lunch and recess in order to do my homework or extra science. Besides, my parents were very old-fashioned, and they didn't allow my sister and me to date in high school. They insisted we keep our focus on academics and athletics. It worked so well that if a boy asked me out, I'd say, "I can't date you, but you can be my lab partner."

That said, I was also an athlete: tennis, track, swimming, softball and cross-country. I would do the normal swimming, compete with the swim team, and then go and run my ten miles after that.

My high school was in a very exclusive, upscale suburb outside of Philadelphia. I remember the lines of Mercedes when parents came to pick up their kids. My dad pulled up in a little pre-owned Honda. But I always walked out proud because I knew my dad was smarter than all the dads in the car line. My parents had poise, elegance and intellect — the kind of sophistication that money can't buy.

I think growing up in an immigrant household gave me a kind of moral center that allowed for cultural dissonance with my peers. Kids at school would complain about their parents, saying, "My parents told me not to do drugs, yet they do drugs." I was thinking to myself, "Your parents do drugs?" I couldn't get my head around it. My parents practiced what they preached, and I felt that honorable. It was unthinkable to me that parents would have double standards. To this day I have no tolerance for hypocrisy and hypocrites.

When it came time to choose colleges, my parents insisted that we pick one nearby and live at home. I was disappointed that I couldn't apply to the Ivy League schools. From the time I was a little girl my heart had been set on going to Harvard, and I liked to wear a Harvard T-shirt. Actually, I did secretly apply to Harvard, and when my mom found out she yelled at me about it. She made it clear that her girls would live at home until they got married, which meant that we weren't going anywhere outside the radius of our suburb. Natalie and I ended up attending a small private college close to home.

In my freshman year of college I was finally allowed to date. I never attended frat parties, nor did I join a sorority. Instead, I focused on my studies as a pre-med student. I was very serious and determined to become a doctor. At the same time, I met my future mentor, Dr. Margaret Aranda. Dr. Aranda was a critical-care attending physician from the University of Pennsylvania, and unlike most physicians, she was exceptionally pretty, single, and brainy — not what you would assume an Ivy League doctor to look like. She saw in me a girl who was mature beyond her years and willing to work endlessly to achieve her dream. Dr. Aranda rewarded me with her trust by appointing me to a role as a medical researcher for the Department of Anesthesia at the University of Pennsylvania, conducting studies and publishing research in critical care and pain medicine. My best days were spent with her and the cardiac surgeons who recognized in me the future surgeon that I aspired to be, especially when they let me scrub in to observe surgeries. I was convinced that my lifelong dream of being a cardiac surgeon was coming true.

****

The medical research opportunity led to my meeting the love of my life. After leaving Dr. Aranda's office, I passed by Scott for the first time. He immediately caught my eye. Scott was a general surgical resident in his last year of training at the University of Pennsylvania. He was nine years older than I — and he was about to become what I wanted to be, a cardiac surgeon. The chemistry was immediate. Besides having the same career aspirations, we both were high achievers who wanted to make a mark in academics. Scott had unique surgical skills and was already published — an unusual success given his age. His research had even been featured on the cover of a prestigious cardiac surgery magazine. But then Scott shocked everyone at Penn: Despite his being one of the most qualified cardiac surgery fellowship candidates to be accepted into the upcoming year, he changed his specialty to cancer surgery, deciding that he saw his calling in helping oncology patients with complicated cases. Scott is a very kind and caring person who loves taking care of people. Unlike typical surgeons, Scott isn't the least bit arrogant, although with his accomplishments, he could have been. What began as admiration and instant attraction gradually turned into love.

Before meeting Scott in my last year of college, I had had only two boyfriends, both whom were successful and came from well-to-do families. But what made Scott different is that he knew what it meant to struggle for everything. He was raised in a working-class family and was the first one to go to college, not to mention all Ivy League schools. Scott has qualities that reminded me of my father — quiet, kind, elegant, devoted. We were — and still are — soul mates made for one another.

After graduating from college, I was accepted into a post-bacc program at Hahnemann University Hospital. The curriculum allowed one to take medical school classes at the downtown campus and, if you excelled, to apply to the medical school. I was getting honors and was excited to be on my way. Without giving it much effort, I also found myself doing what I also enjoyed: lending my contacts and connections to a variety of causes/campaigns for leaders whose needs could be easily resolved with a couple calls.

Being a "community leader" was the explanation given to me for a once-in-a-lifetime opportunity: an invitation to a very special dinner in Italy. The iconic politician Tom Foglietta, the Philadelphian former congressman, had been appointed the U.S. ambassador to Italy. I was one of many guests invited to his diplomatic residence in Rome, Villa de Taverna, where he hosted a Thanksgiving dinner for all the royalty of Europe. This royal gala also included Secretary of State Madeleine Albright, who gave a tremendous speech, among other icons in the diplomatic world. Despite being completely engrossed in my medical career, that unique experience exposed me to a whole new world. This unforgettable introduction to diplomacy left an unquenched desire; I longed for more.

After we'd dated a year and a half, Scott proposed to me. I immediately said yes. We were in love. Despite Scott's backbreaking hours as a surgical resident and my overloaded schedule running between two hospitals as a full-time student and as a medical researcher, we planned a beautiful and meaningful wedding.

We settled down in a spectacular townhouse in Center City Philadelphia and resumed our work and studies seamlessly. In many ways, it was an unusual and perfect marriage. Although our work was long and unending, we saw each other several times a day, since we worked in the same place. Our life in Philadelphia was very busy and filled with promise. And then Scott got was assigned to the Moffitt Cancer Center in Tampa, Florida, for his surgical oncology fellowship training.

Whatever your station in life, marriage, quite literally, changes things — sometimes dramatically. In our case, the change was not only emotional but geographic and, for me, professional and personal as well. I had been on a successful journey with my own medical studies. My resume was shining from years of publishing research at the University of Pennsylvania. In addition to my professional goals, I had developed a wide network of social and political relationships in Philadelphia; moving to Tampa meant relinquishing all that. The fellowship at Tampa's Moffitt Cancer Center was simply too important for Scott to decline. My presence in Tampa was an accident of fate. Like many married wives, I put my studies on hold so that Scott could pursue his career.

Tampa was like living in a foreign country. I had to get used to the slower pace and slight accent. I consoled myself with the fact that it was only temporary. My hopes and plans were understood: In two years we'd move back to our "real" lives in Philadelphia. I even had a calendar and I marked off the days with big X's.

Suddenly, I learned I was pregnant. We hadn't expected to start our family quite yet. In fact, I never really thought about anything more in life than being the best cardiac surgeon in the world — but we were thrilled. I had to accept the fact that we would have to put my goals on a longer hold. I knew I needed to find something to do or I'd go stir crazy, especially with the busy life I'd left in Philadelphia, running hospital to hospital, from classroom to lab room. I needed something to do to keep that hamster wheel spinning.

In Philadelphia I had begun thinking about developing some medical patents that came to mind from my observations during surgery at Penn. One, for example, was a biodegradable sealant to address surgical leaks, since leaks were among the persistent problems in surgery. Any honest surgeon will tell you that they go to bed after surgery praying there's not a leak. My patent would provide a foolproof seal that would dissolve on its own when the site had healed. So now that I was stuck in Tampa, I successfully designed and developed that patent with the lay name "Leak Guard" — which I hope will become the standard of care used during all surgeries.

And since I was "out and about" and not in the hospital 24/7, it seemed that everyone we befriended had a family member with cancer, and couldn't help but to ask us for medical advice or some background about their cancer. I decided that instead of constantly explaining the same facts or answering the same questions, I would gather a group of medical students (many whom Scott had taught) and author a cancer book to explain their specific disease, diagnosis, prognosis, necessary tests, expected complications, etc., in lay terms. That way a patient is informed enough to ask the doctor intelligent questions and understand his or her options and risks — without having gone to medical school. We had regular meetings and wrote 20 chapters on different cancers.

For income — because Scott's fellowship training didn't pay much more than the national stipend of $39,000 — I was investing in and developing real estate. I realized that if you have a brain and a good work ethic in this city, the opportunities are endless. Therefore, I was driven to keep busy until the day we would return to the Northeast — home. Later, the media would derisively refer to me as a "socialite," which I always felt was not only sexist, but an insulting diminishment of my medical achievements and lifetime accomplishments.

I was a couple of months pregnant with our first daughter in September 2001 when Scott and I traveled north to Baltimore for his required national surgery oral exams.

On the morning of September 11, we were watching TV in our hotel room before Scott went next door to the conference hall for his exam when the news came on that a plane had hit the World Trade Center. A chill went down my spine and I turned to Scott. Knotting his tie, Scott looked very stressed — as any person taking oral exams would be. Still not knowing what was going on, he headed out the door to meet the ten professors who were going to grill him for the next hour. Later, Scott appeared in the doorway, his face ashen. I looked at him with the heinous news: "A second plane hit the other World Trade Center. It's got to be terrorism." Scott replied, "Let's get out of here." "What about your exam?" My eyes were wide.

"Done," he said. "The doctors in that room hadn't even heard about it. It was like the room was hermetically sealed. I didn't tell them. I wasn't going to try and get sympathy points."

The car radio was playing eerie warnings from officials for all but emergency personnel to stay off the roads because of the mass casualties and chaos. "They're asking for emergency personnel and surgeons. I have to go there," said my husband, who had just taken the most important test of his career. I didn't even try to stop him. I agreed that we had to do what we could. We didn't even consider the potential danger. It was a gut instinct, a desire to help, hence our mutual decision to pursue medical careers. We continued driving north, and at some point we could see smoke billowing far ahead. Scott dropped me off at my sister Caroline's, and we hugged tightly before he drove off toward New York City.

I felt extremely emotional. I was pregnant, eager to welcome new life, and all I could think of was how many people had lost their husbands, wives, fathers, and mothers that day in an unimaginable terrorist attack. I thought about my own family — about my infant self who had survived bombings even before I was conscious of being alive. Why one person survives and another dies is a mystery of life.

It seemed that in no time at all Scott was back, exhausted and discouraged. He'd been sent to a stadium where they were expecting to treat hundreds, maybe thousands, of injured. But there weren't any people who could be fixed or saved. With tears in his eyes Scott described standing amid smoke-filled air with other medical workers, waiting for the injured, until it slowly dawned on them that they wouldn't be coming. They'd been buried in the rubble. A few days later, when the airports reopened, we flew home.

Later in the fall Scott and I were invited to a hospital charity dinner that would literally change our lives. We were seated next to a wonderful couple, General Michael DeLong and his wife, Kathy. Mike was the deputy commander at Central Command, serving under General Tommy Franks. Through Mike and Kathy's generous introductions to the leaders of the command, Scott and I were suddenly immersed in a new social circle. The image of the Twin Towers was never far from our minds, the wars in Iraq and Afghanistan were front-page news every day. Now, as an expectant mother, I looked at the future in a very different way. When I met Mike and Kathy, I thought, "My God, these are the people who are saving our country. These are not generals just pushing papers behind a desk. These are war commanders. These heroes dedicated their lives so that my family and every American can live in this nation in peace, freedom and democracy" — values my family had never taken for granted.

In the aftermath of 9/11 I began to see Tampa with new eyes. As our country geared up for war and retaliation, Tampa was at the center of the action. I hadn't realized that less than ten miles from our home was MacDill Air Force Base, headquarters of the military Central Command (CENTCOM), the nerve center of international defense efforts. Most of the US military would fly through MacDill on the way to Iraq and Afghanistan. So naturally all the military leaders would also visit the base. This was where some of the best minds in the nation resided and were dedicated to keeping us safe.

The military was all so new to me, since I didn't know anything about the services, culture, leaders, etc. God knows, I'd grown up in a home that focused on my future as a doctor. But since meeting our new friends Mike and Kathy, I looked at the military with interest, even commonality.

I found the military leaders we met to be serious, careful and thoughtful. They weren't the bad boys. Far from it. I began to see that we had a lot in common in our upbringings: honor, integrity, dedication, loyalty, academics, athletics and character. And we shared something else in common — a deep commitment to peace in the Middle East. Hearing these Irish-American blue-eyed men speak Arabic thrilled me. Our "small talk" consisted of long hours discussing Arab history.

At first, our immersion into the foreign military culture of the U.S. Central Command was gradual, like dipping a toe into an unfamiliar pond. It wasn't just the ubiquitous desert-camouflage uniforms that nearly everyone wore at MacDill; it was the bristling military presence on the base; the breathtaking military hardware — even the way soldiers and officers spoke to one another. They were possessed of a warrior argot that seemed designed to thwart penetration by the outside world. General Franks and DeLong invited us to informal dinners and small social gatherings at their palatial homes on the base, the events catered by military chefs and served by handsome young soldiers. Before long, we were frequently asked to attend dinners, concerts and other CENTCOM events on and off the base.

The massive MacDill air base was not only the locus of critical decision-making by commanders of the nation's two most recent wars. It welcomed military representatives from a variety of nations in the international coalition to help the United States military topple Saddam Hussein and transform his former dictatorship into something akin to a democracy while also supporting us in cleansing Afghanistan of the deadly influence of Al Qaeda terrorists and their enablers in the Taliban.

Most people do not know that our coalition is the largest military union in the world. It comprises up to 62 countries. Later I was honored to serve as the coalition's first honorary ambassador.

Surveying the situation, I thought to myself, these generals were also A students and top of their class and could have done anything, but they chose a life full of duty and service. None of them got paid much or lived the way people of comparable status did. I was struck by their sense of duty and service. But since they were willing to make these sacrifices, that elevated them in my eyes.

Given the incredibly demanding nature of their jobs — the commanders were literally on the job 24/7, especially as a result of the time differences between Tampa and Afghanistan and Iraq. The CENTCOM leaders rotated in and out of the command every few years; but each departing commander made sure to introduce Scott and me to their successors. Increasingly, Scott and I began hosting small dinners to "double date," as well as some military events. Eventually, we hosted many events related to the coalition.

As the years passed, it became clear that we were in Tampa to stay. Scott had a dream practice, and we'd had three daughters within four years. And even though I still believed I was going back to medical school to achieve my lifelong goal, I was becoming increasingly involved in support services for our military. Our troops and their families relied on civilian support, and I was thrilled to help in any way I could. With so many wives left behind during deployments, I was able to offer them services and community to ease the isolation. Often I arranged events. And, of course, through it all, I continued to be a useful civilian resource to the top brass and the outside world.

One of the generals told me that Scott and I provided some much-needed "connective tissue" between their highly regimented, demanding lives and the diplomatic world. In my case, being as forthright and outspoken as I am, I wondered if maybe I possessed some kind of emotional intelligence that they could use as a prism through which to view issues of diplomacy and interpersonal relationships that were broader than the lens afforded by their military lives. There was nothing scandalous or controversial about our friendships.

These relationships were the foundation on which Scott and I would build our friendship with David and Holly Petraeus. It would be one of the most gratifying periods of our lives and, in the end, one of the most disappointing, disheartening and terrifying.

Chapter 3: Safira

In the prologue, I mention how things that were so unimportant become meaningful in retrospect. It seems improbable that seating arrangements at dinner, and the conversations that ensued, would become so critical to later parts of this story. My family — the Kelley family — had a pure and true friendship with the Petraeus family. Unfortunately, the FBI represented me disingenuously and leaked rumors about me to justify its unwarranted investigation into my email communications. In so doing, they cheapened years of family memories, holiday gatherings and special celebrations that our families shared.

The weekend before March 11, 2008, Scott and I received a phone call from Admiral Bill Fallon asking us to be immediately available to go to Donatello's restaurant in Tampa. We canceled our previous plans and headed out to the restaurant. Donatello's is a classic Italian restaurant. We walked into the room to find Admiral Fallon crestfallen and his wife, Mary, in a somber mood. Attempting to break the tension, I tried to offer some lighthearted banter. It fell like a brick. The martini in his hand was trembling while we stood at the bar. Breaking through the niceties, Bill announced: "I invited you here because I have some bad news that I would like to share with you before you hear it from the news." He conveyed to us his feelings about the situation. We were left with the understanding that he felt pressured to retire.

Later that evening, when we were sitting at dinner, he said, "The name of the soldier who is replacing me is David Petraeus. He was a commander in Iraq. We have a history. Rumor has it we don't get along, when, in fact, I'm fine with him. There was gossip that I called him 'chicken shit.'" Although he denied calling him names, Fallon did have a past with Petraeus. He went on to explain that Petraeus had gone around Fallon to talk to President Bush directly, rather than going through the proper chain of command. Troops found Petraeus to be ambitious and career-minded, even at the cost of the command structure. Clearly, Petraeus' reputation preceded him — in both good and bad ways.

Soon after, Jeri-Anne Martin, the chief of protocol at CENTCOM in 2008, called me with new a request. "Our new commander, General David Petraeus, just arrived and would like the honor to have his first dinner with you and Dr. Kelley," she said. Of course, we were delighted.

We invited the new commander and his wife, Holly, to dinner on October 25, and I put in a call to Charlie Crist, Florida's governor, and asked him to join us in welcoming the new CENTCOM leader.

From: Jill and Scott Kelley shared email
Sent: Monday, October 06, 2008 9:32 PM
To: Martin, Ms Jeri-Anne H. (DoD)
Subject: Re: Dinner invitation for General Dave and Holly Petraeus with
Dr. Scott and Jill Kelley

Jeri-Anne,

I hope you are well? It was a pleasure, as always, speaking to you on Friday.

As per our discussion, Dr. Kelley and I wanted to know if the General and his wife, Holly, were available for dinner on Thursday, October 23rd?

Please tell me if their calendar allows for dinner that evening?

Thank you again, and looking forward to seeing you at the ceremonies on
October 31st.

Jill

Jerri-Anne passed along my invitation.

From: Martin, Ms Jeri-Anne H. (DoD)
Sent: Tuesday, October 21, 2008 9:55 AM
To: Jill and Scott Kelley shared email
Subject: RE: Dinner invitation for General Dave and Holly Petraeus with Dr. Scott and Jill Kelley

Jill,
....
will pass to General and Mrs. Petreaus that dinner will be for 6 with

Governor Charlie Crist ...General Petreaus' personal security detail will
likely be calling you. I'm sure the same from Governor Crist's office.

....

With warm regards,

Jeri-Anne Martin
Chief of Protocol
U.S. Central Command
7115 S Boundary Blvd., Bldg. 540
MacDill AFB, FL 33635
Comm: (813) 827-XXXX
DSN: (312) 651-XXXX

Scott and I liked the Petraeuses instantly. Holly was warm and genuine, with a smart edge and a down-to-earth manner that came from thirty years as a military wife. I learned she was intelligent, multilingual and sophisticated. David had the straight-laced demeanor and carefully combed hair you'd expect from a spit-and-polish commander, but as the evening progressed, he loosened up and I found him smart, with a dry wit, and a bit sarcastic. But without a doubt, Holly was the better half.

We began with my ritual of popping a jeroboam of Veuve Clicquot while we snacked on a maza (tabouleh, hummus, baba ghanoush and grape leaves, with thin triangles of pita).

Then it was off to Bern's Steak House, which is George W. Bush's favorite haunt when in Tampa. I had reserved our usual dining room downstairs, fittingly called the Champagne Room. On the chef's advice, I had designed an eight-course menu featuring fresh oysters, caviar and, of course, steak. I wanted everything to be perfect, and it was.

At the steakhouse, I sat near David Petraeus and Charlie Crist, and the talk turned easily from education to values to leadership. There were no uncomfortable questions about Afghanistan or Iraq. As the evening progressed, the conversation grew more relaxed.

While Charlie talked about campaigning in the morning with Sarah Palin, David, perhaps a bit tipsy from the champagne, asked an unscripted question to Charlie: "Why aren't you married? What's wrong with you?" I kicked David under the table and said "Google it" under my breath in an attempt to tell him to back off the topic, since rumor had just spread (in the local paper) that Crist was gay. I quickly changed the topic to a subject of common interest. My husband's eyes grew wide, as if to say 'Did you really just kick the new commander?' Accident or not, that was a test: He was either going to like me or hate me for my subtle attempt to save a conversation from becoming a disaster. As it turned out, Petraeus appreciated my forthrightness.

David asked all sorts of questions about our life: How did we have such a fancy house at such a young age? How did I get into commercial real estate development? Where did the ideas for my medical patents come from? How did I know international leaders?

At that dinner, we found that we had a lot in common. David had also been on the pre-med track, and he also liked the finer things in life. After that evening, we regularly went on double dates, and Holly and I met for lunch often.

David recognized early on that I was more than a hostess or simply a supporter of our troops. I was glad that I didn't need to express my niche as I sometimes find myself doing with new replacements at the command. David just "got it." He appreciated the fact that my father had schooled me in Middle East history and international affairs. Petraeus, like his predecessors, appreciated that my Lebanese roots prepared me to understand the language, culture, and ideology of the AOR (area of responsibility) for Central Command.

He also appreciated that I am an extrovert who can bridge conversation with almost anyone at any time. He recognized that my natural gifts and abilities could be useful to his mission of strengthening international support for the coalition when diplomats came to visit Central Command. My presence at official dinners was helpful to diplomatic progress.

Often, we found it difficult to have our double dates in public because too often people came up to meet the general, shake his hand, or make a comment that interrupted our dinner. Too many ears were tilted in our direction, which stilted conversation. So, for the most part, we returned to hosting the commanders in the privacy and security of our home. In the safety and comfort of our living room, David and Holly could relax. Our house became home away from home — to the point where we hosted their family and extended relatives visiting Tampa, and they celebrated the holidays with us. David would call me if he wanted help to organize a surprise birthday for Holly at my house, or if his mother-in-law needed to be picked up, or his son needed a care package delivered to him at Army Ranger school. The friendship in the family became one of trust.

Over a number of months, David observed me in many situations — formal occasions, casual gatherings, large receptions, and private dinners. I became aware of how much I enjoyed the trust he placed in me to host events for CENTCOM officials and to extend the gift of hospitality to the representatives of our foreign allies living in Tampa. Together, we came up with the idea of inaugurating and co-sponsoring an annual coalition appreciation reception at our home for all sixty-two senior national representatives of the international coalition who were assigned to MacDill. CENTCOM's protocol team organized the details and arranged the flags of the coalition participating nations perfectly around my home. The events were a huge success! We sent along the itinerary and the CENTCOM chief of protocol responded enthusiastically.

From: Jill and Scott Kelley shared email
To: Martin, Jeri-anne H Ms CIV USAF USCENTCOM CCDC/CSP
Cc: Drozd-Patterson, Joanna P SFC ARE USA USCENTCOM
CCDC/CSP; Mendoza, Tonya L Ms CIV USAF USCENTCOM
CCDC/CSP; Scott Kelley personal email ; Sister Natalie personal
email ; Jill and Scott Kelley shared email address
Sent: Sat May 15 09:35:56 2010
Subject: Re: Coalition Appreciation Reception

Music by University of Tampa Jazz Quartet

1600 Arrival of Guests
     Receive name tags (for non-military personnel)
     Proceed through Receiving Line

     Meet Hosts: Dr. Scott and Mrs. Jill Kelley

     Present hostess gift to ALL guests
     (Tiffany's lapel pin of the American Flag)
     Assisted by: Mr. Maged Asouty, General Manager of Tiffany's

1645 Emcee: Dr. Scott Kelley

     Introduce Ms. Jessica Best, Opera Singer of Opera Tampa to
perform:
       -Opera Carmen by Bizet
       -O Mio Babbino Caro (Holly Petreaus' favorite opera song)
       - America the Beautiful
       - God Bless America

1700 Emcee Dr. Scott Kelley
     Introduce Ms. Lisa Casalino, Soloist to perform:
       - National Anthem

     Mrs. Jill Kelley
     Welcome remarks
      Thank the Coalition
     Present momento to General Petraeus

     Remarks by General Petraeus

1730 Continue mingling
1900 Event ends / Guests depart (no departure line)

Fyi
- Alec Bradley Cigar Bar
- Bern's Steakhouse Caviar Bar
- Ice Vodka Bar (ie Bloody Marys, vodka Martini's etc)
- Champagne Bar
- Ocean Prime Specialty drinks Bar
-Cary's Fresh Squeezed Lemonade station
-International Gourmet cheese station

"Events by Amore" will butler:
Jumbo Shrimp Cocktail, Lolipop Lamb Chops, Salmon cakes, Jerk Chicken, Sliced Filet Mignon, Lobster BLT, Dungenese Crab California rolls, Smoked Salmon with Truffled Egg Salad on black bread

----

In her response, she indicated her excitement and promised to pass along the invitation.

From: "Martin, Jeri-anne H Ms CIV USAF USCENTCOM CCDC/CSP"
Subject: Re: Coalition Appreciation Reception
Date: May 15, 2010 at 10:10:15 AM EDT
To: Scott Kelley personal email account
Cc: "Drozd-Patterson, Joanna P SFC ARE USA USCENTCOM CCDC/CSP" "Mendoza, Tonya L Ms CIV USAF USCENTCOM CCDC/CSP" Scott Kelley personal email, Sister Natalie personal email

…. We will pass it on to the boss.
Vr/ Jeri-Anne Martin
Chief of Protocol

Eventually Petraeus decided my annual coalition appreciation reception should be timed in conjunction with Gasparilla, Tampa's version of Mardi Gras. It is a pirate-themed "invasion" of the city, beginning with a pirate armada on the bay followed by a parade along Bayshore Boulevard. David was new to Tampa and just learning about Gasparilla, but when I told him the parade passed by our house, he thought it would be a real treat for the representatives from the coalition countries to experience this Tampa festival in a first-class setting. The kind of camaraderie that develops with this type of event is a win for diplomacy — especially since internal turmoil and politics can sabotage progress.

By the second annual coalition appreciation reception, David was out of the country and missed the Gasparilla festivities. When we weren't together, he emailed me where and what we were doing (of course, he usually had something cooler going on than Gasparilla):

> **From: Jill and Scott Kelley shared email**
> **Sent: Friday, February 06, 2009 5:01 PM**
> **To: Petraeus, David H. GEN USA**
> **Subject: Thank you for your kind words**
>
> **David,**
> **Thank you for your email. Truthfully, I am taken back by such kind words from someone that I have the highest regards for.**
> **Nonetheless, I want to thank you and Holly for our friendship, but more importantly I cannot express to you, the honor of being in your company.**
> **I am sorry we will miss you tomorrow at our Gasparilla party.....you will be missed :-(**
> **I look forward to your safe return, and having a great dinner on March 10th.**
> **That said, please start working up your appetite for another fabulous dinner together again.**
> **Bon Voyage!**
> **Jill**
>
> ----------

His response showed that our families were growing close. He asked me to ensure that Holly had a good time. He also shared his challenging work schedule with me.

> **From: Petraeus, David H. GEN USA <petraedh@centcom.mil>**
> **Sent: Friday, February 06, 2009 6:04 PM**
> **To: Jill and Scott Kelley shared email**
> **Subject: RE: Thank you for your kind words**
>
> **Maybe we can do something special when our daughter is there, ... In Munich now... London yesterday. Paris, Brussels, Washington, Qatar, Uzbekistan, and Washington again before we next set foot in Tampa. ....**
> **- Dave**

Obviously, I was impressed with his itinerary, but I was also getting excited about Gasparilla.

> From: Jill and Scott Kelley shared email
> Date: February 7, 2009 at 12:36:09 PM EST
> To: "Petraeus, David H. GEN USA" <petraedh@centcom.mil>
> Subject: Will Do!
>
> David, WOW How Awesome of a trip!
> I absolutely will take Great care of Holly! ....
> The Norwegian General that sat next to me at your home,is bringing
> his whole family, plus his brother wife and their children as well, they
> just flew in from Norway, and wanted to see Gasparilla (so this party
> is getting bigger by the minute)!
> We have dinner plans with you and Holly, Scott and I for March 10th
> ....
> Take care, Please be safe!
> Jill

Petraeus enjoyed calling people by alternative names and titles. It was an ongoing joke, but it was also his personal way of complimenting people and encouraging positive behaviors.

Our conversations were typically a mix of serious and not-so-serious. And our signature lines were usually playful. Over the course of several casual emails, Petraeus jokingly came up with the inflated title of "Minister Plenipotentiary and Extraordinary" for me, but truthfully, I didn't care what he called me. I simply wanted to use my abilities to support our military goals across the globe.

> From: Jill and Scott Kelley shared email
> Sent: Tuesday, February 02, 2010 12:05 PM
> To: Petraeus, David H GEN MIL USA USCENTCOM CCCC/CCCC
> Subject: Re: Forgotten discussions at Gasparilla
>
> Hope your have safe travels, Holly and I are lunching tomorrow ....
>
> Your Ambassador to CentCom, Civilian Liaison, or the magic name I haven't
> guessed correctly yet,
> Jill

He played with my title by embellishing further:

On Feb 2, 2010, at 10:55 PM, "Petraeus, David H GEN MIL USA USCENTCOM
CCCC/CCCC" <david.petraeus@centcom.mil> wrote:

Apologies for delay, ...We'll figure out the
terms of reference for our new "Minister Plenipotentiary and
Extraordinary!"
....
Best - Dave

David introduced me by many titles over the years, but more and more frequently he began to call me his safir, the Arabic word for ambassador. I didn't say anything the first couple of times, and then I corrected him. "Actually, it's safira, since I'm a woman," I explained. "Though you don't see the word used often because there aren't many female ambassadors in Arab-speaking countries."

He looked at me, and then grinned. "Works for me."

And safira it was.

And so I found myself with an unofficial title but meaningful position and responsibility: the general's ambassador, or safira.

As I was his safira, Petraeus regularly kept me informed of his travels, and complained about work just like everyone else.

On Oct 13, 2010, at 1:35 PM, "Petraeus, David H GEN US ARMY
COMISAF"<david.h.petraeus@afghan.swa.army.mil> wrote:
Europe is a drag, Jill. .... Am sure #10 Downing will lack spark
without the safira... And Rome will be a bust,
....

Later, the photos that were sent me (from that same trip) tell a slightly different story!

Many times when a world leader came to Tampa, David invited me to join him. With sixty-two countries in the coalition fighting the war against terror, we welcomed many foreign leaders to CENTCOM. And as they came and went, David saw that I could encourage camaraderie within this unwieldy but vital international team. There were many exchanges with dozens of nations to keep their support in a seemingly effortless fashion during such an unpopular war. I tried my best. We tried our best. I did my best by speaking their language, understanding their culture and, most important, making them feel at home.

To keep up with all the events, David and I began to email each other frequently. Those early emails were even-toned and without much expression, but as our friendship grew stronger, our emails multiplied and the topics expanded to include a wide range of topics — from war to politics to our joint passion for fitness and athletics.

I'm well aware that some people might think our friendship a little strange — after all, David was a man and I was a woman and we were both happily married to other people. But I believe that men and women can be friends if that friendship is founded on mutual respect, and I came to regard David as one of my best friends. I wasn't as close with him as my twin sister, or husband, but he was someone with whom I could share my ideas, values, and thoughts. I felt that I could be myself around him. General Petraeus could be competitive in a way that other people might consider "showing off," but I was the same way. We were both alpha personalities, and we clicked. Neither our friendship nor the honorary role of "safira" was hidden from either of our spouses. Quite the contrary: spouses were included on emails.

> On Dec 16, 2011, at 9:50 AM, "Petraeus, David H Former COMISAF"<david.h.petraeus@afghan.swa.army.mil> wrote:

> Dear Hol -- and Safira -- Sandhurst was great. ....

> Now enroute to London for the night (dinner at COS' house with "C").

> All best/much love - David

As the years passed, when he entrusted me with a task I never said no, and I never went to sleep until it was done. He used to joke that I was "scorched earth" because I could be so relentless in completing a task or mission.

I knew everything David did in a day — we communicated from 5:00 a.m., since we were both early risers, until the last email of the day. I also had an intuition about situations, and sometimes I'd tell him to be wary of this person or careful around that one. Maybe it was a sixth sense or a woman's intuition on steroids, but when he'd ask my opinion about people I'd had dinner with, I could always tell him what they really needed and what he could do to reassure them. I could sense if they were being sincere. And as an extrovert with an affinity for foreign relations and cross-cultural dialogue, I loved meeting people and building relationships with leaders from all over the world — just as he did. And we had nothing to hide (or, more precisely, I had nothing to hide)! So we cc'd spouses on many of our goofy emails.

> **From: Jill and Scott Kelley shared email**
> **Date: June 9, 2011 9:39:02 AM EDT**
> **To: Anne Petraeus , Holly Petraeus , David Petraeus**
> **<david.h.petraeus@afghan.swa.army.mil>**
> **Subject: Back in Tampa...**
>
> **Hello from Tampa!**
> **I arrived last night, and now getting ready for my book meeting tonight!**
> **Fortunatley, the my row 1 seat on Delta (DC to Tampa) had no one seated next to me -wooo-hoooo!!!**
> **So I got lots of editing done on the flight....**
> **Scott said to me before I left to the Ritz, "do you want to stay with your sister in DC and I'll meet you up there Friday night, instead of flying back and forth"**
> **I responded "Thanks love, but I CAN'T cancel my med student research meeting......**
> **....**
> **I attached the yummy pix from Central!**
> **(try not to drool)**
> **I wish we took pictures of my "fresh rhubard" Martini or your beautiful "Cuccumber & mint" gin!**
>
> **Can't wait for Saturday at Marcel's!!!!!**

Now I have to get back to finish writing my last cancer
Chapters before our editing board dinner tonight....
Love
Jill

Petraeus commented on how it was good that I returned to
Tampa to work on the medical book. In his responses, he regularly
recounted his daily work activities and his plans for working out:

> On Jun 9, 2011, at 10:10 AM, "Petraeus, David H GEN US ARMY
> COMISAF"<david.h.petraeus@afghan.swa.army.mil> wrote:
>
> Thx for going back to Tampa to accomplish your assigned mission.
> What a sense of duty, Safira!
> ....
> Being decorated by the highest Italian medal tonight. Then dinner at
> Amb's residence,which is spectacular. Mil and spy chiefs will be there.
> Great 10K run route for tomorrow ....
> ....

I enjoyed the banter and continued:

> From: Jill and Scott Kelley shared email
> Sent: Thursday, June 09, 2011 7:26 PM
> To: Petraeus, David H GEN US ARMY COMMISSAR
> Subject: Re: Back in Tampa...
>
> Rome!!!!!! You mean my "home"
> ....
> Commander, You are SUCH a tease!!!!
> (I'm totally drooling)
>
> And the highest medal? ....
>
> But, Thank you for finding the moment during your surreal trip, to
> appreciate your Safira's sense of "duty"
> ....
> Remember I told you that Ambassor Folietta (from Philadelphia)
> invited me to join him there for a "Royal" Thanksgiving?
>
> ....
>
> Soooo, now that your "rolling like a Rockstar" in Rome ....

His recounting of the events showed that he enjoyed his time in Italy.

> On Jun 9, 2011, at 5:20 PM, "Petraeus, David H GEN US ARMY COMISAF"<david.h.petraeus@afghan.swa.army.mil> wrote:
>
> OK, Jill, the ceremony was tremendous. Extraordinary setting.
> ....
> Then the subsequent dinner at Villa Taverna, the Amb's incredible residence that you know well .... You'd have loved the women there -- haute couture, slim, and etc.. A few a bit younger than their escorts. But, none the equal of the safira!
> ....
> Anyway, you'd have loved it.
> ....
> Best -- Malik D
> ....

Petreaus would often use "Malik" as his signature, it is the Arabic for "king." Holly Petraeus continued to be cc'd and included throughout the string of emails:

> From: Jill and Scott Kelley shared address
> Sent: Friday, June 10, 2011 2:34 AM
> To: Petraeus, David H GEN US ARMY COMMISSAR
> Cc: Holly and David Petraeus personal email AOL email address
> Subject: Re: Safira in suspense.....
>
>
> Holly,
> Did you pass out and hit your head too?
> ....
> Dave,
> You seriously are a Malik!!!!
> ....all I'll be thinking about is how I should be in Rome right now....
>
> ....
>
> However Malik, after 1 year under General Order-1...Rome is the place to
> "undo" all the "cruel and unusual" punishment GO-1 truly is!
> ....
>
> Please enjoy running the enchanted Spanish Steps for me!

(FYI a restaurant right there the Prince of Italy took me and LOVED was
called "Tre Scalini" its wonderful right there in facing the fountains
-try it for lunch if you can)

....
Off to my research meeting....
Love
Jill

****

I've always enjoyed conversing with men. I've always had male friends, probably because I have a lot of natural qualities and characteristics that many men identify with. I speak my mind and always have been competitive and athletic. I'm ambitious, driven and direct. While embracing the full spectrum of femininity, I aspire to be a strong women. In fact, at a reception I even overheard one of the commanders trying to summarize the difference between my twin sister and me. He told the other general, "If you want someone warm and affectionate, you befriend Natalie. If you want to go to war you bring Jill."

Some people might wonder how I could have male friends and yet remain loyal to my husband. I don't think it's a fair question. Scott knows that I am completely devoted to him. He's so much more than a friend — he's my soul mate, my husband, my lover, my strength, and my life. He's the reason I feel so safe. I know that I have his unconditional support. He's everything to me.

That's not to say that things couldn't get tricky at times, because I can momentarily forget the way other people perceive relationships between men and women. I always try to be careful about appearances. For example, one time General Petraeus suggested that I stay at The Fairfax, his favorite hotel in Washington, but I continued to stay at my favorite D.C. spot. Holly was glad I was so conscientious about avoiding misperceptions. Living in a suspicious world, we knew that we would all be better off if we refrained from giving anyone a reason to fire up the gossip columns.

General John Allen was also aware of his position and how sensitive matters could get, and he was always on the "up and up" in all of our email exchanges. (That is why he was ultimately cleared of any findings of misconduct in our email exchanges.) In 2011 there was troop misconduct that caused a flurry of emails condemning leaders for their actions. Keep in mind that most military officials have an unclassified email address in addition to a classified one. These military email addresses are, officially, a matter of public record, so members of the public can direct-mail military leaders, and they often do. When things get hairy, staffers will be dispatched to read and delete emails that are nuisances. This occurred in 2011. Here was our exchange from/to non-military email addresses.

-----Original Message-----
From: Jill and Scott Kelley shared email
To: John Allen AOL email address
Sent: Tue, Nov 8, 2011 9:39 am
Subject: Got your message..

Hello John.

I got your [voice] message.

What's going on?

Is it limited to your Email?

Was something said?

He responded:

On Nov 8, 2011, at 9:07 AM,
John Allen AOL email address wrote:

No ... sorry to alarm you! Someone posted a video of some troops killing an animal with a baseball bat. ....

The people who posted the video, which has gone viral globally, has posted my unclassified e-mail address, ...

....

My team has been monitoring my account ....

....

Didn't want you/us to be misunderstood by the people now monitoring my account.

....

Now … I don't mean to claim that I am unaware of the fact that I am an attractive woman. I do realize that being a woman can be helpful sometimes, just as it can be a hindrance in some situations. The generals were aware and careful too.

Here's one exchange that highlighted that point. Ambassador Ryan Crocker was a career diplomat who had served honorably and effectively as the U.S. ambassador to Afghanistan. He was a trusted and respected statesman for the generals, successfully bridging diplomacy with the leaders of Afghanistan. General Allen was sorry to see Crocker step down from his post in July 2012, which was done for medical reasons. Director Petraeus let me know that he intended to bring former Ambassador Crocker to one of the dinners that I was organizing.

> From: Jill and Scott Kelley shared email account
> Sent: Wednesday, August 15, 2012 10:51 PM
> To: Allen, John R Gen USMC COMISAF
> Subject: Re: (U//FOUO) [Unclassified // For Official Use only]
>
> Dave told me today that he's trying to bring AMB Crocker to my Coalition
> Partner Ambassador Dinner!
> That would be super cool to meet him. I've always wanted to meet him
> -since he's the epitome of Ambassadors!
>
> He thought this would be a great opportunity for Ryan to meet me!

General Allen's playful response showed that he understood how different people respond to my appearance. (Not that I believed he was serious about Crocker's volatile blood pressure.) Keep in mind: These emails were sent to and from an email account shared with my husband.

> From: "Allen, John R Gen USMC COMISAF"
> <john.allen@afghan.swa.army.mil>
> Date: August 15, 2012 at 2:40:25 PM EDT
> To: Jill and Scott Kelley shared email
> Subject: RE: (U) (U//FOUO)

UNCLASSIFIED

**Look ... we're working to keep his blood pressure under control.
Meeting you will not do that unless you're wearing your AFG burqa.
....**

Avoiding criticism and misunderstandings was one reason Scott and I paid for everything we did with the generals — I always paid for my own hotel and meals, and for my plane flights. (A later rumor that I hitched rides on military jets with General Allen was absolutely false.) I never wanted others to have to pay for anything, unless there was an official reason. I certainly didn't want others to get in trouble paying for me; that wouldn't be fair to anyone. I was honored just to be with them and to be able to make a contribution.

General Petraeus' amazing contacts opened what seemed like a universe of new doors for me. One of the first introductions he made was at a dinner he had arranged for me at the Four Seasons in D.C. with the prime minister and the defense minister of Lebanon, which led to my being able to take my family on a trip to Lebanon for the first time since my birth.

We were at the end of our Lebanese trip, relaxing in our hotel room, when I happened to look at a TV and saw something about Petraeus and "scandal" and something about General McChrystal suddenly resigning. (Allegedly because of remarks his aides said to Rolling Stone Magazine, that were critical of the White House.)

President Obama ultimately relieved General McChrystal as commander of the war in Afghanistan and tapped Petraeus from CENTCOM.

Until that moment in my hotel room, never had an announcement about the war affected me so deeply. I sank to the sofa in our suite as my heart pounded almost painfully in my chest. I couldn't believe every news station was showing a picture of Petraeus with the president on the White House lawn with the headline "SCANDAL." I couldn't understand the urgency or drama of this so-called scandal! All this breaking news because an aide to General McChrystal allegedly told a magazine that he thinks the president's advisor is a clown? The world must think we overreact and destroy great patriots over nothing, despite the service they've given. Sadness hit me: Scott and I were losing our friends Holly and David too soon.

Feeling sentimental about our friendship, I wrote a heartfelt email to David and Holly, saying how much we'd miss them. Holly, not allowed to follow David to Afghanistan, would be transferred to Virginia, the commander's American home, and she, too, was feeling sentimental. She and wrote back:

> Begin forwarded message:
> From: Holly Petraeus AOL account
> Subject: Re: Together on your birthday this weekend!!
> Date: July 12, 2010 at 1:47:48 PM EDT
> To: Jill and Scott Kelley shared email,
> david.h.petraeus@afghan.swa.army.mil
>
> Dear Jill, Thank you for your lovely email. We, too, have valued the friendship with you and your family. …. We have a lot of wonderful memories from the past year and a half and I'm sure there will be more in the future, even if we won't be neighbors anymore. :-(
> ….
> Love, Holly

We flew home that night, and Holly texted me the next morning. "David is coming over to tell you goodbye."

That had to be one of the saddest days of my life. David's driver pulled up outside and waited as he came in to see us. My family sat in our living room, and he hugged the girls goodbye. By that time he had become "Uncle David" to them, and they hated to see him go off to war. He asked me to take care of Holly for him, and I promised him that I would.

David and I had always spoken frankly, and there were things I wanted to tell him privately before he left. "I need you to listen to me, David." He asked his bodyguard to wait outside and sat down. I stood across from him and spoke with a serious but respectful tone, beginning with how other world leaders truly perceive him and his unique leadership. "One thing everyone knows but doesn't talk about, though, is that our president feels threatened by you and your international influence. I think he wants to keep you far away in Afghanistan to avoid your becoming a presidential hopeful."

David sat quietly, listening but not responding. He didn't argue. He knew that several political donors had reached out to me, promising over $20 million to fund his campaign if he chose to run. Now I warned him that he was being handed a shit sandwich, and was in danger of being left holding the bag for this long-unwanted war. He'd be worse off if his last mission were to be remembered as overseeing a failing war.

David finally looked up, agreeing with his eyes, but silent, since he had no choice and his military plane was waiting for him to take off. We hugged as I told him we would miss him. With sadness he took one last picture with me and the girls, and then he went back outside to his car and his driver took him to the airport. I can still see him moving down our sidewalk, lengthening his stride as he moved toward his car. A soldier walking away from friends and toward his duty.

If I ever thought we would lose touch with David while he was in Afghanistan, I was proved wrong. We emailed as often as ever. I reported on daily life back at Tampa, and he spoke of life at the command center in Afghanistan. I think David enjoyed leading the troops in Afghanistan, but I could see that he missed his ordinary life and missed Holly. He was able to return home on a few occasions, and he always made sure that he committed a night for our "double dates." We loved catching up on everything that had happened since we'd last seen each other. Sometimes it seemed as if I knew more about his thoughts and everyday life than I had when we lived a couple of miles away from each other in Tampa.

David's star only rose during his time in Afghanistan. He was the ultimate military leader, so important to our national defense that he was in the enemy's bull's-eye. Later, documents found in Osama bin Laden's Pakistan compound revealed that David had been the target of an al Qaeda assassination plot while there. According to The Washington Post, Petraeus was singled out because he was "the man of the hour ... and killing him would alter the war's path."

As I'd predicted, General Petraeus was in the center of what often seemed an impossible situation. There was little agreement about the best course in Afghanistan — doubling down vs. withdrawing. David believed we were making progress against the Taliban, but not everyone agreed. People wanted an immediate solution. In November 2010, as he prepared to travel to Lisbon for the summit of NATO leaders, I could tell he was under a great deal of stress, his normally unflappable demeanor a little more tense.

Back at MacDill, Lieutenant General John Allen, who had been General Petraeus' deputy commander, stepped in to temporarily fill Petraeus's shoes at CENTCOM before General James Mattis took command in August. I got to know both men quite well, and I was doing my part as a goodwill ambassador to CENTCOM and serving as "the connective tissue" to cement relations between our military brass and the foreign leaders who came to Tampa to visit with them.

General John Allen was not only a consummate warrior and commander but a Virginia gentleman. He was a soldier-scholar who was as comfortable sipping tea in a Bedouin tent with a bunch of grizzled desert sheiks as he was prowling the halls of Congress. General Allen was one of the few men in Washington who could honestly say he had genuine friends on both sides of the aisle. In Iraq, General Allen had overseen and directed the highly successful "Anbar Awakening," in which he recruited Sunni sheiks, whom he invariably addressed as "brothers," to fight against elements of al Qaeda in Iraq's lawless Anbar Province. He was the first Marine Corps officer to be inducted as a term officer in the prestigious Council on Foreign Relations after having overseen all of the Pentagon's vast operations in Asia and the Pacific.

His interests ranged far and wide. General Allen and his wife, Kathy, became good friends of ours, and we often entertained them at our home. Kathy is a warm, supportive woman, the love of John's life. Their love shined through. They often held hands and are clearly delighted with each other.

Just like his predecessor, John spent Christmas at our house with his family, and John and I developed a friendly relationship. John had been mentored by David, so it only seemed logical that I would be able to serve as a goodwill ambassador for both men.

Soon after General Jim Mattis took his position as CENTCOM commander, I coordinated with Jeri-Anne Martin to once again host a welcoming dinner, this time for Mattis. I was immediately charmed by him — and I could see why he was known as one of the most popular generals. He engaged me in a warm conversation about my culture. He explained that he was very familiar with it because he had practically been adopted by the Lebanese community while he was serving in Norfolk, Virginia. He said that, based on his experience in the military, behind every successful negotiation there was a Lebanese person. He also told me that his most trusted interpreter was from a Maronite Lebanese Catholic family, just like my family.

General Mattis became close friends with Scott and me. In spite of his tough military bearing, he is the sweetest man alive. Never married, Jim easily related to us as family, and I was often moved by his warmth and caring. He treated me as if I were a beloved daughter. He came to refer to me in our conversations and correspondence as "young Jill," and even after the worst happened, General Mattis always stuck by me and encouraged me. I was honored that he acknowledged my longtime role with other dignitaries and the command.

General Mattis was quite upbeat and loved his gang and the folks he worked with. However, he was very vocal when he was disappointed or disgruntled by politicians and civilian leaders who didn't have a clue or a plan about the military yet put our troops in harm's way for their own political agenda. He was a general's general.

General Allen had quite the opposite personality, but in a complementary way. He wasn't vocal; he was very private. He didn't share his feelings with others. But he loved the trust and responsibility of his job and the leaders he was serving.

****

In March 2011, General Petraeus came back from Afghanistan for his first round of congressional testimony on the status of the war.

On Friday, March 18th, Scott and I flew to Washington, where David honored us with the highest civilian award for community service, the Outstanding Public Service Award, bestowed by the chairman of the Joint Chiefs. Later that evening, Scott and I met David and Holly for dinner in Washington. David arrived late, and whispered that he'd just left the White House and met with the president about a "new job." His look was of a little kid being given a treat. He told me that the initials consisted of three letters.

"HHS?" I guessed. "FDA?" I was kidding around.

"No, No," he laughed. "Jill, it's at Langley."

I knew he meant the CIA, and I thought he'd be great at the job. But I couldn't resist a gibe: "When are you going to make some money? You've put in enough service."

Not even my teasing could diminish his excitement. But what he was most pressed about was that the president had made his appointment contingent on David's retiring from the military. Coming out of uniform and entering civilian life for the first time in thirty-seven years would be a big transition for him. I noticed that he was a bit wary of the contingency, but I reminded David that James Bond, a civilian, wears tuxedos that are very dapper. He smiled. From then on my nickname for him was "JB."

When we went out again for a double-date dinner a second night, Petraeus told me that, with his new job, we could work together on his diplomatic endeavors. I was thrilled. At that dinner we talked about his replacement as commander in Afghanistan. He seemed genuinely interested in my opinion. I told him I thought it should be Lieutenant General Allen, which would require accelerating his rise to a fourth star.

He tried at first to tell me how impossible that appointment would be, since General Allen had only three stars. But I gave a two-minute impromptu dissertation on General Allen's merits, pointing out that not only was he loyal to Petraeus, but this relationship could foster an important partnership between the military command and the CIA, especially regarding covert missions. He finally agreed, saying, "OK, I trust your opinion about John's leadership and capabilities, so consider it done. I'm coming home."

General Petraeus came home to stay at the end of July 2011. He'd been nominated as CIA director, but had yet to be sworn in. "By the way," he said, "I have a meeting with Duk-Soo Han, the Korean ambassador, next week. I think my safira should be there. He's honoring me with the highest medal given in Korea." I told him I wouldn't miss it.

That same week, I attended General Petraeus' formal retirement ceremony from the U.S. Army. It was a beautiful ceremony on a brilliantly sunny day at the parade ground of Fort Myer, near Arlington, Virginia, with almost a thousand people in attendance. The guest list ranged from U.S. officials, generals, and ambassadors to well-known foreign statesmen.

When I arrived, I was very touched to find out that David had seated me with his family. It seemed as if he had returned to the U.S. draped in laurels, and his future seemed very bright, indeed.

The retiring general's speech at the ceremony was emotional and inspiring. He spoke of his great pride and affection for his fellow soldiers, and he also spoke of the contribution of civilians.

In his speech, David praised the woman who had been by his side through it all — his wife, Holly. With his words I turned to smile at Holly, who deserved every accolade possible. She smiled back and there were tears in her eyes. I knew she was looking forward to this new adventure — to living a life where her husband would come home from work every day, without the constant fear military spouses endure when their husbands or wives are overseas in dangerous lands.

The dinner at the Korean ambassador's residence the following week was spectacular, and I was quite impressed with the ambassador, who had earned a Ph.D. In economics from Harvard and was very charismatic. I was even more honored when David introduced me to the Korean envoy as his ambassador in the United States. David went on to say that I was a behind-the-scenes person with many contacts within the intelligence, military and political arenas, not to mention the economic opportunities that I could promote with the new Free Trade Agreement through my financial friends. Three months later, I received this correspondence:

From: [Consul name redacted] Gmail
Date: January 30, 2012 5:33:52 PM EST
To: Jill and Scott Kelley shared email
Subject: Question from the Korean Embassy

Dear Ms. Jill Kelley,

My name is [redacted], consul at the Korean embassy in Washington DC and I
am writing to ask you a question.
(Ambassador Han Duk-soo gave me your contact information.)

…. issues such as the FTA….
We have heard of your interest in Korea, efforts to strengthen US-Korea relations and cooperation on US-Korea issues such as the FTA. Thus, we are currently looking into appointing you as Honorary consul
of Korea….
….
It would be very helpful if you could let us know whether you are interested in holding such a position. ….
Best regards,
[Consul name redacted]
Consul
Korean Embassy

Although many people have made derisive comments about my role of Honorary Ambassador to CENTCOM and the Korean Embassy, I took them very seriously. I also took my role of friend seriously. I was friends to people who were doing unbelievably important and difficult jobs.

> On Jun 7, 2012, at 11:10 PM, "Allen, John R Gen USMC COMISAF" <john.allen@afghan.swa.army.mil> wrote:
> Classification: UNCLASSIFIED
> Caveats: FOUO
>
> Go to sleep, Jill.
>
> The crisis is called "... the war." Karzai is furious ....The future of how we wage this conflict will hang in the balance of the next few hours and how I'm able to shape the environment around this crisis before Karzai returns.
>
> Just another day in AFG ... another day in paradise.
> ....

> -----------
> From: Jill and Scott Kelley shared email
> Sent: Friday, June 08, 2012 7:49 AM
> To: Allen, John R Gen USMC COMISAF
> Subject: Re: (UNCLASSIFIED)
>
> Be easy on yourself. It is what it is....
>
> It's not you, or does it reflect in your leadership.
> ....
> It is what it is.
> You can only apologize for the tragedy.
> That's exactly what it is. A tragedy.
> I'm sorry.

> -----------
> On Jun 8, 2012, at 2:09 AM, "Allen, John R Gen USMC COMISAF" <john.allen@afghan.swa.army.mil> wrote:
>
> Classification: UNCLASSIFIED
> Caveats: FOUO
>
> I am honored by your friendship.
> ....

I continued to engage with him since he seemed to need a friend that evening. We had a back and forth about his present location, which was Afghanistan. He had just returned from Logar Province.

> **From: Jill and Scott Kelley shared email**
> **Sent: Friday, June 08, 2012 5:26 PM**
> **To: Allen, John R Gen USMC COMISAF**
> **Subject: Re: (UNCLASSIFIED)**
>
> **The news just said you're heading to the Pentagon today to announce the**
> **civilian deaths that occurred last night**
>
> -----------

Maintaining his humor, or perhaps expressing his total exhaustion, he replied:

> **On Jun 8, 2012, at 8:59 AM, "Allen, John R Gen USMC COMISAF"**
> **<john.allen@afghan.swa.army.mil> wrote:**
> **Classification: UNCLASSIFIED**
> **Caveats: FOUO**
>
> **No ...**
> **But perhaps I'll be recalled to the US and fired. I can only hope.**
> **....**

Another email shows his sweetness. He was, and is, a beloved friend in my life. He and Kathy considered me to be a "third daughter." Though sometimes he called me "Sweetheart," it was in that Southern gentleman sort of way. Nothing untoward has ever passed between us. I believe that General Allen is a man of honor and, most important, a great patriot that *personifies* "semper fidelis."
He was also exhausted.

> **On Aug 29, 2012, at 1:57 PM, "Allen, John R Gen USMC COMISAF"**
> **<john.allen@afghan.swa.army.mil> wrote:**
> **UNCLASSIFIED//FOR OFFICIAL USE ONLY**
>
> **Jill ... I really don't want to do anything big. I just want to come home**
> **from the war and rest for a few days.**
> **....**

We all just wanted to envelop General Allen with our support.

From: Jill and Scott Kelley shared email
Sent: Wednesday, August 29, 2012 10:29 PM
To: Allen, John R Gen USMC COMISAF
Subject: Re: (U//FOUO) RE:

I understand, habibi.
I hope to at least see you.

By this point in the war, every email from General Allen broke my heart.

On Aug 29, 2012, at 2:09 PM, "Allen, John R Gen USMC COMISAF" <john.allen@afghan.swa.army.mil> wrote:

UNCLASSIFIED

That will certainly happen ... the spotlight of attention is most uncomfortable for me.
....

I'm tired, Jill ... an AFG just shot four more of my troops ten minutes ago. This is just sucking the life out of me.

I've got to mange this crisis.
....

I was shocked and dismayed.

From: Jill and Scott Kelley shared email
Sent: Wednesday, August 29, 2012 11:06 PM
To: Allen, John R Gen USMC COMISAF
Subject: Re: (U//FOUO) RE:

Oh my God.....
I'm so sorry John. ....
This isn't fair to you, or your brave men out there.

Please stay strong John. I'll take the burden while you give them hope.

They need your motivation and emotional support....
You're everything -to all of us.

He seemed to genuinely appreciate my gesture, but the tragedy was still unfolding:

On Aug 29, 2012, at 2:40 PM, "Allen, John R Gen USMC COMISAF" <john.allen@afghan.swa.army.mil> wrote:

UNCLASSIFIED

....Your friendship means the world to me.

3 of my troops just died of their wounds.
....

I couldn't turn away.

From: Jill and Scott Kelley shared email
Sent: Wednesday, August 29, 2012 11:20 PM
To: Allen, John R Gen USMC COMISAF
Subject: Re: (U//FOUO) RE:

So sad. My heart is broke.
It's not fair! I'm so sorry.

I wish I could be there for you....John

A true gentleman, he responded to kindness with kindness:

On Aug 29, 2012, at 3:11 PM, "Allen, John R Gen USMC COMISAF" <john.allen@afghan.swa.army.mil> wrote:

UNCLASSIFIED

I do as well, Sweetheart.
....

Moved, I wrote back:

From: Jill and Scott Kelley shared email
Date: August 29, 2012 at 4:05:48 PM EDT
To: "Allen, John R Gen USMC COMISAF"
<john.allen@afghan.swa.army.mil>
Subject: Re: (U//FOUO) RE:

John,
I really want to thank you for your 'innumerable' sacrifices you've made, and continue to forfeit, to serve our country for this many years.
I can never thank you enough, or adequately show my appreciation to you, COMISAF
Thank you from the bottom of my heart. I'm eternally grateful.

Semper Fidelis
Sincerely,
Jill

Chapter 4: The Change

This is the end of the beginning, or the beginning of the end. This is no longer a story about two married couples with an amazing friendship. It stops being a story about patriotism. It stops being a story about ambassadorial facilitation. This is where things began to get weird. I noticed a change in Petraeus and, unbeknownst to me, my life was about to change, too.

After General Petraeus returned from Afghanistan, I noticed a marked difference. He seemed much younger and fitter than he had before he deployed — and more stylish, too! He was listening to different music, and tried to encourage me to listen to some of his newfound favorite artists like Enya. Before Afghanistan, I would have described David as a complete nerd. Now, something had changed.

(actual note he jotted down his new choice in music for me to listen to)

David had always been a fitness buff. For as long as I've known him he's worked out every day, usually twice a day, pushing his body to its limits. I'm athletic, too, and we've always bantered back and forth about how many miles we can run, how toned we are, and how much body fat we're carrying, but his emails after Afghanistan revealed a new level of body consciousness.

Typically he'd run 6-10 miles a day, at a pretty fast pace.

From: "Petraeus, David H GEN US ARMY COMISAF"
<david.h.petraeus@afghan.swa.army.mil>
Subject: RE: Dinner with McRaven
Date: August 10, 2011 at 9:26:47 AM EDT
To: Jill and Scott Kelley shared email

6 hard miles, Jill. Sub-7s for most of the way. Left another Agency
guy
in the dust. Then 20 chinups... Get ready!
....

He also urged me on in my workouts.

From: "Petraeus, David H GEN US ARMY COMISAF"
<david.h.petraeus@afghan.swa.army.mil>
Subject: RE: TGIM
Date: August 15, 2011 at 8:36:44 PM EDT
To: Jill and Scott Kelley shared email

7.4 miles ....
Not surprising that you're putting the girls there to shame! Pls
Warn me before you break the sound barrier. Sonic booms are hard
on the
ears!
....

He was also interested in fitting into his slim-fit tux, like James Bond.

From: "Petraeus, David H GEN US ARMY COMISAF"
<david.h.petraeus@afghan.swa.army.mil>
Subject: RE: RE:
Date: September 8, 2011 at 10:20:49 PM EDT
To: Jill and Scott Kelley shared email

Biked 30 mins and later ran 6, ...
And will fit into the tux, no worries!
....
Your workout?
....

Like many people, he enjoyed the endorphin rush of a good work out.

From: "Petraeus, David H Former COMISAF"
<david.h.petraeus@afghan.swa.army.mil>
Subject: RE: RE:
Date: March 28, 2012 at 4:23:14 PM EDT
To: Jill and Scott Kelley shared email
....
And, yes, the gym has been demolished. A monster must have been loose in it!
....

And, yes, he also poked fun at himself for being competitive with his athleticism.

From: "Petraeus, David H Former COMISAF"
<david.h.petraeus@afghan.swa.army.mil>
Subject: RE: RE: RE:
Date: March 28, 2012 at 5:24:14 PM EDT
To: Jill and Scott Kelley shared email

The genetic mutant is back in his cage!
....

Immediately after David became director at the CIA, Scott and I were invited to a private tour of CIA headquarters and Director Petraeus' office, followed by a dinner with David and Holly. We ate at his new favorite restaurant, The Prime Rib, an elegant (jacket required) steakhouse that has a history with former directors. We sat at the "director's table," number 55, and David sat in the big armchair known as the "director's chair." I could tell he was enjoying his new life: new house, new job, new suits, and a new high-profile lifestyle.

In October, we were invited to the annual dinner celebrating the Office of Strategic Services, the forerunner of the modern CIA, where Petraeus gave a short speech honoring our mutual friend, SOCOM (U.S. Special Operations Command) Commander Admiral Eric Olson. Director Petraeus was wearing a new tuxedo. I watched with a bemused smile as he modeled his new tux for us, popping a bottle of champagne in his new home office, before we all entered the multitude of SUVs whisking us from the back door of the event. He seemed to have put on a new personality along with his new James Bond tuxedo.

In November, David substituted his 59th birthday party for an engagement party for his daughter Anne and her fiancé at Plume, the tony restaurant in the Jefferson Hotel not far from the White House. We were honored to join the happy parents celebrating Anne's engagement. Not wanting to miss a chance to relax with a nice bottle of champagne, a week later we belatedly celebrated David's birthday at The Prime Rib.

Official work was a part of many diplomatic fancy dinners. In December, the prime minister of Iraq was to dine with Petraeus in London. Petraeus called upon his wife and his safira, intending for us to entertain the prime minister in D.C. Everything was in motion for a highly anticipated dinner at the Blair House, but the State Department intervened. It was echoed that Secretary Clinton's office had called to express a lack of enthusiasm. I soon learned my seat was revoked, as was Holly Petraeus' seat. When I told the commanders on the base in Tampa, their response was somewhere between annoyance and "not surprised." The sentiment they conveyed to me was: "Between the State Department and the White House, we'll never have any progress or peace, since they only care about an election."

One exchange showed the tension between the State Department and CIA:

On Dec 9, 2011, at 1:36 PM, "Holly Petraeus" wrote:

Dear Jill, Change of plans …. The State Dept now is in charge of the dinner ….David doesn't want to push on this since his agency is not in charge.

….

Love, H.

\-\-\-\-\-\-\-\-\-\-\-\-\-\-

Personally, I would have been thrilled to meet Secretary Clinton, since I admire her.

> From: Jill and Scott Kelley shared email
> Date: December 15, 2011 at 9:35:05 PM EST
> To: Holly and David shared email
>
> ....[Petraeus said] Sec Clinton asked him who I was.
> He said his response, and description of my "affect", made her interested in meeting me ....
>
>
> Jill
>
>
> --------------

Apparently, too, the Prime Minister was interested in meeting with us.

> On Dec 15, 2011, at 9:00 PM, "Petraeus, David H Former COMISAF"<david.h.petraeus@afghan.swa.army.mil> wrote:
>
> .... I thought the PM would be angry that I hadn't brought Holly and you by to see him; however, it just would have been presumptuous given Sec Clinton and all the others there.... Good session with MOD Barak of Israel yesterday, too, as well as with the Yemeni and Turkish... Productive.
>
> ....Will rep the Queen .... tomorrow and then meet with MI-6, ...Then on to Kabul!
>
> All best....

As the year progressed, with Holly and David now living near Langley, we established a cadence of once-a-month "double dates" in addition to other diplomatic, philanthropic, work-related functions we attended. We really did have a close, familial, strictly platonic relationship, as couples often do.

For Christmas that year, we flew to Virginia to spend the holiday with the Petraeuses at their home. I first learned about David's biography at that Christmas dinner.

It began as a festive family dinner that turned into a "did that really happen" moment when David began serving the turkey with the words "So, I have a new biography coming out in January."

"Oh, really?" I remarked as I raised my plate for seconds. "Did you get any money from it?"

He shook his head. "No." He explained that the author was writing about him, but he'd cooperated fully.

I was curious. "Has this author written biographies before?"

"Her name is Paula Broadwell — she's never written anything before."

"Then why in the world would you let her write your biography?"

"He didn't allow it," Holly said, speaking up harshly from across the table. Her eyes blazed; clearly, Holly didn't like this.

David shrugged. "At first, the author told me that it was for her Ph.D., but in the middle of working on it, she said she'd decided to sell it and make it into a biography. I had no choice; she said she already sold it to a publisher."

Witnessing David stumble through an explanation about the biographer, I was so stunned about the situation that I didn't say much of anything. I simply stared at him in utter disbelief. Dozens of great writers would give anything for a chance to write his biography, but this woman, whoever she was, had found a sure way to convince him. David always had a scholarly side, so her "I'm-writing-a-dissertation" approach would have appealed to him. But had she really not considered selling the project until she was halfway through it? Or had she simply postponed revealing her real intentions?

The scenario Petraeus described never seemed credible. I have since learned that as early as June 2010 — before Petraeus even went back to Afghanistan — Broadwell approached a Washington Post reporter and asked about agents for a book she was writing on General David Petraeus. The Post reporter gave her the names of four New York literary agents, and within forty-five minutes of emailing them, one had responded enthusiastically. Of course, I don't know when she had begun working on her manuscript, so I can't say when she changed her mind.

Others noted that she wasn't the ideal choice to be Petraeus' biographer. A professor at Harvard said that when the biographer's name was revealed there was shock among the national security faculty at Harvard because "she just didn't have the background: the academic background, the national security background, or the writing background!"

Now, looking back, I found it strange that Petraeus had spent nearly six months working with a biographer in Afghanistan yet had never once mentioned her in any of his emails or conversations to me. He told me all kinds of details about his daily routine over there. Sometimes he told me what he ate for breakfast and lunch, for heaven's sake.

"All In" was released in January. I didn't know. In fact, I'd forgotten all about it. The only thing I didn't forget was that that was the first time I'd ever seen Holly visibly angry with David, thinking he had been duped by a story about "some Ph.D. thesis" — a bait-and-switch that turned into a biography.

Chapter 5: The A Team

In January 2012, while Paula Broadwell was out promoting her book, Petraeus went about his life as if nothing bad could ever happen. Little did we know.

In January 2012, I was able to reunite General Allen and General Petraeus for the first time since President Obama had split them from Central Command in 2010. The dinner was unforgettable. Of course, they both got their digs at me for all the sarcastic comments and grief I'd given them from halfway around the world. It was the best night ever with my two best sets of friends: the Allens and the Petraeuses.

We always had a great time at these dinners: Conversation flowed, wine flowed and we joked around with one another. One of the traditions of the evening was to take a photograph. I tilt my head a lot in photos. Well, Petraeus and Allen used this as an opportunity for some lighthearted ribbing. That night, they insisted on taking two photographs: one with my head tilted, and one with all of our heads tilted.

I attached the photos with my emails:

From: Jill and Scott Kelley shared email
Date: January 15, 2012 at 7:11:40 PM EST
To: John Gen MIL USMC USCENTCOM Commander Allen
<john.allen@afghan.swa.army.mil>, Kathy Allen AOL email address,
Holly and David Petraeus AOL email address
Subject: #3

Speaking of no more Head-Tilt......
What's happened to my seat mates?????
-at least give me a chance to open my eyes....before you "set your necks"

Not Nice, boys! Grrrrrrrrrr.....!!!!!!!

From: Jill and Scott Kelley shared email
Sent: Sunday, January 15, 2012 7:25 PM
To: Kathy Allen; Allen, John R Gen USMC COMISAF; Holly Petraeus

Subject: Last photo

Now.....EVERYONE is straight
That's much better!

Thank you for being part of an unforgettable evening with great food,

fun friends, and rare wines...

Looking forward to making many more memories together!

Thank you again John & David for your Leadership - but most importantly
our friendship.
Love, always
Jill
Classification: UNCLASSIFIED
Caveats: FOUO

General Allen sincerely thanked me for hosting the event.

On Jan 15, 2012, at 8:13 PM, "Allen, John R Gen USMC COMISAF"
<john.allen@afghan.swa.army.mil> wrote:

Classification: UNCLASSIFIED
Caveats: FOUO

….What a great evening.

Hope to see you in MAR.

....

John

I responded:

From: Jill and Scott Kelley shared email
Date: January 15, 2012 at 11:22:34 PM EST
To: "Allen, John R Gen USMC COMISAF"
<john.allen@afghan.swa.army.mil>
Cc: Kathy Allen AOL email address, Holly and David Petraeus AOL
email address
Subject: Re: Last photo (UNCLASSIFIED)

Please don't thank me....it was both my pleasure and honor!
It's the least I can do to show my appreciation for your countless years
of dedication and service to David....
And now for your glorious Command of the most famous war in
history.
Thank you, COMISAF

We all look forward in seeing you in March, inshallah!

Hopefully, the "head-tilt" will make you excited to come home and do
it again! It's very catchy! Hehe! :-)

Please travel safe, and keep these photos as special memories when
you're back in Kabul.
Be safe, John. Allah maak!

Sincerely,
Jill

In January 2012, we felt like the A team, on top of the world.
To be honest, it's both sad and eerie to see the happiness captured in
these photos. Scott and I truly believed everything was great, and our
passion and undying patriotism were our shields against evil. Only
later did we witness the domino effect of betrayals and experience the

way political motivations could ruin the standing of respected generals, thus putting the country at risk.

At the end of January 2012, Scott and I held our annual coalition appreciation reception to celebrate Gasparilla with the troops and the brass at MacDill. It was quite an event. The U.S. and foreign military couldn't have had a finer time. News crews were in the flotilla and in towers along the parade route, and helicopters filmed the event from the air as crowds gathered to catch beads and watch the pirate krewes stumble down Bayshore.

Of course, since CENTCOM organized my coalition appreciation event, I wanted to make sure that I had permission to represent them. Out of respect for protocol, I always ran my speech past the commander before the event. General Mattis came back with a response I found gratifying, especially coming from a man who doesn't mince words. As can be seen in the email below, I also forwarded him an old copy of my resume that the Pentagon had on file, since protocol dictates that each embassy's protocol office receive a resume before an introduction.

> **From: Jill and Scott Kelley shared email**
> **Sent: Friday, January 27, 2012 10:14 AM**
> **To: Mattis, James N Gen MIL USMC USCENTCOM CCCC-CCCC**
> **Subject: Re: RE:**
>
> **Glad you liked my Bio!**
> **Last night was lovely. The UK Ambassador is a big fan of yours...we hit it off!!!**
>
> **I'm practicing my speech for tomorrow.... since almost 60 Nations will be representing themselves at my home**
> **-for my 3rd Official Appreciation Reception.**
>
>
> **My speech is pretty heavy... and will stress the importance of Coalition's zealous advocacy and support to the US Military - especially in the War in AFG and the global war on terror.**
> **Let's hope I don't forget my lines! :-)**
>
> **I hope to see you soon, Jim-and thank you for everything you do, to preserve everything we have.**
>
> **Your friend,**
> **Jill**

General Mattis was incredibly gracious to me. He really boosted my confidence, and he reiterated his promise to make me an official honorary ambassador.

> **From: "Mattis, James N Gen MIL USMC USCENTCOM CCCC-CCCC" <james.mattis@centcom.mil>**
> **Date: January 27, 2012 12:24:19 PM EST**
> **To: Jill and Scott Kelley shared email**
> **Subject: RE: RE:**
>
> **Dear Young Jill: You won't forget your lines....We need to make you "official"....You're making more peaceful waves than any foreign ministry on earth. Best, Jim**

During the Gasparilla reception I spoke with every person at our gathering. I thanked coalition members for their service and assured them: "My home is your home." My speech to the gathering was full of the gratitude I felt for the troops, and our feelings of patriotism:

> Dr. Kelley and I are honored, once again, to host the coalition's top foreign delegates, that represent over 60 nations from around the world.
>
> I want to begin with stating my immeasurable gratitude to the coalition and multinational forces for their selfless service to our United States military.
>
> I stand before you, and stress the importance of your nation's zealous advocacy and avid support to the U.S. military — especially in the time of war.
>
> The coalition's steadfast dedication is essential to stop terrorism and spread peace and democracy around the world. On behalf of Central Command, I wholeheartedly thank the 60 nations that make up our amazing coalition. I am humbled by your presence today.
>
> That said, I also welcome my civilian leaders, my guests here today. Your representation is the visible sign of our great

democracy even being in the midst of a long war... and dangerous Arab Spring setting the world on fire, we still uninterruptedly maintain the peace, freedoms and democracies that protesters around the world are dying for.

However, we must never forget that our freedom does not come without a price. This great privilege comes with the daily cost of our U.S. soldiers' undying commitment, endless dedication, and heroic acts to defend our borders far and wide.

Dr. Kelley and I offer our eternal gratitude and sincere appreciation for the immeasurable sacrifices of our U.S. troops. It is only because of you that we remain free, the home of the brave.

I dedicate this 3rd annual coalition appreciation reception to Central Command and the Special Operations soldiers. We are both humbled and yet honored by your presence...Thank you, and God bless America!

In February, General Mattis congratulated me after I had represented the CENTCOM coalition at the embassy of New Zealand:

From: Jill and Scott Kelley shared email
Sent: Sunday, February 05, 2012 8:14 PM
To: Mattis, James N Gen MIL USMC USCENTCOM CCCC-CCCC
Subject: Thank you!

Jim,
I hope all is well on this epic Super Bowl night :-)

I wanted to thank you for the great privilege last night representing Central Command -to it's dedicated Coalition.

Surprisingly, the Host already heard about Mrs. Kelley -since his past SNR's wrote home about my support to the NZ troops stationed at CentCom :-)

As you could predict, the Kiwi's were a pleasure to meet. They were whole heartedly warm, welcoming, and truly grateful for my company. Surprisingly, we had many things in common, but the most important similarity -was our allegiance and commitment to our success in AFG

Last night was quite an honor (and pleasure) to thank the NZ Military in person, for their steadfast service to our US Military and our mission around the world.

Needless to say, I wish you were there, since the dinner was excellent, our message of our appreciation was brilliantly conveyed, and the memory was truly unforgettable.

Without said, thank you for the humbling honor to allow me to continue building and re-enforcing our essential relationship (and mission) with over 60 Nations around the world.

Your Ambassador-at-Large
Jill
ps DCDR Harward was an absolute RockStar!

With humor and praise, he responded.

On Feb 5, 2012, at 8:27 PM, "Mattis, James N Gen MIL USMC USCENTCOM CCCC-CCCC"<james.mattis@centcom.mil> wrote:

Dear Young Jill: ...And trust me, my fine Ambassador, your reputation has circuited the world and is the subject of discussions near & far, as New Zealand demonstrated last night. ....Thanks very much for being there and for thanking them as only an all-American lady can do so well--their lads have been in the fight with us since December 2001.
All my best .... Back in a couple weeks. Jim

Flattered, I responded in kind:

From: Jill and Scott Kelley shared email
Date: February 6, 2012 at 8:35:59 AM EST
To: "Mattis, James N Gen MIL USMC USCENTCOM CCCC-CCCC" <james.mattis@centcom.mil>
Subject: Re: Thank you!

Thank you for your priceless email....your opinion mean the world to me, Jim

Incidentally, I was telling the Kiwi's that, in my past 10 years supporting Central Command, I find Gen Mattis is the most acute, insightful, and intelligent of all the Commanders.....
And it's more extraordinary to see such brilliance and cognition -on such an unpretentious General.

....

Thank you again Jim -for everything!
We look forward to seeing you when you return.
Please be safe...

Your (proud) Ambassador,
Jill

General Mattis was true to his word to make me the official honorary ambassador to CENTCOM. He finished up the business General Petraeus had left over when he left for Afghanistan. On April 19, 2012, CENTCOM made me the official honorary ambassador.

From: "Martin, Jeri-anne H Ms CIV USAF USCENTCOM CCDC-CSP"
<jeri-anne.martin@centcom.mil>
Date: April 16, 2012 at 12:18:17 PM EDT
To: Jill and Scott Kelley shared email
Subject: FW: Invite

Dearest Jill,

I finally received approval on the invitation write up from the DCDR's office.... Call me at my desk ....

All the best,

Vice Admiral Robert S. Harward
Deputy Commander, United States Central Command
requests the pleasure of your company at
a recognition ceremony in honor of
Mrs. Jill Kelley
as United States Central Command and Coalition
Honorary Ambassador
on Thursday, the nineteenth of April
at twelve o'clock
Main Conference Room
MacDill Air Force Base, Florida

R.s.v.p. (813) 529-0402   *Attire: Uniform of the Day*
Email: protocol@centcom.mil   *Civilian Casual*
..

Chief of Protocol
U.S. Central Command
7115 S Boundary Blvd., Bldg. 570
MacDill AFB, FL 33635

Tel: (813) 529-XXXX / DSN: (312) 529-XXXX

The need to make me official was partly financial and paperwork-related: When the Pentagon would itemize official Defense-funded dinner meetings with visiting dignitaries, there were always questions related to my being the only civilian in attendance. But I was led to understand another reason many wanted to me to be their official honorary ambassador was to sidestep the ineffective State Department guys.   The command felt that, being at war, the military's progress was not being served by the State Department's seemingly domestic political agenda. Simply put: It was felt that the sterile State Department guys weren't going to win friends or grease the wheels of diplomacy when their goals weren't aligned with our military strategy.

It was a wonderful event, the culmination of all of my hard work.   And there was a large turnout — much bigger than I'd expected. I was a bit nervous at how people would respond to the creation of this new role, but I was welcomed and thanked by many, including General Allen.

On Apr 19, 2012, at 11:26 AM, "Allen, John R Gen USMC COMISAF"
<john.allen@afghan.swa.army.mil> wrote:

You'll be great ... as you always are. Poised. Articulate. Loving. A strong leader. ....

The room was packed with representatives of the U.S. and foreign military. I rose to give my speech, with my husband and parents beaming in the audience.

I'm honored to be here today, among so many heroes! I've met each one of you when you each arrived for your tour at Central Command, and I immediately thanked you for bravely serving your respective nations against a common enemy with the United States. I then told you "my home is your home." And after 10 years of supporting the U.S. commanders and coalition, my home officially became the ambassador's residence for the U.S. and foreign troops.

I do this because I love my country. And most of all, I appreciate each one of your countless sacrifices, undying dedication, and heroic acts in Afghanistan and throughout the world. Undivided, we will defeat the enemy.

That said, I stress the importance of the coalition's continuous support and service — despite the distractions of an election year and the propaganda that shakes confidence of our mission. Your commitment is essential in our mission to bring democracy and peace around the world. And in order to prevail in our mission, we must remain dedicated to our credence and genesis.

As your honorary ambassador, I will remain committed to advancing international exchange, cultivating global trust, and promoting camaraderie within the command.

With General Praestegaard, I will zealously promote the U.S. and coalition's relations, protect and preserve their interests and efforts.

But before I end my speech, I have to express my eternal gratitude to General Mattis and, especially, Admiral John Harward. Without your unwavering support, this day would NOT be a reality. I can only imagine what that SEAL did behind closed doors! Thank you, Admiral Harward.

I would also like to thank my husband, Dr. Scott Kelley — my better half, and soul mate — who has supported me and my love for diplomacy and our country. Thank you for your love and support, Scott.

And last but not least, my parents. They have been my foundation for greatness, determination and integrity. Without them, I would be not be the person I have become.

Thank you again for the honor to represent the largest, greatest military superpower in the world. I am humbled by the privilege, and title.

Thank you.

I choked up a little as I saw tears run down my father's face. It was very moving. Then I added a small speech in classical Arabic for the Middle Eastern nations in the coalition. I told them that as their new ambassador, I would emphasize the importance of cross-cultural and interfaith dialogue in order to foster a greater understanding, tolerance and acceptance between the USA and the Islamic world. And I thanked them for aligning with the USA in fighting the "common enemy." And I urged them not to let any "agenda or propaganda" shake their confidence in commitment in Afghanistan or in the global war on terror. Admiral Bob Harward got up and spoke. He explained how it had been decided to designate this new position, and why the CENTCOM unilaterally chose me. He told the audience about how General Petraeus and I had pioneered this effort to build bridges between the U.S. and its international allies, and how this effort was especially important in a time of war. He also spoke of how I had continued the work after Petraeus left. I was very humbled and flattered by his warm endorsement.

The reception afterward was truly spectacular. I shook hundreds of hands in the receiving line, and cut the huge cake, which looked like a wedding cake. Afterward, a member of the CENTCOM team took my parents for a VIP tour. It was a wonderful day for my parents. We took them to the yacht club for dinner and celebrated with a huge feast and many champagne toasts. Throughout dinner, they couldn't stop telling me how proud they were to see their daughter so poised, elegant, and articulate. They told me I had stood so tall and composed when I delivered my speech — like a true ambassador. At dinner, my mother reminded me of a comment I'd made to her during my trip to Villa Taverna, Rome, with the American ambassador when I was 23 years old. "Do you remember when you said, 'Mom, I want to be an ambassador one day'?" she said. I looked at her with a smile and said, "I can't believe you remember that." "A mother never forgets her daughter's wishes and always hopes to live long enough to see them come true," she replied.

That evening, emails continued to roll in by those who had witnessed and supported my new appointment.

> From: "Petraeus, David H Former COMISAF"
> <david.h.petraeus@afghan.swa.army.mil>
> Subject: RE:
> Date: April 19, 2012 at 4:26:05 PM EDT
> To: Jill and Scott Kelley shared email account
> Cc: Holly Petraeus AOL
>
> Mabruk, Jill. ....Thanks again for all that you have done -- and will do. Congrats again -
> ....

Jerri-Anne was also congratulatory:

> From: "Martin, Jeri-anne H Ms CIV USAF USCENTCOM CCDC-CSP" <jeri-anne.martin@centcom.mil>
> Subject: Re:
> Date: April 19, 2012 at 6:21:46 PM EDT
> To: Jill and Scott Kelley shared email account
>
> Jill,

.... congratulations as our first USCENTCOM Coalition Honorary Ambassador!
....
Your friend,
Jeri

Jeri-Anne Martin
Chief of Protocol
Sent by blackberry
(813) 966-XXXX

Admiral Harward was also generous in his praise.

From: "Harward, Robert S VADM MIL USN USCENTCOM CCDC-DCDR" <robert.harward@centcom.mil>
Subject:
Date: April 19, 2012 at 1:01:02 PM EDT
To: Jill and Scott Kelley shared email account

Ambassador Kelley, Congratulations and well deserved.   Bob
....
Robert S. Harward
Vice Admiral, USN
Deputy Commander
U.S. Central Command
Comm - 813.529.XXXX DSN 5XX
SVOIP - 302.529.XXXX
DRSN - 80.529.XXXX
Cell - 813.422.XXXX
NIPR: robert.harward@centcom.mil
SIPR: robert.harward@centcom.smil.mil

General Mattis, despite being in Baghdad, weathered-in by a dust storm, was kind and amazingly timely with his congratulations:

From: "Mattis, James N Gen MIL USMC USCENTCOM CCCC-CCCC" <james.mattis@centcom.mil>
Subject: RE:
Date: April 19, 2012 at 9:25:50 PM EDT
To: Jill and Scott Kelley shared email account

Congratulations, Jill! ...I wasn't there physically but was there in spirit with you on this special day and I'm sure that the speech in Arabic will be long remembered ....
Well done to you and thank you for all that you do for the Coalition.   Building friends and allies, one at a time....   All my best to you, Scott and Natalie, Jim
....

A few days later, General Allen was continuing the fight on the war on terror. In this funny email from him, cc'ing his wife, Kathy, we joked about a game changer in the war strategy by using his "new" (official) Madame Ambassador to gain the enemy's love.

On May 9, 2012, at 2:30 PM, "Allen, John R Gen USMC COMISAF" <john.allen@afghan.swa.army.mil> wrote:

Classification: UNCLASSIFIED
Caveats: FOUO

I'm beginning to think these Al Qaeda fellows are never going to warm up to me.

DUBAI, May 9, 2012 (AFP) - Al-Qaeda head Ayman al-Zawahiri rejected
the US apology over the burning of Koran copies at a base in Afghanistan, urging all Muslims to support the Taliban, SITE Intelligence Group reported Wednesday.

.... Zawahiri criticised Obama's apology.

"After each of their crimes, they pretend to be sorry....
The American Crusaders and their allies showed over and over again their hatred and envy of Islam, the book of Islam, the prophet (of) Islam," Zawahiri said.

....
Zawahiri delivered a similar message in March, urging Afghans to rise up against "Crusader pigs" after US Marines were shown in an Internet
video urinating on the corpses of Taliban militants.
....

Sensing that he was trying to locate the silver lining in the cloud, I replied:

From: Jill and Scott Kelley shared email
Sent: Wednesday, May 09, 2012 11:09 PM
To: Allen, John R Gen USMC COMISAF
Cc: Kathy Allen AOL email address
Subject: Re: Qaeda chief slams US sorry for Koran burning
(UNCLASSIFIED)

No....I'm not feeling the love yet!

Our banter continued for a bit:

On May 9, 2012, at 2:43 PM, "Allen, John R Gen USMC COMISAF"
<john.allen@afghan.swa.army.mil> wrote:

Classification: UNCLASSIFIED
Caveats: FOUO

My guess is if they met you they'd like me even more
....

As always, I continued to express my support:

From: Jill Kelley
Date: May 9, 2012 at 3:15:54 PM EDT
To: "Allen, John R Gen USMC COMISAF"
<john.allen@afghan.swa.army.mil>
Cc: Kathy Allen AOL email address
Subject: Re: Qaeda chief slams US sorry for Koran
burning (UNCLASSIFIED)

Let's do it!
My bags are packed!
:-)

Even though I'm upbeat and uplifting, I took my role of ambassador very seriously, even as the stalker madness began to unfold. Despite the stresses, I hosted several events while fulfilling the role of CENTCOM honorary ambassador well enough to garner recognition. The king of Jordan enjoyed the company that General Mattis, Scott, and I provided; and he obviously enjoyed some of the ideas that I put forth, too.

On May 20, 2011, at 11:28 AM, "Mattis, James N Gen MIL USMC USCENTCOM CCCC-CCCC" <james.mattis@centcom.mil> wrote:

Dear Jill: Regret that I won't be in Tampa on Tuesday, but I know you'll do just fine without me there. You remain our best Ambassador....
.... Jim

From: Jill and Scott Kelley shared email
Sent: Saturday, May 21, 2011 11:02 PM
To: Mattis, James N Gen MIL USMC USCENTCOM CCCC-CCCC
Subject: Re: Thank you!

Bummer x2!
I would have been honored to join you in DC!

Nonetheless, I promise to carry the torch for you, Commander
....

More curently, if you read today's NYT   (and the other papers) it covered the King's meeting with the President.

It's exactly what he and I were discussing over dinner at your house! Scott read the newspaper first, then handed it to me and said "look Jill, the King really did like your perspective. He articulated your argument verbatim" Surprisingly, the King used my take, to convey his strong message to the President Pretty cool stuff!! -glad to see there's an Arab nation trying to be a gatekeeper for peace.
Jim wherever you are, please be safe!

Your friend
Jill

Mattis responded with encouragement:

**From: "Mattis, James N Gen MIL USMC USCENTCOM CCCC-
CCCC" <james.mattis@centcom.mil>
Date: May 22, 2011 at 7:24:34 AM EDT
To: Jill and Scott Kelley shared email
Subject: RE: Thank you!**

**Like I say, young Jill, you are a GREAT ambassador. Keep advising
Kings and Soldiers, we'll have a better world with your refreshing
advice guiding some folks. You're a Natural at this stuff.
…. My best to Scott and Natalie. Jim**

Chapter 6: James Bond

"The Spymaster" may have fancied himself James Bond, but I was never a Bond girl. Before I go further, I feel the need to take a side trip to explain how the special "Sayida Safira" (Madame Ambassador) had unusual access to the director of the CIA. It was a bona fide title, and my role was vetted.

At the end of summer in 2011, the U.S. Senate held a hearing to vet Petraeus for the role of director of the CIA. Everyone expected it to be a slam dunk: He was qualified and well-respected. Apparently, though, this session was unusually long.

During a break in the closed confirmation hearing, a senator emerged and began to leak information. He cozied up to a reporter whom he knew and trusted. This particular journalist specializes in stories related to the intelligence community.

Unbeknownst to me at the time, I was the snag in Petraeus' confirmation hearing. According to the reporter, in the vetting process, Petraeus had revealed that I was his confidante, so the committee and CIA needed to take the extra time to vet me before confirming Petraeus. In swift order, I was vetted and cleared, and Petraeus became director of the CIA.

Still, the reporter was shocked to hear my name for the first time that day. This reporter had covered the "intelligence beat" for over a decade without ever hearing my name. To hear an unknown name in such an unusual and important setting stood out; the reporter was intrigued and genuinely surprised.

A few weeks later, this same reporter was approached by Paula Broadwell. In that meeting, Broadwell asked the reporter what was known about me since she (Broadwell) was supposed to interview me "for the chapter on leadership" per Petraeus' request. The reporter divulged to Broadwell that a source stated "off the record" that the vetting took extra time to account for vetting me, but that everything (obviously) passed muster. Broadwell anxiously began to ask more questions, and the reporter simply said that I was Petraeus' "confidante." Miffed at the odd line of questioning, the reporter recommended that maybe Broadwell should go and interview me as Petraeus had suggested.

Much later, David confirmed that he had, in fact, mentioned my name to Paula Broadwell for the biography's chapter on leadership. He wanted her to interview me and speak about my relationships with the diplomatic community, with particular focus on cross-cultural dialogue with our coalition allies. He said that when the mistress was confronted with the characterization of me as Petraeus' confidante, and saw a photograph of me, she became overwhelmed with feelings of jealousy.

Again, I never knew that I'd been brought up during this vetting process. David simply didn't mention it, so I don't even know if he knew that I was the reason for the delay. Regardless, we were approved for correspondence and approved for a close professional relationship. I was unknowingly vetted at the highest levels and I passed. After Petraeus assumed the command of the CIA, we were determined to continue our mission of peace and diplomacy in Washington, D.C., through his new position at Langley.

Director Petraeus was a success, in part because he wore an array of hats at the CIA. Not only was he the spy chief, but he was also acting as a diplomat, statesman, spinmaster, and CEO. Throughout his early tenure, he kept me apprised of many of his successes, including attaining better investment terms for the Silicon Valley companies that team with the CIA. (Yes, the CIA invests in a for-profit business.) Petraeus did his job exceptionally well. I had the highest respect for his "petraen" leadership in Silicon Valley. In our daily banter about his activities, I expressed that I'm not as keen on Venture Capitalists as David was. (But since then, I've gained a new respect and become friends with many VCs and indeed journalists who changed my perception in the years since I wrote this email.)

:

From: Jill and Scott Kelley shared email
Sent: Wednesday, February 29, 2012 2:55 PM
To: Petraeus, David H Former COMISAF
Subject: Re: OUT OF OFFICE REPLY Re: RE: RE: RE:

Ugh! VC's?
I meet with them all the time in NY.....
You'll quickly realize they're all naysayers, and pretty much talking heads -they can't think outside the box!

Petraeus' excitement about the partnership opportunities was contagious:

> On Feb 29, 2012, at 3:10 PM, "Petraeus, David H Former COMISAF"<david.h.petraeus@afghan.swa.army.mil> wrote:
>
> They provide $9 in venture cap for every dollar we put in to our firm... More after tonight!
> ....
>
> ---------

He convinced me:

> From: Jill and Scott Kelley shared email
> Date: March 1, 2012 at 2:55:35 AM EST
> To: "Petraeus, David H Former COMISAF"
> <david.h.petraeus@afghan.swa.army.mil>
> Subject: Re: OUT OF OFFICE REPLY Re: RE: RE: RE:
>
> Awesome!
> Wish I was there...
> Sounds neat.
>
> But you should know that you're truly extraordinary, David.
> You never cease to amaze me!

****

April 2012 brought Florida sunshine, Easter egg hunts for my children, and the delivery of Easter baskets to the Petraeuses' house in Virginia. By this point, Scott and I had been friends with the Petraeuses for years, and we enjoyed our monthly double dates. We decided to make our Easter dinner at Bourbon Steak in the Four Seasons in Georgetown. I took my usual seat by David, and Holly sat, as usual, at my right. Natalie sat at David's left. Also in attendance were David and Holly's adult children.

The families gathered around a bare table, nicely appointed with modern flair, but without linens. The wine flowed easily. We all enjoyed good times as old friends. David and Holly brought their son, Stephen, to dinner since he had just come back from war. My sister brought her boyfriend.

At the table, David and I bragged about our recent athletic accomplishments since we were "calling each other out" to a race. We tested each other's muscles to see who had the hardest quadriceps, while our spouses looked on in tolerant amusement, as they understood our athletic competitiveness. Perhaps a bit tipsy, David got a little enthusiastic comparing our quads. Bear in mind that at all times, we were seated with our spouses along with my sister and David's son. They all know that David and I constantly joke around like this. I can only speculate that situations like this could have been misinterpreted by others, including Paula. At that time, I enjoyed a private life and never even new who Paula was. To this day, I've never met her.

Back to the dinner, there was too much alcohol flowing that day. Leaning toward me, David sloppily spilled wine on my dress. To tell the truth, I thought little of it. David was just blowing off steam. The next day, I sent an email with photos to Kathy and John Allen.

From: Jill and Scott Kelley shared email
Date: April 8, 2012 at 8:20:58 PM EDT
To: Kathy Allen AOL, John Gen MIL USMC USCENTCOM
Commander Allen <john.allen@afghan.swa.army.mil>
Subject: Happy Easter

Happy Easter!
We were out with David & Holly last night and speaking about you!

Please wish your family our best!
Love
Jill

As you can see, these Easter photos were familial in nature. There were no table linens, just good food and plenty of wine glasses. Everything, quite literally, was "in the open" with our family members present. You might also note that the photos show my sister and I posing our best sides by leaning on an arm to get an angular line for the photo: I admit I'm a bit vain sometimes. You can also tell that Petraeus was a bit squinty-eyed from too much wine!

That dinner was to be our last together in peace. It really was a fine dinner, with nothing weird or unusual about it. But that didn't last long. Within a few days, David began to get weird and cryptic. He really wasn't being himself. I was willing to overlook it at the beginning.

A few days later, on April 14, 2012, a subdued David Petraeus sent me an email that I didn't think too much about at first:

"Petraeus, David H Former COMISAF"
<david.h.petraeus@afghan.swa.army.mil> wrote:

Two key points: first, we enjoyed very much the friendship between our tribes and deeply appreciate all that you/S have done for us, the coalition, and so on -- and love the girls, of course; but, second, can't repeat events of the latter part of the dinner last Sat night. OK?
....

To: "Petraeus, David H Former COMISAF"
<david.h.petraeus@afghan.swa.army.mil>
From: Jill and Scott Kelley shared email
Date: April 14, 2012

Yup! But no need to apologize for spilling your drink on me, Bond. No big deal.

Originally, I chalked up his odd response to some sort of hangover guilt — that feeling you get when you realize that you drank way too much. Furthermore, when people are tipsy, they sometimes lose their motor skills. Petraeus is no different than the rest of us. I remember several dinners where David spilled his wine. Even spilling wine on my dress wasn't a surprise. I have a good dry cleaner; it wasn't anything worth worrying about, so I moved on quickly.

It turns out there was a subtext to David's email that I didn't know about at the time. This relaxed evening with friends turned out to be fateful. How could any of us know what was about to happen? It barely makes sense even in retrospect.

Chapter 7: The Stalker

*In this chapter, I am unwittingly sucked into an alternative universe.
I think I'm in a spy novel — or a horror movie. Someone's tailing me
and knows the itineraries of the top brass. I'm told I'm being watched
and photographed. Is it a stalker, an assassin, or a rogue terrorist?
My efforts to figure out what's going on uncover all sorts of odd
dynamics. Only later will I come to understand the gravity, the very
serious nature of my initial interactions with the FBI.
I have come to believe that agents within the FBI did identify the
stalker fairly quickly. But, for whatever reason, someone decided to
allow the director of the CIA to continue to be compromised, his
emails to be improperly accessed, and innocent people to be stalked
and terrorized. The political intrigue began here, and still isn't done.*

In 2012, Washington, D.C., was experiencing the third-warmest May on record. The balmy setting lifted most people's spirits — including mine. As coincidence would have it, I was in Washington on May 11, emailing Kathy Allen about something or other, when all of a sudden I received an email from John, who was in Kabul.

> **From: John Allen AOL email address**
> **Date: May 11, 2012 at 2 at 2:29 PM**
> **To: Jill Kelley**
> **Subject: Re: Strange note**
>
> Jill ... I received a strange note from someone with an e-mail address
> called: kelleypatrol. It was a gmail.com domain. The message said
> something like: "Be careful at dinner, she'll play with you under the
> table as she has other generals." It was unsigned. ....I was sitting at
> my computer when it came up on the government account and I
> deleted right away. ....
>
> Let's stay on AOL for now.
>
> ----------

This was literally the first time I'd ever heard of this. I was truly taken by surprise.

> **From: Jill and Scott Kelley shared email**
> **Date: May 11, 2012 at 2:33:41 PM EDT**
> **To: John Allen AOL email address**
> **Subject: Re: Strange note**
>
> **That's so bizzare!**
> **Can you find out who sent it??**
> **Can you call me in 25 min?**
>
> ----------

I didn't really realize that I had asked for a trace, but that's what I had done, in effect. He was reticent:

> **From: John Allen AOL email address**
> **Date: May 11, 2012 2:59:56 PM EDT**
> **To: Jill and Scott Kelley shared email**
>
> **Subject: Re: Strange note**
> **I don't think it would be a very good idea for me attempt to trace an address, Jill.**
>
> **....Only person ever opened on our e-mails is Kathy. Our correspondence is innocent anyway. Would seem to be someone from Stateside who has some sense of the crowds in which you move.**

General Allen responded almost immediately to my request that he call me. I could tell by his voice that he was worried. "I'm not concerned about this silly business of touching under the table" (since John knew David and I were childish when it came to flaunting our athletic prowess), he said. "I'm really worried about this upcoming dinner. No one's supposed to know about it. No one even knows I'm coming to the States." I asked John if he was concerned about my safety. "Yes. You don't have security to protect you. And since you have three young precious children at home, I think we should cancel this dinner."

Later in the day, John forwarded me the original email. I couldn't sit still. I really wanted General Allen to trace the email since it was clearly someone tracing my comings and goings, including diplomatic dinners with top Generals.

He still wouldn't trace it, but he did figure out how to retrieve it from the trash.

On May 11, 2012, at 2:40 PM, John Allen AOL email address wrote:

Found the note. It was titled "Jill Kelley" and read: "Just don't let her play with you under the table at your dinner this month like she does to charm other four-star officers, Ambassadors, and officials... "

It was sent by someone who knows we're having dinner this month. Very strange

....

Obviously, I was mortified. But I was also deeply curious and concerned.

From:Jill and Scott Kelley shared email
To:John Allen AOL email address
Sent: Fri, May 11, 2012 11:16 pm
Subject: Re: Strange note

Can you trace it?
That scares me!
First of all, it's NOT true. So want to know who knows of my dinners

The upcoming dinner was to be a big deal. It was a really important diplomatic dinner — not a gathering of old friends over some nice food. This one was top secret, since it involved a war commander. Terrorists would have salivated to know General Allen's itinerary. The dinner was set for May 22, 2012. Its purpose was to introduce General Allen, who was to replace David in Afghanistan, to the United Kingdom's top intelligence, military and diplomatic officials — essentially the war leaders, because England had the most weight in choosing the post for Supreme Allied Commander of NATO forces in Europe. The British ambassador had invited his minister of defense and the head of MI6, the British foreign intelligence service — the equivalent of the CIA — and the commander of the British forces. Kathy Allen was also to be in attendance.

This sort of assessment is common for Europeans, who tend to want to evaluate both the man and his wife in a dinner setting, rather than the sort of individualistic and formal interviews to which Americans have become accustomed. The Brits are the most influential of the NATO allies, and the dinner was a way for them to meet John informally. Impressing the British "cousins" can be immensely helpful in overcoming any NATO objections to a new American commander in Brussels.

General Allen pondered whether or not to cancel the dinner because of this puzzling email. Many regarded John Allen as the most effective commander of the U.S. and coalition troops during our decade-long war in Afghanistan. I knew how much this dinner meant to him. Being tapped as the Supreme Allied Commander of NATO forces in Europe would be a fitting capstone to his brilliant career. Safety was paramount, but this dinner was a golden opportunity.

I definitely did not want to cancel this dinner, and with it his opportunity to be evaluated for the position of commander of NATO forces. "OK," he replied. "But I'll come armed. Kathy and I will pick you up at your hotel, and I'll escort you." I swallowed hard. Just the fact that John thought I needed his protection made me nervous, but it was also comforting.

Later, I discovered that David Petraeus must have also received stalking emails with threats. On May 11, David suggested that we move our double-date dinner, at which we would celebrate Scott's forty-sixth birthday, to the Cosmo Club, a prestigious private club in D.C. This was an unusual choice, because David liked to people-watch and let his hair down, but the Cosmo Club is old school and doesn't have that kind of atmosphere.

That night was just weird. I was not seated next to David, at his request. Even Holly was surprised at the new and unusual seating arrangement, since this was the first time in years that he hadn't insisted on sitting next to me. And it was most unusual when he didn't drink at all that night, except for Scott's birthday toast. Meanwhile, all night long, David was preoccupied, looking over his shoulder in a paranoid way.

After dinner, he suggested that we take a tour of the grand library, located on the third floor. He led us to the back elevator, effectively dodging his security detail. Without saying a word of explanation to his security, he looked at us and simply said, "Let's get in the elevator and see how long it takes the security detail to find me in case something happens to the director of the CIA. Let's ride it to the bottom floor and see how long it would take for them to locate me."

While in the elevator with Natalie and me, he referenced our upcoming shared birthday the following month, suggesting we would be turning forty, when we were in fact turning just thirty-seven. Why did he think that this was going to be our landmark birthday? (We would later learn that it was Broadwell, a lady we'd never met or heard of, who was turning forty.) Natalie and I were becoming very disconcerted by his odd behavior and weird questions.

When the ancient elevator finally reached the bottom floor, David stepped out and looked at the watch he had been testing. Seconds later, his security team was running down the steps to catch up with the director of the CIA.

What was on his mind that he felt that there was a threat requiring him to test his men out?

Despite General Allen's selfless suggestion to call off the important British ambassadorial meeting, I kept it scheduled for May 22. General Allen flew in from Afghanistan, his plans shrouded in secrecy. No one could know his itinerary, since he was the commander of international security of the allied forces. Still worried by the odd email, he had requested extra security. Three armored black Suburbans wheeled up under the porte-cochere at the Ritz-Carlton in Washington's West End, just across Rock Creek Park from Georgetown. Kathy Allen stayed in the Suburban while General Allen met me in the regal, marble-framed lobby.

It was a short ride from the Ritz to the British ambassador's residence. The spectacular white-glove affair took my mind off my fears. It went off without a hitch. Afterward, we repaired to a handsome sitting area, and as we were getting comfortable, a liveried butler entered with a silver tray full of a variety of scotches. I politely declined, but the minister of defense insisted. "Come on, Jill," the minister cajoled. "We hear you have the reputation of being tougher than any man." Foolishly accepting the challenge, I requested some kind of single-malt and took a tiny sip.

I was certain our hosts would do all they could to help pave the way for General Allen's appointment to NATO. Elated after the dinner, I emailed General Mattis, who was in Bahrain, and raved about the success of the evening. I felt I had done a good job as the honorary ambassador.

> From: Jill and Scott Kelley shared email
> Sent: Wednesday, May 23, 2012 10:29 AM
> To: Mattis, James N Gen MIL USMC USCENTCOM CCCC-CCCC
> Subject:
>
> Dear Jim
> Last night was spectacular!
> I represented you in the bests possible light -as your "proud" special
> Ambassador.
>
> As you predicted, David Richards and I absolutely hit it off!!!
>
> Actually we laughed so hard about our good friend Graeme!
> He told me stories that, I promised to never repeat! I'm sure you have
> a couple of those takes as well!
> I LOVED it!!!!
>
>
> After dinner was over, we retired in the living room over a glass of
> Scotch (no! I don't drink Scotch, but Richards dared me and said
> "tough guys drink this" ......so I "had" to make realize he's
> challenging the wrong Ambassador! :-)
>
> And 2 more Visitors end up joining us, one guy "General John"
> (I think as his name, Richards was his predecessor) And another guy
> John Sawers. Who, well you know who he is!
> (I didn't until he tried telling me, and I thought he was lying)
>
> I didn't get to speak to Sawers that much, since Richards and I were so
> deep in discussion....that we didn't come up for air!
> (the good news is, he agreed with many of my thoughts....so I know
> he's a bright guy! Hehe!)
>
> As you could imagine, John Allen thoroughly enjoyed the dinner.
> He couldn't stop thanking me enough for arranging the evening and
> new friends (which reminds me, AMB Westmacott looks forward to
> me with You next!)
>
> It was a perfect evening. I wish you could've been there.
> I think Richards will shoot you an email telling you that "we've" met!
>
> Thank you again for being my favorite topic of the evening!
> We all think the world of you. You're awesome!

Your proud friend
Jill

ps I overheard John Allen describe me as the CentCom Commander's
right hand, and special envoy to CentCom (in Tampa and in DC) Very
nice of him to speak words of glory to the other Guests

He replied with his typical kindness. His response was cheery
and bright:

On May 23, 2012, at 2:08 PM, "Mattis, James N Gen MIL USMC
USCENTCOM CCCC-CCCC"<james.mattis@centcom.mil> wrote:

Dear Young Jill: What a note--your spirit shines through. ...Sounds
like an evening to remember...You're my right hand, left hand and
brains, young Jill. All my best from Bahrain....

As I basked in the success of the British ambassador's dinner,
the strange email was far from my mind. The next morning, however,
I refocused. I put in a call to Fred Humphries, the MacDill Air Force
Base FBI counterintelligence agent. Fred and his wife, Sarah, were
casual friends we'd met from our work together on the base, and we
occasionally dined together at base events. In 2011 he had nominated
me to attend the FBI citizens academy in Tampa. (I attended every
day of the course, except the one when we had SWAT team training
to shoot guns.)

I trusted him. Fred was a highly decorated veteran and a man
of great integrity. He wasn't your stereotypical FBI agent. Deeply
religious, he regularly attended Bible studies and sprinkled his
conversations with "bless-you's." A tall, strapping guy, Fred had been
awarded two of the bureau's most coveted honors, the Director's
Award, for his work on helping prevent the "millennium bombing
plot" that al Qaeda had set in motion to target Los Angeles
International Airport, and the FBI Medal of Valor, for having used his
service pistol to shoot a knife-wielding motorcycle thug who was
threatening a line of stopped cars holding civilians and kids outside
the entrance gate to MacDill.

Among his other responsibilities, Fred handled
counterintelligence work at the MacDill Air Force Base, which

largely meant keeping an eye on the foreign representatives of the international coalition to make sure they weren't purloining any U.S. military and intelligence information. It was delicate work that kept Fred constantly on the go and alert for the potential for any security breach.

On the phone, I told Fred about the email John had received.

"What do you think this means, Fred?" I asked, reading the "hands under the table" comment.

"It might mean passing money under the table," he suggested. "You know, an under-the-table deal?"

"Well, that's crazy," I laughed. "You know I don't take money for my role at CENTCOM; it's 'honorary,' which means I don't get paid."

"You probably don't have to worry, then," he said. "The stalker is misunderstanding your role, and will probably lay off." He advised that I put it out of my mind.

That wasn't so easy, but I hoped Fred was right. In any case, I didn't have time to worry about phantoms in emails. I was busy with my kids and husband, since school break was approaching the following week.

****

On June 1, 2012, Scott sent the Petraeuses an invitation to surprise me for dinner in honor of my birthday. It was sent from Scott's private email account — one we do not share. Unfortunately, the Petraeuses were away, and unable to attend.

Two days later, June 3, was my thirty-seventh birthday. Scott and I were doing the best we could to have a relaxed birthday dinner with my twin sister, Natalie, and her fiancé in Georgetown. We were dining at Café Milano, a well-known watering hole for diplomats and politicians, which was one of our favorite spots in Washington. The Italian menu was wonderful, and the setting warm and inviting. We enjoyed our meal, and toward the end, Scott made his apologies. He had to leave to catch a flight back to Tampa for his morning rounds the next day. I was planning to stay in town another couple of days, as my new acquaintance, the British ambassador, had invited me to the embassy to join the group celebrating the Queen's Jubilee and watching the festivities on big plasma TVs. As the three of us were finishing up our dinner, I received a call from Scott. He was getting ready to board his plane at Reagan National Airport.

"Jill," he said, "I just got an email from the stalker. The address is from someone calling himself 'Tampa Angel.'" He told me the email subject was "Jill Kelley's behavior." He read it to me with a shaking voice.

From: Tampa Angel <tampa.angel@yahoo.com>
Date: June 3, 2012, 9:05:04 PM EDT
To: Scott Kelley MD personal email
Subject: Jill Kelley"s behavior
Reply-To: Tampa Angel <tampa.angel@yahoo.com>

As her husband, you might want to examine your wife's behavior and see if you can rein her in before we publicly share the pictures of her with her hand sliding between the legs of a senior serving official (while at a DC restaurant). (You might actually question why she travels to DC so often, and ensure she is supervised when alone with senior government including
SOCOM and CENTCOM officials.)
Furthermore, you might want to suggest she stops sending inappropriately suggestive emails to senior military and public officials and foreign Ambassadors with whom she has contact. You might want to read her sent email file to verify her behavior. (We would caution against sending such emails to official government email accounts.)
Her continued inappropriate and suggestive behavior will otherwise become an embarrassment to all. This info genuinely shared in the hope that such embarrassment for all, including spouses, such as info in national headlines, may be averted.

All I could focus on were the alarming bits:
- Publicize pictures
- Embarrassment to all, including spouses
- National headlines
- Senior military and public officials and foreign ambassadors with whom she has contact

I was petrified. I hadn't done anything wrong! These had to be deeply religious men from the Middle East, or perhaps Pakistan. But most important, these guys regarded my service to our military as a threat to their terrorist agenda.

Could the stalker be at Café Milano, having waited for Scott to leave for the airport? All kinds of thoughts raced through my mind. Café Milano was not just a trendy restaurant. It was also the place where a hit man paid by the Iranian government had planned to murder the Saudi ambassador to the U.S. Call me paranoid, but even paranoids, as someone once said, have enemies. Could it be an assassin?

"How would anyone know your private email address?" I asked in dismay.

Scott thought for a moment, then came up with an answer: A day earlier he had sent an email (from his private account that we don't share) to Petraeus asking if he and Holly could join us for dinner the following week to celebrate my birthday. I turned white. Not only was the stalker hacking General Allen's email, which was bad enough; now he was reading the email correspondence of the director of Central Intelligence. Our lives could be in grave danger.

I turned around in fright and secretly took note of suspicious men sitting alone at some tables. I was really spooked.

We paid the bill and fled the restaurant, but not before scanning the room to see if there might be a hit man on the premises. The only problem was, what does a hit man look like? None of us had any earthly idea.

Back at the hotel, I called General Allen in Kabul in a panic to tell him the stalker was now secretly emailing my husband and threatening to "publicly shame" the leadership of our country and to be an embarrassment for all — including the spouses.

He was very concerned by this threat. He advised me to call Fred Humphries, the CENTCOM FBI counterintelligence agent, and tell him everything.

General Allen and I thought the stalker could be a security threat — a rogue terrorist or some foreign agent who wanted to start an international conflict by smearing the reputation and honor of these world leaders with the threat of going to the media with false leads.

"You need security," General Allen told me. "This isn't just about you, but a threat to shame U.S. generals, public officials and foreign ambassadors."

I decided to meet with Fred when I returned to Tampa. I had another ambassadorial event in D.C. that precluded my arriving in Tampa before Tuesday, June 5. I had barely landed back in Tampa when Scott received another email from Tampa Angel, with the subject line "Re: Jill Kelley's behavior."

> From: Tampa Angel <tampa.angel@yahoo.com>
> Date: June 5, 2012, 8:26:11 PM EDT
> To: Scott Kelley MD private email
> Subject: Re: Jill Kelley"s behavior
> Reply-To: Tampa Angel <tampa.angel@yahoo.com>
>
> **Would you like to know whom she has fondled? How do you think she became an Ambassador?**

Then, just in case Scott had missed the first email, its text was repeated below.

Scott and I speculated that the sexist tone of the email suggested it maybe came from someone who thinks women shouldn't work or women are incapable of having a relationship with leaders of the opposite sex, so must be sleeping their way to the top. What a chauvinist. My credentials are real; I worked hard to earn every opportunity. I am well-versed in Arabic history and speak several languages; but I thought I was dealing with gender bias from an anti-coalition stalker.

I continued to speculate about the stalker's identity: a male foreign agent? a terrorist group? Who wanted to start an international scandal besmirching the honor of our military and political leaders?

I also contacted Admiral Bob Harward; he advised me to do what I'd already planned: go to Fred Humphries, since he was the FBI agent on our base.

> **Subject: correction**
> **From: Jill and Scott Kelley shared email**
> **Date: Wed, 6 Jun 2012 17:20:21 -0400**
> **To: Robert Harward**
>
> **I apologize but the correct email is:**

tampa.angel@yahoo.com
(no apostrophe s)

And other email is correct as I stated:

kelleypatrol@gmail.com

**I am being very clear, PLEASE don't respond to their email.
Just find out who it is?**

Admiral Harward was clear about the correct course of action:

**From: Robert Harward
Date: June 6, 2012 at 5:33:49 PM EDT
To: Jill and Scott Kelley shared email
Subject: RE: correction**

**I would go to the police or your FBI contact on this.
....**

The next day I again called Fred, my primary FBI liaison and friend, and spelled out my concern. "It's not just about me," I said. "I'm worried that there's some jeopardy for John, David and other generals and ambassadors, as the email clearly threatened."

Agent Humphries took the threat seriously. One thing he said stayed in my mind: "If someone took you for ransom, he would have access to all these people — CIA, CENTCOM, SOCOM." (The Pentagon's elite Special Operations Command, SOCOM, was also based at MacDill, and virtually all its activities were cloaked in the highest level of secrecy.) "Those are all the leaders a terrorist would want to get to."

Fred told me he couldn't personally handle the matter, given our friendship, but he asked me to come into the Tampa FBI field office to make a report to another agent. Once I arrived, Agent Humphries introduced me to Agent Adam Malone, a special agent in the Tampa cybercrime unit. Agent Malone was a young man, about my age. With the increased emphasis the bureau was placing on cybercrime, he had a full plate.

Right off the bat I told Agent Malone about my privacy concerns. I didn't want my personal emails to be read by everyone or made public. He reassured me about the way the FBI worked. As a victim, he said, everything I shared would be completely confidential. He assured me that my name would never be publicly disclosed.

Agent Malone said he'd make a couple of calls to contacts at Yahoo to do an email search and try to determine the identity of the person or people writing the emails. Although I wanted to know the stalker's identity, I was shocked that Agent Malone could make a call and gain access to such information so quickly. (That concerned me; I wondered if he ever did that to get his ex-girlfriend's emails or his neighbor's emails — and, who knows, he could do that to me when I walked away from the table.) That said, at the time, agents thought the stalker was a foreign national, not an American citizen. Malone speculated that this stalker could be trying to retaliate against me for my work with the coalition; perhaps someone was intent upon kidnapping me to exploit my direct access to the most powerful military and intelligence leaders.

I understand why Admiral Harward and General Allen urged me to go to the FBI; we lived in dangerous times, when terrorist threats were real.

The most alarming aspect of this threat was the fact that my appointment as an informal ambassador was known only among the folks I directly worked with. My access and appointments came with no pay or publicity, and outside of the cloistered world of the coalition and CENTCOM. It was not, I believed, generally known that I worked as an informal ambassador for the U.S. military. In fact, one influential ambassador made a comment to another foreign representative that "Only those who need to know Jill Kelley know her." In short, I was a secret.

But our fear was real — palpably real. I felt alone and vulnerable, even in my own house. One day in early June, the phone rang when I was in our bedroom upstairs, getting ready for my daily ten-mile run. For some reason, the vibrating cellphone petrified me. I had read somewhere that the Mossad, Israel's intelligence agency, had executed a Palestinian terrorist by somehow calling him on his cell, then blowing it up. Could that be possible? The phone continued to vibrate, and I looked out the window at my three girls playing on the lawn. I ran downstairs and outside. Until we knew what was going on and the stalker was caught, the girls would have to remain inside.

The emails became relentless. They were also increasingly troubling. On June 7, Scott received a third startling email from Tampa Angel:

From: Tampa Angel <tampa.angel@yahoo.com>
Date: June 7, 2012, 7:54:13 PM EDT
To: Scott Kelley MD personal email
Subject: Re: Jill Kelley''s behavior
Reply-To: Tampa Angel <tampa.angel@yahoo.com>

Did you ask Jill about her promiscuous and adulterous behavior yet? It does not seem the nature of her inappropriate emails have changed this week. She is still the most self-centered narcissistic person we've ever seen (a sign of insecurity).

I called Fred Humphries. The emails were laser-focused on me in a way that continued to lead me to believe that someone had a huge problem with my being a woman working with men. Agent Humphries suggested that I file an official complaint to get a search warrant to figure out who was sending the emails.

Upon filing the complaint, we were advised by Adam Malone, the FBI cybercrime expert, to change all our passwords. General Allen, Deputy Commander Harward, General Mattis, and Scott and I all did it.

Adam and Fred felt they had a case, since the stalker had alluded in his email to having taken photographs, which amounted to physical stalking, not just the cyber kind. They also felt the threats had reached the level of blackmail, with the email's promise of "embarrassment for all, including spouses, such as info in national headlines" that "may be averted." What particularly struck the FBI agents was the fact that the stalker had access to the comings and goings of the general's schedule. Obviously, an unauthorized individual had accessed official information. That was the clincher. That's why the FBI cybercrime unit opened an official investigation.

Agent Malone explained that he needed to have access to the email header of the specific stalking email in order to trace the IP address, which would allow him and his colleagues in the cyber unit to identify the anonymous sender's identity. That sounded reasonable; he reiterated that he could investigate the "specific email that that the stalker had sent to analyze the header to determine the IP address to identify the suspect."

But then he asked for access to my other private email account, which had never received any threats. I declined to give them any access to any other email accounts we have. Agent Fred Humphries witnessed my refusal to comply with that request.

To calm our anxiety, the following weekend Deputy Commander Bob Harward called to invite Scott and me out for a drink. I was very anxious about going out because of the threats, but I felt safe because Harward was a Navy SEAL and expressed concerns about my safety. We decide to meet in the nearby area of SoHo in Tampa, a young happening part of town, located on Howard Avenue.

When we met — Harward had just flown in from yet another of his seemingly endless visits to Washington — he told me how glad he was that the FBI was investigating. And not only that, he said, he had also ordered a separate investigation, by the Navy's Criminal Investigative Service. "Everyone is on this, Jill," he told me. "We've got your back."

I guess my nervousness was evident, because Harward was trying to lift my mood by jokingly taunting the stalker: "Tampa Angel! Come out, come out, wherever you are!" All joking aside, Harward simply could not understand why the FBI hadn't already identified the stalker: "This is a matter of National Security! People's lives could be in danger!" he said.

We were very careful beforehand not to have any electronic communication regarding our night out in SoHo, since Harward hadn't brought his bodyguards. I hadn't emailed either David Petraeus or John Allen about the outing, since we knew the stalker was still on the loose.

The following Monday morning, Tampa Angel struck again.

Scott got an email with an unsettling subject line:

From: Tampa Angel <tampa.angel@yahoo.com>
Date: June 11, 2012, 7:29:57 AM EDT
To: Scott Kelley MD personal email
Subject: Ask Jill about suggesting "doggie style" to Harward...
Reply-To: Tampa Angel <tampa.angel@yahoo.com>

Scott was driving to the hospital, about 7:30 a.m., when he opened the email. He nearly lost control of the car. Then he called me.

"Did you say anything funny to Harward about sex?" he asked me. "About doing it doggie style?"

I was flabbergasted. I was puzzled. Clearly I was being watched. And this stalker was trying to convince my poor husband that I was having an affair.

The only time I had used the term "doggie style" was in a nonsexual context. Scott was right there with us. I reminded him of the context. I had ruthlessly teased Harward about his lacking athletic prowess. In actuality he was a SEAL who had surpassed every other SEAL in history in athletic prowess. But while were talking about competitive swimming I cracked a joke: "The stroke you compete in is doggie style." Now, OK, you might say "doggie paddle"… that's fine. I said "doggie style" instead, but I said that with the appropriate, nonsexual gesticulation. I actually paddled. Everyone knew what the heck I was talking about in the moment.

But Scott was clearly disturbed by the vulgarity of the stalker's accusations, even though he didn't believe any aspect of the continuing accusations.

"Scott," I said, "this is really creeping me out. This is not just something to defame me or embarrass me. This person is trying to ruin our marriage." I took a deep breath. "Scott, I don't know why this guy is taking me on, why it's so personal. I'm not doing anything wrong!"

Somehow, we both calmed down, but now we were really worried. The stalker, whoever he was, was clearly maintaining some kind of visual surveillance on me. And despite the fact that Admiral Harward and I had not communicated via email, the stalker still knew that Scott and I had met up with Harward the night before. Which meant he was probably physically stalking us, too.

As the week progressed, I had several functions sponsored by the State Department to attend. This was the first time I started to question if my sense of mission and duty was worth the personal turmoil. My family and my sanity were being threatened. Celebrating Father's Day in Orlando, all I could think about was how my husband was being dragged into the stalker's web. I was worried that the innuendo would actually hurt our relationship. It wasn't fair to any of us. I was at my wit's end.

Eventually, I heard from Agent Malone. The FBI's cybercrime wizards had run checks to trace the Tampa Angel emails, but they had come up empty. The sender, he told me, "was fingerprintless."

I was discouraged. Were they trying hard enough? If the stalker was considered so sophisticated, shouldn't they be putting much more emphasis on this investigation, considering the named targets?

In the midst of all of this, I emailed General Allen to give him an update. Even an outsider could see that we obviously weren't having an affair. If we were, would General John Allen have encouraged me to go to the FBI? In one email, he reiterated his approval of going to the "police" (FBI.)

On Jun 12, 2012, at 10:09 PM, "Allen, John R Gen USMC COMISAF" <john.allen@afghan.swa.army.mil> wrote:
Classification: UNCLASSIFIED
Caveats: FOUO

Good on going to the police, Jill. It's the right thing to do.
....
John

Much of our email was about other topics, but on this point, I responded:

From: Jill and Scott shared email address
Sent: Wednesday, June 13, 2012 6:23 AM
To: Allen, John R Gen USMC COMISAF
Subject: Re: (UNCLASSIFIED)

....
I'm taking your advice by going to the Police about my stalker. Since, We now confirmed he's following me (besides knew when I'm coming or going -as per his email alerting you about our upcoming UK Ambassador dinner) Fred the FBI Agent (he's a friend) is handling it....

The FBI never informed me that it had already identified this relentless stalker. I can recall how scared my children were about this faceless man who was going to get them because the FBI said he was "fingerprintless." I tried to calm them down, and told them that they could believe in the FBI, and Adam Malone was working hard to make sure nothing happened to us or the generals. But in truth I was terrified, since I believed their lies about not being able to catch him.

Chapter 8: Shoot the Guard Dog

Remember, I was experiencing all of these events in real time. I was convinced that my stalker was a terrorist, someone or some group working against the coalition. In actuality, the FBI already knew the identity of the stalker but chose to allow the director of the CIA to continue while compromised.

On June 18, there was another email.

From: Tampa Angel <tampa.angel@yahoo.com>
Date: June 18, 2012, 3:57:22 PM EDT
To: Scott Kelley MD personal email
Subject: Be sure to watch Jill's hands under the DC dinner table this Friday...
Reply-To: Tampa Angel <tampa.angel@yahoo.com>

They have been seen there before.

Before Scott received this email, I had begun to think I was safer. I hadn't heard from the terrorist stalker for a week. But now, this. It referred to a dinner with the director of the CIA. This was on top of the past email referring to unannounced dinners with the COMISAF (head of the war) and deputy commander of the MacDill Air Force Base. Now I was going to be followed to dinner with the director of the CIA?

All I remember is calling Fred Humphries. I was screaming, petrified: "They know I'm having dinner with Petraeus on Friday. They'll probably kill us both, since they know my communications haven't stopped!"

Fred kept telling me that he was just as concerned as I was. Since General Allen, Admiral Harward and I had already reassured him that we had changed our passwords multiple times, Fred was able to put it all together: The director of the CIA clearly was the only one whose emails were being hacked by this terrorist stalker.

I couldn't move. I was panicked and paranoid. I kept fretting about everything.

I received a phone call from Fred and Adam. "Do you know any person who has been in Aspen, West Point, San Francisco and Charlotte in the last month?" I racked my brain again.

"No," I said, finally.

"Jill, this person is very sophisticated," Adam replied. "I'm very worried about this."

Not nearly as worried as I was, I wanted to say. But I held my tongue. Agent Malone asked me again if he could review the Yahoo email account Scott and I shared. Again, I declined. We spoke a bit longer, and I became increasingly uncomfortable.

"Am I a target of this investigation?" I blurted out.

"No," Adam replied, calmly. He asked again whether he could see our personal emails.

"No," I repeated.

"Jill," Adam said, in what I took as an attempt at reassurance, "it would be against the law for us to disclose any of these emails." Without citing it by name, Adam was referring to the FBI's "minimization" protocol, protecting victims and witnesses.

"Good, then let me be clear: The answer, once again, is 'No!'" I said.

Then, in almost the very next breath, Agent Malone asked me, "Jill, do you think that someone in General Petraeus' family, like his son or daughter, is jealous of your closeness with the director and the fact that you spend all your family holidays together?"

To me, the question was ludicrous and insulting given the trust between our families. Shaken and confused, I cried after I got off the phone with Agent Malone.

Though I was never told at the time, I later learned that the FBI had been able to determine the stalker's identity based upon IP locations at Internet cafes using via Wi-Fi access to send the anonymous emails. The FBI requested a series of airplane and hotel manifests and, using IP addresses and timestamps, was able to match the travel information with Tampa Angel emails to addresses in West Point, Aspen, New York City and San Francisco. Only one name was a "hit": Paula Broadwell. Agent Malone and his team had tracked the identity of the faceless stalker behind Petraeus and other generals: a female, Major Paula Broadwell. The agents Googled her and saw her interview on "The Daily Show" with Jon Stewart doing push-ups after fawning about Petraeus in every other sentence. I was told the FBI had been able to watch a closed-circuit video security camera from a Starbucks in Charlotte, North Carolina, showing Broadwell pulling up in her BMW to send another email to terrorize my family.

That email became her undoing. I texted Fred Humphries:

June 18:
JK: "I just got off the phone with Adam. They sent another email"

No response. The next day, I texted again.

June 19:
JK: "Can you call me"
FH: No, I can't; in meeting.
JK: Could you believe he knows I'm having dinner with Dave on Friday!

I was completely oblivious to Fred's answer to my next text question (since I did not know the suspect had already been identified), which is very telling in retrospect:

FH: Yep.

Unnerved, I just kept trying to make sense of things. I was rattled to the core:

JK: Unreal. I can't believe this. I think I'm going to have a heart attack if this criminal isn't caught.
Can you call me
FH: No, Jill. I can't! Hang in there.
JK: I think I'm going to have a panic attack.
Adam spoke to me, I can't believe how sophisticated this [stalker] is!

When I did finally have a voice conversation with him, Fred was circumspect. Seemingly out of the blue, he called to recommend the new biography on Petraeus' life. I responded by saying I didn't need to read any books about his life. I didn't need to. Then he proceeded to ask me about a book called All In by Paula Broadwell.

Only in retrospect can I see that this was a ruse, a way to figure out if I had had interactions with my stalker. Notice that Fred didn't actually reveal anything. Fred knew that, in accordance with FBI protocol, the investigative officer, Adam Malone, needed to reveal the name of the stalker to me.

That conversation was actually Fred's attempt to clarify that I did not, in fact, know the identity of the stalker. Keep in mind, at this time, I still referred to the stalker as "he," "him," "the terrorist." I simply did not think the stalker could be female, let alone a jealous woman projecting, since she was having an affair of her own!

Actually, Fred Humphries did a lot to protect the safety of the Petraeuses too. He obviously wanted to save Petraeus from any public embarrassment or any potential physical assault. Once he knew that the stalker was an female (he didn't know until months later that she was a mistress), he suggested that I not email Petraeus about the location of our upcoming dinner so that the stalker wouldn't know where to find us in time to spoil things.

On Wednesday, June 20, I was supposed to meet up with Fred Humphries. He texted me to cancel at the last minute:

June 20, 2012
FH: I'm jammed up. Just had meeting on a certain cyber case. Ahem…. So have to raincheck.

Dying of curiosity about the meeting, I pleaded for more information:

JK: Can you call me? After I spoke to Adam, I broke down in tears…. I can't believe this is happening to me.
FH: I think we're making good progress. I can't though tonight. I believe you are physically safe.

Not picking up the hints he was dropping, I responded:

JK: I hope so…. I never underestimate someone that's this persistent and had no regard for bullying, blackmailing, stalking, harassing or especially invading the privacy of a high profile circle – with their reputation as a threat. And the fact that we are being followed and watched is scaring the heck out of me. I'm in great fear that they know where, with whom, and when I'll be this Friday, and my Official dinners all throughout next week.

Trying to calm me down, Fred responded:

FH: Listen to me. I am objective.

Undeterred, I kept up with my panic attack.

JK: I know... but you can't blame me for the panic that's setting in.

He didn't respond. On June 20, I texted Fred again:

JK: The anxiety is ripping my spirits. Can you call me?
He tried to encourage me:
FH: Hang tough. Let's meet tomorrow. I'm on a landline phone with HQ. You will be fine. Many people are working hard on your behalf.

In actuality, that wasn't true. Fred was working on my behalf, but there were others working on Broadwell's behalf. Just as I was never told that Broadwell had been identified as the stalker, I was never told officially that briefs of Agent Malone's investigation had made it all the way up the chain of command to the top of the J. Edgar Hoover Building in Washington, as well as to Attorney General Eric Holder and the office of FBI Director Muller. There were explicit orders instructing Agent Malone and his colleagues in the Tampa cybercrime unit to handle the case "differently" from standard FBI minimization procedure "or else." This meant, among other things, that we were never accorded our privacy rights.

I had no idea that things would only get worse. Soon after Broadwell was discovered to be the stalker, the high-level investigation suddenly seemed to go off the rails when Sean Joyce, the deputy director of the FBI (who we learned had known Paula Broadwell for years), got involved.

Agent Malone and his partner had every reason to be proud of their countless hours of detective work, sniffing through manifests in four different cities, trying to pin down the fingerprintless and sophisticated stalker. They were excited to finally apprehend the suspect.

On their way to the airport, they received an abrupt phone call ordering them to abandon the trip, supposedly on orders of FBI Deputy Director Joyce. The understanding was pretty much "call it a day, and don't ask any questions."

Since I didn't know about any of this, I was relentless in my texts to Fred, pleading for information, hoping beyond hope that he could calm me down. We texted about praying: I was praying for safety at Friday night's dinner. He prayed for me too, but for other reasons.

> June 22 11:30 AM:
> JK: "I hope God heard my sad prayers last night…"
> FH: "He did, and he heard mine for you."
> JK: That makes me cry ☹
> June 22 2:38 PM:
> JK: Done from my meeting… Any progress?
> FH: Stop. Adam and I are getting beat up by management enough.
> JK: Sorry. That's not cool. They probably should be taking it out on the criminal — not the heroes.

Actually, it was much worse than that. After it was all said and done, Fred recalled this tumultuous time with disdain. He got "beat up" by management pretty badly, but there was much worse treatment in store for him, since he wouldn't go along with what the FBI upper management was doing to me. Here's Fred's analogy for that time period:

> FH: The fox slaughters chickens in the middle of the night and the farmer shoots the watchdog for barking an alert.
> What a tangled web we weave, when first we practice to deceive.

On Friday, June 22, the day we were supposed to be having dinner with Director Petraeus, based on Fred's recommendation, I purposely delayed until 3 p.m. emailing where we would meet.

Director Petraeus continued to ask where we would be having dinner. After prolonging my email response as long as I could, I finally emailed "The Prime Rib" at 7 p.m.

Fifty-nine minutes later, Scott received the most chilling Tampa Angel email. The subject line had been designed just to horrify us: He knew where to find us:

From: Tampa Angel <tampa.angel@yahoo.com>
Date: June 22, 2012, 3:59:57 PM EDT
To: Scott Kelley MD personal email
Subject: Prime Rib Tonight
Reply-To: Tampa Angel <tampa.angel@yahoo.com>

Notice the seating arrangement. There is a reason the man at the table won't sit next to her...

I was getting my hair done when the email arrived in Scott's inbox. Without waiting for the hairdresser to finish, I stepped outside, glancing left and right for anyone who might be watching. A group of men in dark suits waited near a car on the street, but they are a common sight in D.C., as many people travel with security details.

I walked back to the Ritz, breathing in deep, ragged breaths. I kept looking behind me, searching for anyone who looked suspicious, afraid that someone might shoot me right there on the sidewalk, even before reaching the dinner that night.

I was extremely scared. I was completely overwhelmed by anxiety because of the stalker's knowledge of the dinner. I screamed into the phone at Agent Malone: "They can kill the director! His security is breached!"

Agent Malone was very selective in answering my calls. answered every other phone call. I finally got through to him, but he was distant and eerily calm. This previously sheepish and unconfident young agent advised me: "Tell the director to change his passcode, because your stalker is accessing his emails."

I was a wreck. I was convinced there was danger, and I expressed my fears to Agent Malone and chastised him for not having his guys protect the director of the CIA and my family, now that we knew there had been a security breach. He was sanguine. He suggested I put my feelings in an email so they could use it as evidence when they identified and charged the stalker.

I frantically texted Fred Humphries, begging for help.

June 22 5:06 PM
JK: Important PLEASE CALL
June 22 5:28 PM
JK: He emailed again. I'm going to have a massive heart attack.

Agent Humphries ignored my pleas. He was trying to be "good" and follow orders based on his chain of command, in what was actually an FBI investigation run amok.

Later, I learned that after they had determined Broadwell's identity, the FBI, an agency that's supposed to enforce the laws, had now began to break them. Agent Malone got orders from bosses in Washington to search though all the emails on my personal Yahoo account. They did this because they wanted to see if I ever had had an affair. (If that was true, why ever would I go to the FBI and bring attention to it?) The FBI was able to attain search warrants weeks after the suspect already had been identified. I was told the FBI never got a search warrant for the Scott Kelley MD personal account, which is the email that received the stalker email. The reason? It wasn't needed. The FBI already knew who the stalker was. Instead, the bureau searched the Jill and Scott Kelley shared email account (again, not the account the stalker had targeted) specifically so it could snoop into my life.

Let me proffer an analogy to help explain why this is a problem for all Americans: Suppose a house is burglarized. The police do a cursory investigation of the crime scene. A few days later, they figure out who the burglar is, but they lie and tell the victim that they don't know the identity of the burglar, in order to keep the case open. Then they go and search the victim's beach house — an un-related location — just to snoop around for evidence hoping to find some salacious details about the victim's life, possibly evidence of an affair.

Therefore, rather than stopping the burglar, they abuse their powers to enable the criminal to continue committing crimes, while using taxpayer money to attempt to gather evidence of immorality on the part of the victim.

The only reason that there possibly could be for this type of overreach is to get trash to leverage against the powerful people I was in contact with for nefarious agendas. I now believe that the FBI didn't care about the harm or damages it might cause to a victim of a crime. The fact that I was a law-abiding citizen, let alone the victim who went to the FBI to report the crime, was irrelevant.

The important thing to understand is that FBI didn't "stumble" on the Petraeus affair at all. The FBI took invasive measures to spy into email accounts. That's how it pieced together the situation and found out about David Petraeus' past extramarital affair. The most shocking part is the fact that Broadwell was engaging in what ordinary people might characterize as criminal behavior. Instead of focusing on the question of *criminality*, they focused on the salacious details of her actions, which had more political currency.

The invasion of our lives, this drama, this investigation, was simply a tool for digging up dirt on political targets. What I'm most dismayed by is that some political appointees within the FBI used taxpayer resources to deliver my friends into the hands of their political enemies. Did we learn anything from Watergate? I naively thought that the FBI was not supposed to be political, that the FBI was supposed to protect Americans. But, you see, that's the thing. I knew I wasn't doing anything wrong, immoral, or illegal, so went to the FBI for protection. How could I possibly have suspected that this situation would turn so ugly?

****

Scott and I arrived at The Prime Rib that evening, nervous and frightened. There were over a dozen security officers around the entrance, and they whisked us inside. The security guards blocked the doors. We waited in tense silence for David and Holly, and they arrived with a double entourage. I thought to myself, all this is because of those emails. It was a sobering reality. David and Holly pulled up in their car, and were rushed into the restaurant and the door was locked behind them.

The main dining room — usually packed on a Saturday night — had been cleared, and bodyguards sat at the vacated tables ready to form a human shield around Director Petraeus, Holly, Scott, and me.

David said nothing, but stood by his seat and pulled out the chair next to him, for me (despite the warning from "Tampa Angel" that the man would not sit next to me). I leaned over and whispered to David, "You have a stalker too? Scott and General Allen and other CENTCOM generals and foreign ambassadors had been receiving emails from a stalker." He lifted an eyebrow, quizzically.

I spilled out the whole story, describing how I was being stalked and had been told not to sit next to him. General Allen and Admiral Harward had urged me to go to Agent Fred Humphries at CENTCOM. Everyone on base was concerned that the stalker might be a terrorist, since all of our comings and goings were known. "They even know we're here tonight," I said. "The FBI told me to tell you that your government email account is being accessed by our stalker."

Now Director Petraeus looked shocked. "How do you know I'm also being hacked?"

"Because my husband got an email from the stalker referring to our dinner tonight," I said. "John, Scott and all the Generals had already changed our passwords and yet the stalker knew we were going to be at The Prime Rib!"

Director Petraeus responded cryptically, "I don't know how to change my passcode. My aides usually do it, but I'll figure it out."

Later, before our ritual of picture taking began, he said, "Let's not take pictures tonight. And from now on, let's be careful about what we say in emails to each other; somebody bad is reading my government account."

I agreed, as it seemed like a sensible way to avoid inflaming the stalker. Once again, I reminded him to change his password. At the same time, it troubled me, as it seemed that someone was remotely controlling the director of the CIA's actions and stifling our correspondence. I hated to see some ruthless, unseen force inhibiting one of the most powerful men in the world.

Three days after the dinner at The Prime Rib, David emailed me that he had changed his password:

On Jun 25, 2012, at 7:34 PM, "Petraeus, David H Former COMISAF"<david.h.petraeus@afghan.swa.army.mil> wrote:

Btw, will have password changed... Suspect that will do it...
....

I still thought it was a male stalker, as evidenced by my response:

> **From: Jill and Scott Kelley shared email**
> **To: "Petraeus, David H Former COMISAF"**
> **<david.h.petraeus@afghan.swa.army.mil>**
> **Sent: Monday, June 25, 2012 11:30 PM**
> **Subject: Re: RE: RE: RE:**
>
> **I agree, I'm truly convinced it's your email he's [the stalker] breaking into**
> **Let me know when you change your passcode...**
> **Because I have something that you asked for.**
> **(please don't tell anyone about this -ie friends or family)**
>
> **Did [the stalker] email you after Prime Rib Friday night?**
> **I wish we took a photo together :-(**
>
> **Just unbelievable that this weasel is taunting the most powerful guy in the world!?**
> **But glad he lost "street credit" when you sat next to me! Hah!**
>
> **Let me know when it's changed.**
>
> **Your SS**
> **Jill**

My signature "SS", means Sayida Safira, or lady ambassador. The next day, I was still feeling the stalker's threat. I tried to call Fred Humphries again.

> June 23: 8:45 AM
> JK: Call me
> June 23, 10:29 AM
> FH: No. I've been put on notice by management. Sorry.
> JK: WTF I can't believe this! I'm sorry. This is not fair to you.
> June 23 2:31 PM:
> JK: I didn't know they really took you off the case. I'm sorry. Can I tell you about yesterday — but phone call
> FH: Not now. My comms are subject to monitoring.

Much later, in person, Fred told me that he had walked into a room by accident to find that my name had been drawn into the center of an elaborate "link chart" detailing the progress of the investigation. You know what I mean by "link chart," even if you've never heard the term before: It's one of those diagrams they use in movies to depict the Mafia don's connections to all of his lieutenants and captains. Arrows emanated from the circle at the center enclosing my name and radiated out like spokes on a bicycle wheel to other circles enclosing the names of VIPs I communicate with: Petraeus, Allen, Mattis, Harward, and other U.S. leaders and foreign heads of state.

When he saw that, Fred started asking himself questions. What's going on? Why are we treating Jill like she's done something wrong? Before he knew it, and before he could don the mantle of whistleblower, Fred was also accused of inappropriate communications and of having an affair with me. He was called into his boss's office. It's my understanding that Humphries' supervisor told him that "[Deputy Director] Joyce was convinced that he [Fred Humphries] was fucking Jill Kelley." Fred strenuously denied it, but the truth was irrelevant and inconvenient. Fred was inconvenient. He was asking too many questions. He cared way too much about doing the right thing.

What makes the allegations so preposterous is that Fred is one of the most religious laymen I have ever met. He peppers almost every conversation and email with comments that underscore his faith in God. Anyone who actually knows Fred would know that he would never have an affair. To accuse him of that … to put his wife and family through that … was unconscionable. It was also a preview of what was to come.

This "femme fatale" fable and set of false accusations was very, very effective at destroying the lives and careers of three great patriots. The bogus narrative was simply a weapon to use to get the witnesses to stand down and shut up until the election took place — a political delay so their boss could be re-elected and their jobs secured.

An internal investigation was launched into Fred's supposed misconduct. Fred offered to take a polygraph regarding the appropriateness of our relationship, but his superiors didn't let him. Later, Fred Humphries was forced to sign an affidavit characterizing his and his wife's relationship with Scott and me. In the affidavit, Fred included a sentence of his own: "Never at any time has this relationship been inappropriate or sexual." As I understand it, the supervisor told Fred that he must remove the sentence or face losing his job. Bottom line: The bureau didn't just manipulate an investigation; it also tampered with evidence. Fred might also have been "burned" by someone in the bureau. Fred's name later appeared on an ISIS website. To protect him and his wife, the government has since installed cameras and listening devices in the Humphries home. Upon hearing of the ISIS threats, his boss allegedly muttered something about how Fred "deserved it for not following orders from the bosses in D.C."

I was also told that the Tampa unit was troubled that the national headquarters of the FBI (in Washington, D.C.) had taken over the case; there was a concern about possible manipulation and corruption of the investigation. Allegedly, the cybercrimes supervisor was so creeped out by this interference that she surreptitiously duplicated and bootlegged everything that had been recorded up to that point in the investigation, to make sure nothing was later destroyed or "disappeared."

The FBI internal message was clear: Get on board with the emphasis on salacious rumors or your career is toast.

For the purposes of clarifying how terrible the FBI was to Fred Humphries, I'll jump ahead in the timeline to September-October. In mid-September Fred was again called into his supervisor's office and his boss said, "The director sent this up my ass." He threw down on the table a photograph of Fred shirtless, which he had emailed to me, claiming it was proof that we had an inappropriate relationship.

Fred was thunderstruck. The photo was of Fred bald and skinny as a result of his successful fight against cancer. It showed him shirtless and was clearly meant as a gag. In fact, it had been sent in a mass email to Fred's wife and numerous other friends, including a reporter at The Seattle Times in 2010. The bald, shirtless Fred bore an uncanny resemblance to the two firing-range dummies on either side of him. The photo was captioned, "Which one is Fred?"

The allegation against Fred, in a wholly different context, might simply have been deemed absurd — if it weren't so potentially damaging to so many. This was a willful misrepresentation of the facts, again to destroy the credibility of anyone who wasn't following the bureau's orders. Fred was outraged.

From: Humphries, Frederick W. II FBI email
Date: February 23, 2013, 4:30:32 PM EST
To: Jill and Scott Kelley shared email
Subject: Re: Fwd: Washington Post

Some day the world should know that all this extraneous, needless and tragic collateral damage ....

This investigation was about one thing and one thing only: a self-admitted cyber stalker. But those at FBI HQ chose to make outrageous allegations ....

....
Unconscienable. ....

V/R,
Fred

FREDERICK W. HUMPHRIES II
Special Agent, FBI
Special Operations Group
(SOG/MST-A)
Tampa Bay, Florida

24/7: 813.253.XXXX
Cell: 813.394.XXXX

Much later, he recounted the whole story in writing

From: "Humphries, Frederick W. II" FBI email
Date: May 17, 2013 at 1:51:26 PM EDT
To: Jill and Scott shared email
Subject: Re: Fwd:

.... It became apparent you and I were the focus of the investigation. ... yet our family friendship was perverted ....OPR (our Internal Affairs) .... determined nothing inappropriate had occurred ....I was told I ... going to be re-assigned to a squad where I will be properly supervised ....

V/R,
Fred

FREDERICK W. HUMPHRIES II
Special Agent, FBI
Special Operations Group
(SOG/MST-A)
Tampa Bay, Florida

24/7: 813.253.XXXX
Cell: 813.394.XXXX

Deeply upset by political appointees at the FBI, Fred decided to confide in a former boss, now a retired special agent in Seattle. Fred's ex-boss relayed his concerns to House Majority Leader Eric Cantor. In September, Cantor unexpectedly called Fred on his cellphone to hear the story directly. Fred described all the sabotage in the investigation and what he believed the evidence supported: the national security breach, the D.C. leaders' knowledge that CIA Director Petraeus had been compromised, the failure to inform the Senate Intelligence Committee, the illegal search of everyone's emails, and the failure to arrest (or even stop) Broadwell.

Humphries told Cantor he had learned that Petraeus had promised Broadwell the role of National Security Advisor. To me, that's an ironic twist, since she would be required to keep the confidences and security of the types of people whom she stalked and terrorized. Fred Humphries nearly choked when he claimed the only way she impressed anyone as a talking head was by acquiring classified information from Petraeus. Fred managed to blurt out a warning to the effect that: "She's dangerous, and the government officials assisting and enabling her with FBI resources are even more dangerous!"

Cantor had his chief of staff call bureau Director Robert Mueller and repeat this very disturbing high-profile conspiracy. He was told that Mueller's office would investigate.

Fred thought everything was going to be OK.

Soon after, Fred was once again called into his boss's office and was threatened with dismissal for speaking to Cantor. A few phone calls went back and forth. Cantor originally offered to file for whistleblower protection, but then he never followed up, unsympathetically offering what amounted to a death sentence for Humphries' career: "I have bad news. I do not want to address this matter before the election because I don't want to make this political, either."

In November 2012, Sidney Blumenthal, acting in his role as confidant to Hillary Clinton, wrote in a memo (released in the recent Clinton email trove): "My operative theory on Petraeus scandal is that it became an October Surprise that failed. …. [T]he scandal … and his resignation would have been the trifecta — leaks, Benghazi, then Petraeus — allowing Romney to argue that Obama had created a national security collapse. It would have overtaken the end of the campaign."

I actually agree with Blumenthal on this point. However, the way that the government officials were able to foil the "October Surprise" was telling. Judicial Watch explained about a confidential memo from Blumenthal to the former Secretary of State suggesting that a grand jury and the Senate Judiciary Committee should investigate whether former Rep. Eric Cantor or his staff violated the Espionage Act by disclosing classified information related to the FBI investigation of former CIA Director David Petraeus." Could this threat of felony charges against Cantor have been the way that he was muzzled? I wonder.

Regardless, Fred was left high and dry when Cantor backed out. He was told that politically elected officials from FBI headquarters ordered that nothing could or would be done until after the election, leaving Fred's career in jeopardy, Petraeus compromised, and the rest of us in harm's way.

I am saddened to report that, at the time I began writing of this book, Fred Humphries, the quiet hero of this tragedy, is still the subject of a hostile and retaliatory investigation.

His upright and ethical involvement in this matter was punished by a storm of retribution and retaliation. Yet he amazes me with his strong faith and ability to pray for grace:

On Jun 23, 2013, at 9:06 PM, "Humphries, Frederick W. II" wrote:

…. I am so pleased and honored to know you and Scott and your beautiful daughters, wonderful parents and sisters. I believe this friendship was anointed by God to face the challenges we have faced. ….I believe we were given a commission from God ….I am grateful to God ….I am honored we were and are found worthy of such great testing, as Paul declared. How easy to witness for our Lord when things are simple and pleasant. We have been provided the opportunity to witness under trying circumstances. What a privilege! I have NO regret. ….Please share with Scott so the evil bureaucrats understand that our friendship is holy and biblical. ….
Fred

Fred's words brought me to tears. I replied:

From: Jill and Scott Kelley shared email
Date: June 23, 2013 at 10:04:14 PM EDT
To: "Humphries, Frederick W. II"
Subject: Re: Just thinking...

We're more honored by your friendship Fred...and humbled that you have remained a man of honor and integrity--before, and after this life-changing ordeal. Your family means so much to us, and I look forward to the day we are liberated with the blessings of the truth.

Thank you again for sharing your faith to keep me strong during these most tested times in our life...

Good night, and God Bless you my friend.

NBC reported about on this in a article entitled: "Agent feared FBI was stalling Petraeus investigation until after 2012 election."[1]

---

[1]http://www.nbcnews.com/news/other/agent-feared-fbi-was-stalling-petraeus-investigation-until-after-2012-f8C11550786

Chapter 9: All Out

Fred Humphries' texts and phone calls were being monitored.

> July 13, 2012, 2:35 AM
> FH:
> We need to talk in the morning. We've reviewed your E-mails. People are trying to make it harder than needs to be.

> July 13, 2012, 7:00 AM
> JK:
> Call me
> Thx

When we talked by phone, it was a short call. He spoke in a surreal, brisk staccato. I remember:

"They read all your emails. Even though you said 'No!' ... Not only did they read your emails, but they read Director Petraeus' and General Allen's too. They said Petraeus and Allen are both coming down after the election! ... They made this simple investigation harder than it needs to be. It's bad, Jill. It's really bad."

He hung up with no further explanation...

Chapter 10: Dirty Little Secret

In this chapter, truth slips around obstacles and cuts a new path. David Petraeus attempts to contain and minimize the situation. He attempts to appease his mistress, and to have me call off the FBI. But it is all too late. This is the unfurling.

Rewinding all of the events and replaying them, I see how foolish I was for not entertaining the concept that infidelity and jealousy might be at the heart of this matter. Paula Broadwell was David Petraeus' dirty little secret ... right up until she wasn't.

Things were getting tense. A formal dinner had been scheduled for June 27 by Arab ambassadors in my honor at the residence of the ambassador from Yemen. I was bringing Admiral Harward as my special guest, since Mattis was out of the country. Needless to say, it was a very significant occasion in our efforts to strengthen our collaboration and work for stability in the Middle East. The guest list was extensive, including ambassadors and representatives from many Arab nations.

In honor of

The Honorable Ambassador Jill Gilberte Kelley
US-Central Command Coalition

"with special guest"

Vice Admiral Robert S. Harward
Deputy Commander of US-Central Command
****

H.E. Abdulwahab Al-Hajjri
Ambassador of Yemen

Requests the pleasure
of
Ambassador ....
To a Dinner
With Arab Ambassadors

On: ***Wednesday, June 27th 2012***
       At: 7.00pm

Place: Ambassador's Residence
4850 Glenbrook Rd, NW
Washington, DC 20016

Rsvp to: Email nadiayemembus@gmail.com
202 965-4760
Directions
Attached   **Invitation is Non-**
Transferable

Then, less than a week before the dinner, I was informed that it had been canceled. It was unexpected. I was told by the Yemeni ambassador's secretary that the ambassador had urgently been called home. I thought nothing of it at first, until I realized the atmosphere around me was getting weird.

Holly's birthday dinner was at the Plume restaurant in the Jefferson Hotel. I was still disturbed about Fred's warning about Petraeus and Allen coming down after the election. I felt I couldn't say anything during the dinner, but I looked at David across the table and he was on edge. I didn't even know what to say. Still, I tried to act as if everything was normal. I stirred up small talk.

David and Holly had just returned from the Sun Valley Economic Forum, a prestigious annual gathering, where they interfaced with the King of Jordan, Bill Gates, Warren Buffett, Rupert Murdoch and a huge lineup of business and media stars. David had participated in a conversation on stage with former CIA Director George Tenet. David and Holly were enthusiastically describing the event at the table, but I was somewhat distracted. David was remote that night, choosing not to sit beside me as he usually did. He was apathetic when I most needed his reassurance. It seemed he had purposely distanced himself, as if I were radioactive.

Holly looked at me and said, "You know, David got a really weird email yesterday while we were in Sun Valley. We had security there, but David and I decided to sneak out for pizza." Afterward, she said, he had received a taunting email saying, "Did you enjoy pizza with your wife?"

My heart nearly stopped.

Holly went on talking. "We were actually very concerned. Our security was concerned because how did anyone know where the director was having pizza, in the middle of Sun Valley? But David played it down. He said, 'Oh, maybe one of the workers tweeted that David Petraeus the CIA director was there.'" Not noticing my shocked expression, she shrugged. "You know how David is. He just doesn't want any drama."

At one point Holly and I excused ourselves and went to the ladies' room together. "Do you remember the email address?" I asked Holly.

"Yes," she said. "It was DavidsAngel@Yahoo."

I tried not to show my horror. For the first time I could link David's stalker's email address to our stalker. Looking back now, I realize the FBI allowed our CIA director to remain stalked and compromised when the bureau knew who the stalker was all along.

We returned to the table and finished our meal, but I was fuming. The connection was obvious, but David's behavior was downright strange. He was the director of the CIA! And he knew about the previous stalking. It didn't make any sense that he'd just ignore it. And why was the stalker now threatening David, but leaving Scott alone all of a sudden? What the hell was going on?

I decided that I was going to confront him the next day, when we had a longstanding arrangement to do a thirty-mile bike race. In spite of all the intrigue, we were going ahead with our plan. He had previously instructed me to go to the bike shop he patronized and get fitted with a road bike and meet him at his house. We'd be driven to a long bike route in Virginia. I'd even emailed Holly a couple of days earlier, describing how I'd been practicing on a road bike and beating myself up pretty good in the process.

I let Holly know I was getting ready for the bike competition. David was also included in the email banter:

> **From: Jill and Scott Kelley shared email**
> **Date: Thu, Jul 19, 2012 3:29 pm**
> **Subject: What time is dinner Sat.?**
> **To: Holly and David Petraeus**
>
> **I think you mentioned that David was flying in, and needed time....**
> **Otherwise we are available whenever you are?**
> **So if 7pm is good for you -then its good for us!**
> **We're excited!!!**
>
> **On a separate note.....today was the first time I rode a "road bike!"**
> **Yipppeeee!!!**
> **It was so awesome! I was soooooooooo fast!!!**
> **(I'm gonna smoke David so bad on Sunday....**
> **It'll be a lesson for all his lame excuses lately! :-)**
>
> **But as I was going fast and furious, I had to stop short at 25 m/hr!!!**
> **(a dumb biker dodged in front of me -so I had to hit my brakes -which I never used yet!**
> **But.....I forgot that I'm strapped into my bike!**
> **(these shoes click into the peddles)**
>
> **As you could guess....I went airborne before slamming into the cement!**
> **Thankfully, a whole bunch of roadies saw my air show!**
> **They couldn't believe I wore clicks on my 1st bike ride**
> **(that's usually advanced -but I always like starting with a challenge -- same reason I wanted to start with stick shift when I learned to drive)**

So unfortunately my arms and legs are are scraped up and black &blue!
I feel fine -you know I walk away thinking "at least I'm alive"
(but a little sore -especially at the toosh from that seat! :-)

Holly interjected a little levity:

On Jul 19, 2012, at 3:36 PM, Holly Petraeus wrote:
Owwww! I do not want you to kill yourself in this mano-a-mano with David....
Looking forward to Saturday if not Sunday!
Love, H.

David continued the competitive trash talk, so of course I responded in kind:

From: Jill and Scott Kelley shared email
Sent: Fri 7/20/2012 5:17 AM
To: Petraeus, David H Former COMISAF

Why?
(if you're asking my speed.....it's a "need to know basis")
And ALL you need to know is that I'm faster than you :-)

You're TOAST!!!!

The next morning, as we were driven together to the trail in one of his security vehicles, David quizzed me about what had happened since last month's dinner, after I had told him I had reported the stalker to the FBI. I began to tell him the update, and he kept saying, "Shh, shh," motioning for me to keep my voice down. He held his hand in front of his mouth so the driver and the security agents wouldn't hear.

Looking grimly at me, he whispered, "Jill, I want you to go to the FBI and say you want to drop the charges. It won't be good of any of us."

"Why?" I whispered. He abruptly spurted "Shh," even though I wasn't talking loudly. He kept hushing me so the security guys in the car wouldn't catch on.

I whispered in a deep low voice, "The FBI are trying to make Fred say he's having an affair with me." He looked at me with wide eyes.

"Shhh…shhh…"

I growled with my whisper, "The more you say 'shhh,' the more these guys' ears are going to open up and heads tilt farther back."

He put his head down and mumbled, "Speak slower and much lower."

"David, it's getting scary," I said honestly. "It's getting creepy. It's taken a turn. I don't even know what to say. Fred's not allowed to talk to me."

He looked pained. "David," I went on, "I think this person is still reading your emails, and I think they're watching you, and doing something, and something bad is going to happen to you. I'm worried. I think they're using this to hold against you as leverage, and you know you have a lot of political enemies — not to mention the boss."

He seemed disbelieving, but I insisted. "I'm telling you, this is like out of a bad movie. I don't know what the hell is going on, David. But it's really scaring me, and I can't even talk to Fred. I can't even tell Fred to stop it."

"Jill! You've got to stop it," he said firmly with an exasperated frown.

I laughed in disbelief, as if he hadn't heard one word I'd said. "I can't even get him on the phone. Fred CANNOT speak to me. Don't you get it?"

At this point, David said, in a very guarded way, that my pursuing the investigation might not be good for him. He didn't elaborate. I assumed he meant because of his status as director of the intelligence agency … as if there were a rogue double agent who had turned on him or the organization who wanted to take control of the matter within his own agency.

It never occurred to me that he might have personal considerations he had been hiding … a dirty little secret.

Our conversation ended abruptly as we arrived at the trail. David's demeanor instantly changed as he turned into the competitive biker. The race was grueling, and David smoked me. There was a moment when I was ahead, but then David sped up and passed me on my left in a whirlwind. I almost fell off my seat when I saw him speed past. It got worse when I got stopped behind a five-minute traffic light and he kept going. And I endured one major face plant. I reminded David that it was my first time on a road bike, but I gave him full credit. My motto: no tears, no tissues, no excuses!

He gloated in the car on the way home, but I warned him that the next time it would be another story. "Enjoy your short-lived glory."

After our bike ride, I sent David a winner's gift of beautiful bike gloves. He wrote me to thank me for the gloves and to catch me up on his recent work events. At the end of a rather long, chatty, breezy email, he tacked on:

> On Jul 26, 2012, at 9:30 PM, "Petraeus, David H Former COMISAF"<david.h.petraeus@afghan.swa.army.mil> wrote:
>
> .... (Btw, got the g-men called off now? Suspect, as you noted, best for all, if so...)
>
> - Dave

After that day I sent "the G-men" an email requesting that they end the investigation. And I followed up with a phone call to Adam Malone stating that the director had asked me to make this request, since he would know what is best.

> From: Jill and Scott Kelley shared email account
> Date: July 19, 2012, 7:44:35 PM EDT
> To: "Adam R. Malone" <FBI email address>
>
> Adam,
> After giving it much thought to our conversation, I have decided to NOT press charges against my stalker.
> Which means, I do not want the person to be arrested -and would like to end this.
>
> I truly appreciate all the work you (and your team) have put into this. And hope you can accept my decision.

....

Sincerely,
Jill

I sent Petraeus a follow-up to his nonstop requests that the investigation into my stalker be called off. He was a bit circumspect about it, referring to it as "my mission." I responded:

> **From: Jill and Scott Kelley shared account**
> **Sent: Sun 8/19/2012 2:35 AM**
> **To: Petraeus, David H Former COMISAF**
> **Subject: Re: RE: RE:**
>
> **I did talk to the guy, and let him know that since the emails have stopped, "please end the matter." He accepted my wishes, but also said it may not be fully in my control since the sender also emailed CCDR [Combat Commander] and COMISAF etc.—which they considered a matter of National Security—making it a broader issue. But I think they'll cooperate and honor my request.**

He was a bit more breezy in his emails than I was around this time. His emails continued to be filled with comments about training, food, and the cool people he worked alongside. He must have really believed that "ending" the investigation would solve everything.

> **On Aug 18, 2012, at 8:53 PM, "Petraeus, David H Former COMISAF"<david.h.petraeus@afghan.swa.army.mil> wrote:**
>
> ....
>
> **Thx for talking to the guy. Again, best for all if it is ended. Pls keep me posted. Reticent about doing much with the SS until certain it won't become an issue in the months ahead.**
>
> **.... peddle hard tomorrow!)**

Chapter 11: My Mission Continues

Despite still not knowing the identity (or gender) of my stalker, I still felt that I had an important mission during a complicated war. I was still an honorary ambassador to Central Command's coalition, as well as honorary consular general to Korea. Having requested an end to the stalker investigation at Petraeus' request, I hoped that everything would just go away so that I could return to a normal life.

As I was dutifully planning the first inaugural D.C. ambassadorial reception honoring all 60 countries supporting our coalition, on September 4 at the Cosmos Club Main Ballroom, the event was being organized by CENTCOM's protocol office and the deputy chief of outreach programs at NESA, the Near East South Asia Center for Strategic Studies. Since these important guests had schedules that are committed far out, I had begun sending emails in July for this September reception.

> **From: Martin, Jeri-anne H Ms CIV USAF USCENTCOM CCDC-CSP**
> **Sent: Monday, August 06, 2012 12:28 PM**
> **To:Subject: Save the Date to 1st Annual Multi-National Ambassadors of the Coalition Appreciation Dinner, 4 September 2012**
>
> **Dear Embassies,**
>
> **Good afternoon. On behalf of Mrs. Jill Gilberte Kelley, Honorary Ambassador to United States Central Command Coalition, please save the date to The 1st Annual Multi-National Ambassadors of the Coalition Appreciation Dinner on Tuesday, September 4th, 2012 at the Cosmos Club. ...The official invitation will be coming to you by mail.**
> **....**
>
> **Jeri-Anne Martin**
> **Chief of Protocol**
> **U.S. Central Command**
> **7115 S Boundary Blvd., Bldg. 570**
> **MacDill AFB, FL 33635**
> **Tel: (813) 529-XXX / DSN: (312) 529-XXXX**
> **Cell: (813) 966-XXXX**

Guests received the following preliminary itinerary:

Sent: Friday, August 10, 2012 1:12 PM
Cc: Jill and Scott Kelley shared email
Subject: RE: Jill Kelly Dinner (04 September)
....

Sequence of events will likely go as follows:

- 1830 Receiving line to meet/greet Guests (recommend Gen Mattis to also be in receiving line)
     Cocktails and passed hors d'oeuvres provided
     Music provided by 3 Piece Ensembles
- 1920 Call to dinner (guests proceed to their seats)
     Head Table: Mrs. Kelley, Gen Mattis, + 6 or 8 TBD (either 8 or 10 at table)
     All other tables are open seating
- 1930 Mrs. Kelley short remarks and introduced Opera singer for the singing of the National Anthem
     Mrs. Kelley welcome remarks and introduces Gen Mattis
- 1945 Gen Mattis remarks (Key note speaker)
- 2000 Dinner is served
     Music provided by 3 Piece Ensembles
- 2100 Mrs. Kelley closing remarks
- 2115 Guests depart (no departure line)

....

When Petraeus confirmed his attendance, an update was sent out to everyone:

From: Martin, Jeri-anne H Ms CIV USAF USCENTCOM CCDC-CSP [
Sent:
Subject: Invitation to 1st Annual Multi-National Ambassadors of the Coalition Appreciation Dinner, 4 September 2012

Dear Embassies,

....
Mrs. Jill Gilberte Kelley, Honorary Ambassador to United States Central Command Coalition wishes your attendance and looks forward to meeting you. She is honored to have another special guest

attended by CIA Director David H. Petraeus. Attached is an updated invitation for your records.

....

Jeri-Anne Martin
Chief of Protocol
U.S. Central Command
7115 S Boundary Blvd., Bldg. 570
MacDill AFB, FL 33635
Tel: (813) 529-XXX / DSN: (312) 529-XXXX
Cell: (813) 966-XXXX

The guest of honor was General Mattis, with special guests Admiral Bill McCraven and Director David Petraeus. And since COMISAF General Allen was in Afghanistan, I asked him to call in through video teleconference to thank the ambassadors for their nations' support.

> **From: Jill and Scott Kelley shared email account**
> **Date: July 24, 2012 5:28:51 PM EDT**
> **To: Bill ADM USSOCOM McRaven <Bill.McRaven@socom.mil>**
> **Hello Bill,**
> **I hope you're having a great summer do far.... I wanted to invite you to be the "Special guest" at my Ambassador Dinner that I'm hosting (in Washington DC) for ALL the**
> **Ambassadors of the Coalition countries.**
> **(@60 Ambassadors)**
> **Jim Mattis agreed to be the Guest of honor, and I would LOVE for you to be the Special guest.**
>
> **(Dave will probably do a cameo)**
> **We have it planned for Tuesday Sept 4th -I hope you are available! (especially since Dave asked me "if I get togther with Bill and Georgeann often" and I regrettably said "not as much as I'd like)**
> **I look forward to hearing back from you -and hopefully seeing you soon.**
> **Sincerely,**
> **Jill**
>
> ------------

When he replied in the affirmative, it was a great honor:

On Jul 30, 2012, at 3:30 PM, "McRaven, Bill H ADM USSOCOM HQ"
<Bill.McRaven@socom.mil> wrote:

Jill, it looks like my schedule is clear! However, I really just want to come as a guest and nothing special. …. I would feel awkward either speaking or receiving additional recognition.

….Bill

I was very happy that Admiral McRaven would be in attendance:

From: Jill and Scott Kelley shared email account
Sent: Monday, July 30, 2012 3:35 PM
To: McRaven, Bill H ADM USSOCOM HQ
Cc: Bill McRaven Google email address
Subject: Re: RE: Re: Fwd:

Wonderful!!!!
I'm honored to have your presence there.
Thank you again, Bill.
Sincerely
Jill

Ever the gentleman, he responded:

From: "McRaven, Bill H ADM USSOCOM HQ"
<Bill.McRaven@socom.mil>
Date: July 30, 2012 at 3:39:09 PM EDT
To: Jill and Scott Kelley shared email address
Cc: "Bill McRaven" at Gmail email address
Subject: RE: RE: Re: Fwd:

The honor---is mine!

Unfortunately, the continued unfolding human drama ruined an important diplomatic opportunity — the first of its kind. Later, I was told by people in the command that rumors flowed that Paula Broadwell had personally intervened to sabotage the event, since it would have put David Petraeus in the same room as me, under official auspices.

Remember: This was something she couldn't do, since a mistress (or ex-mistress) could never be seen in public with him in any sort of official capacity.

To minimize embarrassment and humiliation, the leadership at CENTCOM decided to tell the ambassadors that General Mattis had an unexpected emergency in his schedule.

From: Kelley Assistant
Date: August 21, 2012 at 10:43:11 AM EDT
To: Kelley Assistant
Cc: Scott Kelley MD personal email
Subject: POSTPONED: 1st Annual Multi-National Ambassadors Appreciation Dinner

On behalf of Mrs. Jill Gilberte Kelley, Honorary Ambassador to United States Central Command Coalition, we regret to inform you that due to a unexpected change to General James Mattis' travel schedule, the 1st Annual Multi-National Ambassadors Appreciation Dinner scheduled to be held on 4 September at 6:30pm at the Cosmos Club will need to be postponed. We will inform you once a new date has been chosen, and we hope you will be able to attend.

We apologize for any inconvenience this change may cause. Please feel free to contact Honorary Ambassador Mrs. Jill Kelley

Sincerely,

Ms. Wendie White
Assistant to Honorable Jill Kelley

Even as I was agonizing over my personal security and safety, I was continuing my work for CENTCOM and committing more hours and resources every day. I believed my role to be more critical than ever. I made the opportunity to host the Parliament from Afghanistan. It was important to our cause, since we were losing ground from the political turmoil as we withdrew our troops from the region. We felt that promoting dialogue and gaining the trust of the Afghan Parliament would cement a peaceful and strategic exit to help our transition our troops out of Afghanistan.

In order to build our diplomatic relations with the Afghan parliamentarians, I organized a confidential two-hour question-and-answer session before the dinner. The questions were thoughtful and well-targeted, focusing on our strategic partnership agreement and their nation's concerns. We followed with dinner at my house, where we pulled out all the stops. The conversation at dinner was lively and stimulating. There were many debates. Throughout the meal I spoke Arabic and sent the translators to a separate table. I told them about my personal story, and how committed my family was to the ideals of freedom and democracy that they were exploring.

Buoyed by the success of the event, I wrote to General Allen to tell him about it, included photographs along with previous email correspondences with attendees.

> From: Jill and Scott Kelley shared email
> Date: July 6, 2012 at 1:54:01 PM EDT
> To: B
> Subject: Re: Hi
> -
> I hope you enjoyed the Dinner last night.
> It was a pleasure and honor hosting you, and the rest of your parliament.
>
> I was very impressed with your company, and the impression you left on as the youngest Parliamentarian in Afghanistan's history. Bravo. With your elite education, progressive thinking, and great intention for the future of Afghanistan.....I have great trust in the Democracy that we fight so hard to protect.
>
> Thank you for your generous invitation to Kabul. I look forward to the visit, inshallah.
> I wish you a safe flight back to your country, Allah maak.
> Shukran jazeelan,
> Jill
> ps keep practicing your Arabic. It's very good! :-)
>
> --------
>
> From: B-----
> Date: July 6, 2012 3:09:58 PM EDT

To: Jill and Scott Kelley shared email
Subject: Re: Hi

Jill thank you very much for your kind hospitality and being very kind with us , also a great "Shookran Jazeelan" for comments that you made about me,

I will be very happy to see you insha allah in Kabul and
honestly I am counting the moments to have you in Kabul, insha allh

Here is my self phone in Kabul: 009X-700XXXXXX and I am waiting for your call anything you need from Afghanistan feel free to call me.

And for learning the Arbic perfectly I need a kind teacher like Jill if you accept me as your Arabic language student then I promise to be a good student

Thanks again Habibi anta

From: Jill and Scott Kelley shared email
Sent: Saturday, July 07, 2012 10:08 AM
To: Kathy Allen AOL; Allen, John R Gen USMC COMISAF
Subject: Fwd: Hi

John & Kathy,

I finally received the photos from CentCom today......
The Parliament from Afghanistan left the with an unforgettable memory of the HQ's in Tampa

I'm so glad Jim gave authorized me to bring them through with Car[te] Blanche)

He came in to surprise me! I didn't know he was going to be there!

The Parliament all came prepared with many (well targeted) questions... 2 hours of questions -no kidding)
And thankfully Karl Horst did an excellent job responding to all of them.

However, the Q&A series was followed by Dinner at my home
the Parliamentarians continued to raise their nations's individual
issues and concerns, with the new Strategic Partnership Agreement.....
With [that] said, our dinner was full of compelling conversations and
tons of speculation.

Many of my responses to their criticisms, suspicions and doubts, was
based on our vision of democracy and ultimate mission.
They appreciated the fact that nothing's easy, or perfect... but our best
intentions are there
(again, people don't want advice -they want an understanding)

After a fabulous dinner, and lots of stimulating debates...the
parliamentarians left with the confirmation that their new Democracy
has the steadfast support of the USA -well....as long as they preserve
the integrity in which it was meant to represent
 (my speech was 10 min long about the past historical 2nd world
nations that eventually developed into a "democracy"....but without
the vital responsibility and duties of the Parliament's executive check
.... i.e. the genesis for the revolution in Egypt etc
....

Throughout dinner, I spoke Arabic. And fortunately, because
everyone was Moslem (which means they read the Koran in Arabic)
they were able to communicate with me
 (FYI I put the interpreters at another table in the breakfast room, so
the privacy of the communication creates develops a bond -
Ambassador 101 -lol! :-)

With that said it was an excellent day/evening spent together.

Today I received a number of emails from the Parliamentarians. It
was so special and flattering.
 (below is the one email from the one the youngest, yet most
influencial Parliamentarian -who btw comes from one of the wealthiest
families in Kabul, and unsurprisingly was educated at the London
School of Economics. Very bright 27 year old -Google him!)

Enjoy the photos. Wish you were there!
 Love
Jill
ps John,

this group LOVED you.

Many have met you.....and agreed that you're their most incredible
Leader in history!

The females and male were separated by my middle seat of the
conference roomy
They may be "equal" but they're still separated

My speech with a simultaneous interpreter (not pictured)

General Allen was inspiring in his response:

On Jul 7, 2012, at 2:02 AM, "Allen, John R Gen USMC COMISAF" <john.allen@afghan.swa.army.mil> wrote:

UNCLASSIFIED

Jill ... thank you doing all this. It makes a huge difference overall. Your personal background is hugely valuable for these folks to see/hear.

Democracy is very hard for these newly emerging countries. ...The most important thing a young parliament can do is become a check on the power of the executive branch ... I am pleased that so many of the Members visiting were women. I'm reorganizing all the gender related activities in my HQs to gain better focus and effect. ....

Remember the famous quote from Churchill: "Democracy is the worst form of government ... except for all the others." How true, and no other people in the world have had more recent and calamitous experience with "all the others" than the Afghans. They can be excused for being skeptical, especially when there are so many voices in Afghanistan are saying that democracy is being imposed on ... forced on ... the Afghans by the Americans.

....

John

From: Jill and Scott Kelley shared email
Sent: Saturday, July 07, 2012 3:08 PM
To: Allen, John R Gen USMC COMISAF
Cc: Kathy Allen
Subject: Re: (U//FOUO) Hi

Wow. Great email.
And yes...I know that famous Churchill quote well. It's quite fitting.
Thank you.

I too, was surprised (and impressed) by the large female presence.
I even made a point when we were arguing hard Islamic laws vs Secular gov't, that it's wonderful to see this representation and delineation.
(as much as they are "equals", they still couldn't go swimming at the Hotel.....they had to wait until 2am to all sneak in the pool -with their clothes on!)

As a person very informed/aware of the Moslem culture and ideology, I made a very targeted expression to the female parliamentarians about the importance of their "voice" for their struggle in my speech....
They all had a tear running down their eye.
So with that said, they understand the significance and exceptional responsibility they hold for the future of the Islamic female race.

I mentioned that COMISAF Allen was very versed on ... gender representation and rights during the rebuilding from the War(since you mentioned it once to me) They smiled from ear up ear, to hear that a top US Commander would make the effort for their cause.

With[that] said, the Parliament is a HUGE fan of yours.
You effectively deliver a message of "peace and respect" to these wonderful people.
Thank you and God Bless you for the work you do, and the Future you pave this new Democracy.

Love,
Jill

He acknowledged my contributions further:

From: "Allen, John R Gen USMC COMISAF"
<john.allen@afghan.swa.army.mil>
Date: July 7, 2012 at 9:17:56 AM EDT
To: Jill and Scott Kelley shared email
Cc: Kathy Allen AOL
Subject: RE: (U//FOUO) Hi

UNCLASSIFIED

Thanks, Jill. I deeply appreciate and respect your partnership in this.

....

John

Chapter 12: The Interrogation

I later learned that at this point I was the only one in the dark about my stalker's identity. That was about to change. But before it did, I had yet to face another ordeal.

When I thought things couldn't get more sinister, on August 10, Agent Malone and another agent, who, I assumed, was from the Tampa cybercrime unit, arrived unannounced at my home. I was getting ready to go to the airport to fly to Washington, D.C., for dinner with Holly and David in celebration of my honorary consul appointment to South Korea. (The nomination had been made back in January, but the State Department had taken this long to finalize it.) I was standing with my girls in my driveway, surrounded by luggage, when all of a sudden black Suburbans pulled up, blocking my driveway. Agent Malone got out with another sizable agent with a serious look. It was very intimidating. He ordered: "Jill, come into our car."

"What?" I didn't understand.

"I need you to get in the car," he repeated in a severe tone.

"I can't. I'm going to the airport."

"Well, then, we'll drive you," he said,

"But I need to … I want to…" I felt rattled and scared.

"If you don't come in the car with me, there will be a scene in front of your kids."

I still held back.

"I need to call my lawyer."

"You don't have time to call your lawyer."

"I don't have time to call my lawyer? I need to talk to my lawyer."

I could tell that he was saying I didn't have a choice and was going to ultimately end up in his car.

I didn't understand what this was about, but I felt I was in some jeopardy. Agent Malone wasn't budging and kept telling me to get in the car. I didn't want my girls to be frightened or to see me being treated in this demeaning way. I put a good face on it for the girls and got in.

We were soon hurtling through Tampa with all the vehicle's darkened windows sealed tightly. I was not permitted to call my husband, my attorney — no one. I felt sick about leaving my daughters so abruptly. And Agent Malone's questions did nothing to alleviate my anxiety. But now I was just as scared as I had been by the faceless stalker.

The conversation didn't make any sense to me. Nor did the tone, which was like an interrogation.

"Tell us," Agent Malone ordered, "are you having an affair with General Allen?"

"No!" What an absurd thing to ask.

"Are you having an affair with Director Petraeus?"

"No." I didn't like the direction of this questioning.

"Are you having an affair with Mattis or Harward?"

"No." I was getting irritated and I interrupted him. "Excuse me, why are you asking me who I'm having an affair with? I haven't had an affair with anyone my entire life. Who is my stalker? Let's talk about what the real problem, the reason I went to the FBI in the first place. Please tell me: Who is my stalker?"

He glared at me. "You don't ask any questions. Only we ask questions. Now admit that you are having an affair and this would make it better for everyone involved."

I said, "I can't believe this. What do you mean I don't ask questions? Who is my stalker? Is this guy going to kill us? My family still looks around everywhere we walk not knowing when this guy will go crazy and hurt us. You're telling me they're reading the emails of our director of the CIA and breaching the security of our generals and putting my family's safety in harm's way. But yet you haven't stopped him or arrested anyone, and now you're telling me I can't ask if my family is in danger? My family is terrified and I'm scared to death! The generals are concerned, and David is troubled. Why can't we ask? Why are you holding me against my will? And now you're telling me to lie about an affair? Please tell me what is going because my kids and I haven't slept one night since June 3."

He said, "Again, you stay quiet and you answer our questions. Admit that you're having an affair with Petraeus."

I said, "I'm not having an affair with Petraeus."

"Admit you're having a ..."

"I am not having an affair with anyone." I glared at him. "Why can't Fred talk to me all of a sudden? He's my friend. What's going on?"

He repeated, "You're not allowed to ask any questions." And then, "You'll regret it if you don't cooperate or agree."

"Regret it if I don't agree?" I'm sure my voice sounded hysterical. "I didn't do anything."

My mind was racing. All I could think was, Oh my God, this is getting so scary. How do you beat two FBI agents? How do you even argue? They seemed to have all the power. I had none. They wanted an affirmative answer — that I was having an affair. Did they think they could bully a lie out of me? I wasn't going to lie.

"Is Petraeus blackmailing you to stop this investigation?" Agent Malone asked.

"What? Why would you even ask me that?" I might have added that Agent Malone himself was the one who had seemed to be pulling back from the investigation.

I tried to steady my voice.

"Why? Is this about Petraeus? I would never allow myself to be blackmailed. My family's security is at stake."

It went on like this for thirty very long minutes. Malone asked me where I flying to.

"I'm heading to D.C. to see General Petraeus tomorrow for dinner with his wife, Holly."

Right before the interrogation from hell was over with, Agent Malone said, in an unforgettable, inexplicably snarky tone, "Tell Director Petraeus that we've identified the stalker."

Then Agent Malone and his colleague dropped me unceremoniously at the curbside of the Tampa airport, with no luggage and no time to get back to my house to retrieve it. I called Scott, crying. He could hardly believe the story I told him, but did his best to calm me down. He promised to take care of the luggage and get our children from the house. Neither of us knew what to think about what had just happened, much less what might happen next.

Despite the unexpected interrogation, I made it to Washington on time, and met with my lawyer later that evening.

The next evening at dinner, I was seated once again next to David. He invited me to sit in the "director's chair." He was back to his old self, drinking glass after glass of champagne at Table 55. But it wasn't old times, not at all. The last time we had eaten together at The Prime Rib, Petraeus had had the place cleared out because he thought our stalker was going to attack us there.

We began a whispered conversation inaudible to others at the table.

I shared with David the apocalyptic update: "The FBI basically kidnapped me yesterday and asked to send you a message." His eyebrow raised up, and he hunched his back to creep closer so that Holly couldn't hear what I was about to say. "They said, 'Tell Director Petraeus that we've identified the stalker.'"

I expected him to ask me "Who did they say it was?" But I was shocked by the grievous tone in his response: "It's Paula Broadwell." Just then, he reached for my hand, and grasped it tightly in both of his. This action, designed to put me at ease, instead made me very uncomfortable.

So many thoughts filled my mind in that fraction of a second. I was shocked that he even knew the stalker's identity. I wondered how long he had known. I thought it was a terrorist all along. Even General Allen and the other CENTCOM brass thought the stalker was a man. My mind rebuffed the idea that it was a female.

"Who?" I asked, dumbfounded.

David repeated the woman's name. It meant nothing to me, so he explained.

"She's the one who wrote that biography about me."

It didn't hit me. I had totally forgotten about any biography.

"Do you realize she stalked all the generals and they can't wait to have her in jail for all the panic, security breaches, and threats she's brought on?" I asked angrily. "Why the hell did she target me? How did she even know about me?"

David gripped my hand more tightly. He explained that he had asked Paula Broadwell to interview me for the chapter on leadership. None of this made any sense to me. No one by the name of Paula Broadwell had ever contacted me, and I wouldn't have known what this lady looked like even if she had stepped into the room at that very moment.

Evidently seeing my perplexity, David sought to explain: "When I told her how dynamic and skilled my safira was, she became obsessed with knowing all about you. Then she saw a photo of you, and when she saw how pretty you are, she got twisted." He saw my eyes expand in disbelief. David tried to backpedal: "I tried to end her jealousy by telling her that if she met you she would like you, and you weren't a threat since you're a longtime family friend. I even tried to tell her that you are married to a doctor named Scott. But nothing could stop her."

I didn't know what to say. That was the most disturbing thing I ever heard in my life. Why on earth would a woman I didn't even know put me and my family through the torture and torment we'd endured (and are still enduring) because she was jealous of me? And why would she have entangled David and all his esteemed colleagues in this nonsense? I didn't even want to speculate, because the conclusion was one I wasn't ready to acknowledge.

Finally, I managed to say, "Do you realize she was trying to ruin my marriage?"

"I'm sorry," he said. "She lost control when she became obsessed with you. But as soon as I figured out it was her, I told her to stop the stalking."

My nerves were raw. I felt numb. It felt as if this was the first time ever he hadn't been honest with me. Who was this man I proudly called my best friend, my avatar, my "id", my twin brother? Who replaced the honorable and honest general that I had known for years?

Although I didn't know it then, at the same time that Scott and I had been living through hell (first at the hands of Broadwell, and then the FBI), David's life was equally fraught as he desperately tried to keep the volatile situation with Paula Broadwell from spinning out of control. His relationship with her had begun to deteriorate, and she had become ever more manipulative, threatening David's career and perhaps even his security. Later, I would find out that Paula had emailed David, threatening him in a variety of ways; one of the many stalking emails she sent him was a demand that he not sit next to me at dinner —which explained his bizarre behavior for the last few months. Despite our friendship, he had effectively kept all information about Paula behind a firewall. I was oblivious to the demands she made of the Director of the CIA.

Previously, David and I had made plans to go paddle boarding on the Potomac the next day. We'd been planning it for some time. During dessert, David emailed his daughter Anne to invite her and her fiancé. Anne was an experienced paddle boarder. I think David was glad to have some other people in attendance. After the unusual admission about the stalker, I honestly didn't know what to expect from the paddleboard adventure. Competing against him in another sport was not on my mind — in fact, with all the mixed feelings and the emotional roller coaster I had experienced over the past few months, I felt at the moment like I never wanted to see him again.

"See you at the boathouse in the morning," David said, with tone that was more like "please let me make this up to you" as we bid our goodbyes.

Chapter 13: Cease and Desist

There is a certain strain of narcissistic self-confidence among many people in senior government positions. You might not see it very often. After all, these people are "civil servants," so everything is couched in humility. Sometimes, however, a person will show his true colors with an "I'm kind of a big deal" worldview. It's a dangerous place to be.

General David Petraeus finally revealed aspects of his relationship with Paula Broadwell to me, but he did so without wanting to admit the whole truth. I now think he hoped to be able to clear things up, and make the whole affair go away. For his entire life, he'd been able to declare the stop and start of conversations, inquiries, and actions. He simply wasn't accustomed to anyone embarrassing him, or creating a situation that got out of hand. I don't blame him, really. After all, Paula Broadwell's behavior wasn't anywhere near the honorable and respectable circle that David surrounds himself with.

Jack's Boathouse, underneath the elegant span over the Potomac River linking Georgetown to Northern Virginia, has been renting canoes and kayaks to heat-parched Washingtonians since the 1940s. Sitting on the hard-worn dock beneath the bridge named for Francis Scott Key, the author and amateur poet who penned the lyrics to "The Star-Spangled Banner," I was overcome by a sense of having been both unaccountably blessed and cut to the core of my being by a gnawing sense of dread and unease.

Above me, the spires of Georgetown University stabbed the August sky. Not far away, members of David's ubiquitous security detail busied themselves with preparations for the latest in a series of outdoors adventures that, at times, I imagined, must have sorely tested their patience. This time, it was paddle boarding on the Potomac; but David was a fitness fanatic whose six-minute miles, twice-a-day regimen in the gym and constant quest to push his sixty-year-old body to the limit (even after a bout of prostate cancer and having been shot in the chest in an accident during military field training, plus a broken pelvis) kept even the most hard-charging among his security detail on edge. Paddle boarding was a new one on the security guys, and as they clambered out of their gleaming black Suburbans, earpieces dangling from their thick necks. A Coast Guard vessel bobbed in the gentle chop just east of the bridge, as the loose-security perimeter extended itself around the CIA director before we set off on the river.

David and I had done hard cycling trips together, on the few occasions his hectic schedule allowed, but mostly our visits had been dominated by holiday get-togethers with our families, dinners at our house in Tampa, exclusive receptions hosted by philanthropists in other cities, and, of course, the weekly diplomatic gatherings in Washington.

Sitting on the dock, waiting for the three of them, and replaying the conversation from the night before in my mind, I was angrier than ever. I was appalled at the blithe, by-the-way manner in which David had told me the identity of the stalker who had been terrorizing my family for so long — a woman who was profiting handsomely from his biography.

As I waited for David to join me, and for someone to give us our paddle boards, the sense of dread I felt would not leave me. For months now, it was if a worm had insinuated itself in my life.

Somehow, the worm of distrust had crept in. I had just learned that the stalker, whom I had assumed was a stranger, was actually a woman whom David knew well. As for David, I just wasn't sure what was going on in his mind. Even with me, his warrior demeanor had never cracked. "Sorry" was not in his vocabulary.

Finally, David arrived with his daughter Anne and her fiancé Matt in tow. He was wearing a pair of bathing trunks, and he grinned at me. "Come on, safira," he said. "Let's hit the water. I'll teach you how to paddle board. We'll have fun!"

The Potomac was as warm as bathwater, but it felt good to finally be moving. At Jack's Boathouse, the show of force was still impressive. Besides the Coast Guard boat with its mounted machine guns, some of those on the security detail had clambered aboard Jet Skis.

I laughed. Washington, unlike Tampa, was not exactly a Jet Ski kind of place, if you know what I mean. The typical crowd at Jack's — teenagers, college students out of school for the summer, uncomfortable tourists broiling in the heat — must surely have wondered at the older guy in a bathing suit surrounded by armed men who looked as if they had all been recruited from the NFL. Not a typical day at Jack's, that's for sure.

Anne and Matt took the lead, David waiting for me as I settled into a rhythm on my board, paddling west under the shadow of the Key Bridge toward the rock formation known as the Three Sisters on the other side. The security guys on the Jet Skis maintained a loose, horseshoe-shaped presence around us, close enough to render immediate assistance if necessary, but not so close as to be able to hear our conversation — not that there was much of that, at least at first.

"That was a great dinner last night," David said, finally, waiting for me to pull alongside.

"Yeah," I said, the scene at The Prime Rib still etched in my mind.

David and I paddled slowly, side by side, Anne and Matt ahead of us. David pulled ahead of me on his board and motioned me to follow. "Paddle faster," he said, "so they (security detail) won't hear us."

Questions flooded my mind. I was still reeling from his disclosure of Paula Broadwell's name the night before. Had David known she had been the one stalking us? For how long? And the big question: Were the two of them having an affair? I couldn't bring myself to ask, but my suspicion was aroused. This was the man, after all, who had been emailing me several times a day from Afghanistan and, later, as CIA director, from all over the globe. No detail was too small, it seemed, for David Petraeus to confide it in his emails to his safira: what he had had for breakfast or lunch, how his workout at the gym had gone. And yet David had never, not once, mentioned the name Paula Broadwell in a single email.

Perplexed, I asked David if he knew that the woman had hacked into his email account. After all, I knew that she knew classified information about the dinner with MI6, not to mention the director of the CIA's comings and goings, and that of war commanders.

"Yes," David replied, as laconically as if he were commenting on the weather. "I gave her my passcode and let her read my emails."

This was too much for me, and David must have seen it.

"Jill," he said, balancing on his paddle board, "she lived with me in Afghanistan for six months." I was completely flustered, but

David hastily explained that during the time Paula Broadwell was researching his book, she had spent months with him in Afghanistan. There was more behind David's tone than a mere living arrangement of convenience with this unlikely biographer, I thought.

I was furious, since that answer still didn't make sense.

"Did you guys have an affair?"

"No."

One word, no explanation.

David began paddling away.

I paddled faster, away from him. We went a long distance without talking.

Finally, the four of us started heading back to Jack's, the security guys on the Jet Skis no doubt welcoming the fact that the end of their boss's latest adventure was in sight.

I caught up to David, still seething. At the time, I was angry as much for him as at him. "David," I said, "how could you have trusted this woman with your career and reputation? She's going to destroy everything you worked your entire life for!"

David looked crestfallen. He knew he had disappointed me, and he hates — absolutely hates — to disappoint anyone.

"Jill," he said somberly, "this is out of control. She is so out of control. I don't know what to do, but you need to call off the Feds."

I reminded David, very quietly, as we approached the dock, that the FBI investigation I had originally requested was entirely out of my hands at this point. At that time, I didn't know exactly who knew what, when, or how. But I knew that a lot of powerful people now knew that the director of the CIA's emails had been compromised, and that the person who compromised the emails was acting like a national security threat.

"David, it can't be stopped. It's so much bigger than us. It's so far beyond our ability to call it back in," I said. "I am so worried, David. I am so worried about you and your career." I had a brief flashback to the warning from Fred Humphries on June 13: Maybe Petraeus will be coming down after the election … but will General Allen, too, as Fred heard back in July?

These people, whoever they were, had allowed the mistress to continue to improperly access his official government emails, breach the security of high-ranking officers, compromise the director of the CIA, and terrorize an innocent family.

David — the alpha male, soldier extraordinaire — gave me a look like I had never seen before. "It's over, Jill," he said. "Done."

The very next day, still reeling from the revelation, I emailed Petraeus, so that there would be no doubt that he understood what we had endured. .

> **From: Jill and Scott Kelley shared email**
> **Date: August 13, 2012 2:35:44 AM EDT**
> **To: David Petraeus <david.h.petraeus@afghan.swa.army.mil>**
> **Subject: Fwd: Strange note**
>
>
> **David,**
> **Now that you changed your email passcode. ....below is one of the several emails Paula Broadwell sent to COMISAF Allen right before the evening of our private Dinner with Sir John Sawers, Gen David Richards, and the UK Ambassador.**
>
> **Please read the despicable email below, that she sent to the Top US, and Foreign Leaders- in efforts to ruin my reputation and honor.**
>
> **Thankfully all the US Commanders immediately guarded and protected me**
> **with their diligent actions of instantaneously forwarding Paula's emails, and contacting the FBI.   Their actions and defense was in response to their undying respect and great regards for me.**
> **....**
>
> **David, what Paula has done is heinous.**
> **Please don't underestimate her .... capabilities.**
> **....**
>
> -----------------

Later, I concatenated all of the previous stalker emails. I forwarded emails from General Allen and from Scott's personal email:

> **From: Jill Kelley**
> **Sent: Mon 8/13/2012 1:23 PM**
> **To: Petraeus, David H Former COMISAF**
> **Subject: Fwd: Jill Kelley''s behavior**

Paula Broadwell emailed my husband almost every other day.

This was a very unsettling time for us!
I was terribly frightened about my safety....since the nature of Paula's emails were written to clearly inflict harm.

....to anonymously email the top US Leaders, and Foreign Ambassadors....and then my husband.

As you read below, Paula sent email on top of email, stacked (in case Scott missed one)
But he didn't. The FBI suggested that Scott not communicate or reply.

....

That lady has single handedly caused a lot of destruction in my life.

[All of the stalker emails followed]

Unfortunately, his response was terse and dismissive, despite having learned that his mistress had sent all of these emails to the people loyal to him:

From: "Petraeus, David H Former COMISAF" <david.h.petraeus@afghan.swa.army.mil>
Date: August 13, 2012 at 5:04:41 AM EDT
To: Jill Kelley
Subject: RE: Jill Kelley''s behavior

It stopped, correct?

"Sorry" wasn't in his vocabulary … yet.

Chapter 14: Petraeusgate

That next week I was back on the base for a meeting. When I had lunch with General Mattis I told him that our stalker was a lady named Paula Broadwell. He was indignant. He wanted me to demand that she be arrested for cyberstalking, which included terrorizing my family and forwarding official government emails to a personal account. I told him David had asked me not to, and we dropped it.

I remember pondering out loud to General Mattis about the possibility that Petraeus had had an affair with Broadwell, since it wasn't making any sense that this girl was directing such personal hostility at me. Mattis chewed me out.

"Jill! Why would you question Petraeus' honor and character?" He made me feel bad for entertaining the thought. I never brought up the suspicion of infidelity again.

Later that week I brought up with our buddy Admiral Harward Petraeus' request to not have Broadwell arrested, since Harward used to be in constant touch with Fred Humphries. Later, I found out that Fred was removed from the office after witnessing the FBI's Mafia don-like portrayal of me and it is my understanding that he had to stop all contact with everyone, including the generals. I went on to explain to Harward what had happened to poor Fred Humphries since the FBI headquarters had unconventionally forced its way into the Tampa-based investigation. At that time Fred had been told that FBI Deputy Director Sean Joyce had issued explicit orders instructing Agent Malone and his colleagues in the Tampa cybercrime unit to handle the case "differently" from the standard FBI minimization procedure, "or else." I told him Fred had warned me that the FBI was looking through my emails in search of evidence of the affair they were sure I was having, and that they also gotten hold of private family photos on vacation with the kids. Apparently, some junior agents had made lascivious comments about me wearing a bikini while standing near my children on the beach during a family lunch. My privacy was completely betrayed by government officials with endless (taxpayer) resources, driven by political agendas.

Harward was furious. He wanted answers.

Meanwhile, David, alternately inhabiting the persona of James Bond or Malik (which translates as "king"), was by now ending every email with the same annoying demand. He expected me to be able to end an investigation that had by then been turned on me — not our stalker:

> **From: "Petraeus, David H Former COMISAF"**
> **<david.h.petraeus@afghan.swa.army.mil>**
> **To: Jill and Scott Kelley shared email**
> **Sent: Wednesday, August 15, 2012 9:21 AM**
> **Subject: RE: Countries**
>
> **….And help the malik by ending action on the other thing; won't help any involved and could limit Malik's ability to say chukrun [thank you in Arabic] to the SS and the countries, and to pull this together. ….**

His putting me in this awkward position reminded me what I (and all the generals) had been through. Despite agreeing to his request, I resented David for his seeming lack of concern that Scott and I were being terrorized, first by an anonymous stalker, and now by the FBI.

He did it over and over again:

> **On Sep 24, 2012, at 1:23 AM, "Petraeus, David H Former COMISAF"**
> **<david.h.petraeus@afghan.swa.army.mil> wrote:**
>
> **JB can handle himself ….Again, the sooner we can put that all behind us, the better. Nothing good comes of it for any involved, even the innocent parties -- ao, again, apprec your forbearance, not sharing, etc., etc. ….Will restrict Malik's ability to interact ….. In any event, just need to soldier on and survive... All best**

During the rest of the summer, the investigation dragged on — although the FBI knew that Paula Broadwell had sent the harassing email messages, was breaching national security regulations and was compromising the director of the CIA. David, of course, knew as well. And even more bizarrely, Broadwell still seemed to have me in her sights.

I tried to put the chaos behind me and move on according to my friend's request. Although something or someone had been effective at getting Paula to stop the obvious "cyberstalking," I was still experiencing serious repercussions in what felt like an ongoing campaign of harassment and sabotage of my career. Things really came to a head in September over my attendance at the private Concordia Summit.

I was invited to the Concordia Summit by Ambassador Hakimi of Afghanistan. On September 20, I received this invitation on the letterhead of the Concordia Summit:

> **The Honorable Jill G. Kelley**
> **Honorary Ambassador to U.S. Central Command's Coalition**
>
> **Dear Ms. Kelley:**
> **We invite you to attend the Second Session of the 2nd Annual Concordia Summit**
> **....**
> **On behalf of the Concordia Summit Advisory Board, we would be honored by your attendance as the special guest of Ambassador Hakimi of Afghanistan.**
> **Sincerely,**
> **Matthew A. Swift**
> **Co-Founder: The Concordia Summit**

A week later Matthew Swift, in his role as president of the summit, began grilling me over a speakerphone, after work hours. (I found a speakerphone an unprofessional choice for this improper conversation.) He wanted to know how I knew the ambassador who was bringing me as a special guest, and how I had become the honorary ambassador to the coalition. He contacted me several times, always with suspicion about who I was and whom I represented. The tone of the conversations was very immature for the chairman of a diplomatic conference, and I considered it suspect. I asked him if he was interviewing other invitees of the ambassador this way.

Later that evening, I found out from General Petraeus that Matthew Swift happened to also be Paula Broadwell's PR agent. That explained it all!

General Petraeus divulged that detail to explain his bizarre email to me. In it, he asked if I was telling the Summit Chairman (Matthew Swift) that "I was attending as a representative of CIA Director David Petraeus." I was peeved about the incorrect assertion, especially since he knew I rarely disclose knowing the director, and I certainly wasn't going to misrepresent myself to anyone. I reassured Petraeus that I was doing no such thing, and I couldn't imagine where he'd heard it. Petraeus immediately apologized, regretting that he'd even ask something so absurd; then he disclosed that the chairman of the summit was also Paula's PR agent.

I replied with fury: "Look at the source."

After I hung up the phone and barely had time to process this new information, Matthew Swift called me, blithely announcing, "Mrs. Kelley, I'm very sorry, but we have to revoke your invitation." He mumbled something about how the fire code had changed and there was suddenly no room for me. "The Secret Service is doing seating arrangements and they are a couple of seats short," he said.

Wow. No room now? Secret Service now is being blamed? I called Harward and explained why I couldn't attend the summit. He sighed aloud and said in a sarcastic tone, "The Secret Service, a taxpayer-funded agency, is now in the business of doing seating arrangements at a private, for-profit convention? Do they plan birthday parties, too?"

Another sabotage, once again. I was surprised — but now not surprised, given the source.

Needless to say, it was unnerving. I was the one being harassed, humiliated and embarrassed. I had been the one who had urged the FBI to drop the case against Paula. I had been the one who declined to press charges. I had been the one who kept the whole matter out of the news. And yet she couldn't leave me and my family alone. I was angry, and I fired off an email to David.

I was still disturbed by his initial email questioning me. David reassured me that he trusted my outright denial that I had claimed to be attending the summit as his representative, as Broadwell had conveyed to him. He followed it by his way of saying "let's change the toxic subject":

On Sep 22, 2012, at 12:19 AM, "Petraeus, David H Former COMISAF"<david.h.petraeus@afghan.swa.army.mil> wrote:

Thx, SS. Trust is solid; no worries.

But do be worried about getting ready for your shot at the title. Gonna be ugly. Was a physical animal today.
....

But Petraeus' effort to, once again, convince me to not be bothered by her latest attacks on my professional career, and instead move on and try to pretend that everything was just fine, was futile. I had to just take his head out of the sand:

From: Jill Kelley
Sent: Saturday, September 22, 2012 9:28 PM
To: Petraeus, David H Former COMISAF
Subject:

David, As you know, I was invited by Ambassador Hakimi to this summit. (read the attachment below)

A week later, this Matthew Swift (one of the organizers of the summit, and I suspect the 'agent' you were referring to) calls me several times. He essentially grilled me about how I know the Ambassador, how I became the honorary Ambassador to the Coalition.etc. I thought it was a bit bizzare that he kept calling me.....especially since I was invited by the Ambassador as his Special Guest with his Minister of Foreign Affairs
In no way, shape or manner did I represent myself to this 'agent', that I "represent you".
Three hours later, I got your string of emails accusing me of approaching some 'agent'
I should've immediately put it together Paula is behind this.
 NOW to add insult to injury- this same guy just called me a few hours ago saying "Mrs Kelley, we have to revoke your invitation because suddenly we found out things changed and there's 'no room'!"
 (Ironic, right)
 So then I said "Really. That's very strange......Almost unbelievable!!!"
      Then I said "Now I have questions for you Matthew.....do you remember our conversation yesterday?
He "Yes! Very clearly"
He said "Do you want me to read me back my notes verbatim?"
When he repeated our conversation.......-NOTHING that you accused me of yesterday was even in his notes -he said he would share them with you!
I asked Him who else knew Jill Kelley was attending, or was debriefed about our conversation.....
And after a short list, he said "Paula Broadwell!"
Why wouldn't you tell me she had anything to do with this conference?

Or behind the latest drama???

....

It's particularly frustrating since I already paid for my airplane tickets, hotel deposit, and private driver....that is All non-refundable-in addition to the humiliation this will cause to me in front of the AFG Ambassador and Foreign Minister that invited me?

....

David, this girl's constant intrusion in my life, ...

After all I'm doing to stop her arrest.....she STILL continues to pull stunt after stunt, AFTER her episodes of emailing my husband. What does she want????

You generously gave her the rights to your Biography....one of the most iconic and legendary Leaders in our history, even though she has never written a biography before.

Other renowned authors would have killed to have such a chance....Instead, she sends anonymous emails the top US Leaders and DC Ambassadors (and tries to ruin my marriage)....all of which has now exposed you to the FBI-

This is how she shows her appreciation for "confiding" in her?

You know how much I care about you (and your family) and need to warn you that there's a lot you don't know about her --- the FBI has subpoenaed all her emails, I can't tell you more in email

David, she dug her own grave ....

It's not easy to being the one asking to drop charges -when her other email victims are asking for full prosecution.

.... you need to know she's NOT your confidant ....

She's a huge liability to your career....

I worry that your request may instead make the example out of You - since I won't let them arrest her (they want to proceed -but I keep refusing to press charges.... we need to discuss the most recent turn of events)

I think you known me long enough, that you know I will always support you, never embarrass you, and be loyal to you.

Please, please ask her to leave me alone. I don't want to be part of any of the drama.

Your friend,

Jill

PS: read my (now repossessed) invitation below.....please realize my invitation had nothing to do with any ties or representation of you!

After he saw how offended I was to have been dragged into this inexplicable drama, he followed up with an emasculated email:

> From: "Petraeus, David H Former COMISAF"
> <david.h.petraeus@afghan.swa.army.mil>
> Date: September 22, 2012 at 9:45:45 PM EDT
> To: Jill and Scott Kelley shared email
> Subject: RE:
>
> "Petraeus, David H Former COMISAF"
> <david.h.petraeus@afghan.swa.army.mil> wrote:
>
> Got it, Jill, thanks. Very sorry for the drama, trouble, issues, etc. Fully understand your perspective. Still think it best to avoid further pursuit, as it will undoubtedly drag all down. Appreciate your understanding of that, however, difficult it may be. ....

Again, David ended every email with the default response: So sorry … don't make waves, then change the subject. And what bothered me the most was his foolish assertion that "this is over." I was getting tired of it. I didn't appreciate being patronized. Each time I accepted his hollow assertions, I kept getting sucker-punched. I shot off emails conveying that point, to no avail:

> From: Jill and Scott Kelley shared account
> Date: September 24, 2012, 7:12:16 AM EDT
> To: "Petraeus, David H Former COMISAF"
> <david.h.petraeus@afghan.swa.army.mil>
> Subject: Re: RE: RE: RE:
>
> David,
> You need you be honest with me, and answer if this is over?
>
> Clearly you did not end this....since this weekend's humiliating/embarrassing turn of events
> -which I'll have to go into significant damage control with your colleagues (once again) due to her latest ambush.
>
> I falsely believed that the last time I came under her attacks (when she was anonymously emailing/stalking your colleagues and my husband) that you had put an end to it?

Perhaps you don't realize that "I am the one that wants to put this all behind us".......but everytime I think it's over, SHE does something new!

....

As much as I love You, Holly, and your family.....I cannot fall victim to Paula, again -just because we're friends.
I realized that's probably what she wants. And if I must, I will concede.
(....but realize what you don't know about her, can eventually end your career)

I plan on calling everyone today, and make up some bad excuse for my absence with the Ambassador on Thursday...
This is so unreal.

David, I ask that you put an end to this.

David's email was again terse:

On Sep 24, 2012, at 2:11 PM, "Petraeus, David H Former COMISAF" <david.h.petraeus@afghan.swa.army.mil> wrote:

Caught me by total surprise.   Assured nothing further....

****

That weekend Admiral Harward invited me and Scott to Charley's in Tampa for dinner. It's a nice family steakhouse that serves big steaks on a wood-burning pit. A few Navy SEALS were at the restaurant, so they came over to pay homage to Admiral Harward.

We were there to meet up with Michael Gottlieb, a trusted colleague of the generals'. Gottlieb was the associate counsel to President Obama and the White House liaison on military matters. Gottlieb had just flown into the Tampa International Airport from the White House. Harward was peppering the conversation with profanities while describing the latest Concordia/Broadwell ordeal, when Gottlieb arrived.

Harward was personally invested in this drama, since his name had been brought up in one of Broadwell's stalker emails (and some vulgar comment she made about Harward, me, and "doggie style").

So Harward brought Gottlieb up to speed with the latest developments with the stalking drama.

Both Gottlieb and Harward actually knew Broadwell from Afghanistan, but Gottlieb couldn't recall her immediately. Harward said something like, "Yes, you know this gal: the broad with the crazy eyes? The one who was obsessed with trying to interview us for her book on Petraeus? It's her!"

Harward included all the key examples of improper behavior in the drama, including that Petraeus' email was being improperly read and forwarded by Paula Broadwell, and that her access of the CIA director's email had enabled Broadwell to stalk the generals and my family. Harward complained (loudly) that the FBI wasn't stopping her or even interviewing her after they had identified her in June.

At that meeting, Harward also told Gottlieb that Paula Broadwell's terror campaign was still going on, since she had just been involved with canceling my Concordia invitation from Ambassador Hakimi.

Harward let Gottlieb know that General Mattis was pissed about the possible FBI mishandling of the case, noting that Fred Humphries, our FBI contact, had been pulled off the case and was forbidden any contact with us.

Gottlieb said he'd look into it.

At Admiral Harward's urging, I followed up:

From: Jill and Scott Kelley shared email
Sent: Monday, September 24, 2012 10:42 AM
To: Gottlieb, Mike
Subject:

Dear Micheal,
....and he said to reach out to you so we can have breakfast or an early lunch together?
(I would have to leave at 12:45pm for another appointment)

Please let me know if you're available.
Again, it was a pleasure meeting you!
Sincerely
Jill

On Sep 24, 2012, at 10:45 AM, "Gottlieb, Mike"
<Michael_J_Gottlieb@who.eop.gov> wrote:

Hi Jill! Great to hear from you. What time do you arrive on Friday?
....Best - Mike

Michael J. Gottlieb
Associate Counsel to the President
mgottlieb@who.eop.gov
(202) 456-XXXX (desk)
(202) 744-XXXX (mobile)

A few days later, FBI Agent Adam Malone finally interviewed
Broadwell. I was told that during this first interview she lied and
denied having had an affair with Petraeus. Instead, she spent her
interview spinning an elaborate explanation for her actions: She
speculated that Petraeus was in love with me, and she feared that
other generals wanted to have an affair with me. She did what she did
(stalking and intimidation) hoping that her drastic tactics would keep
them away from me to protect them.

I was later informed that Malone came back to the Tampa
offices and reported that he felt sorry for Broadwell. He boasted that
he was smitten with her. The supervisor laughed it off, claiming that
"Adam always falls in love with his female suspects!" When Fred
Humphries heard this, he gasped and expressed his disgust, in no
small part because his wife had been hurt and their marriage was
being severely tested by the false allegations that Humphries had had
an affair with me.

****

October was a bittersweet month for Director David Petraeus.
On October 13, his daughter Anne was married in a warm and happy
ceremony in Washington, D.C. My family and I were invited to the
wedding, but Paula Broadwell's invitation had been revoked by
Petraeus, and she was furious. I learned from FBI sources later that,
like some ill-willed spirit, Paula followed me around the wedding site,
and some feared she might physically assault me. I was told Paula
was also sending David vindictive messages to keep him in a state of
fear. And by now, Petraeus also knew that his mistress was known by

his bosses, who might hold this extramarital affair over his head like a sword of Damocles.

The election was approaching and everything began to become more clear, including an outrageous newspaper headline, "Petraeus Throws Obama Under the Bus," almost pitting Petraeus against the president. I felt as if this was the first move in the endgame: marginalize Petraeus. I sent the following email:

From: Jill and Scott Kelley shared email
Sent: Friday, October 26, 2012 6:48 PM
To: Petraeus, David H Former COMISAF
Subject:

Dave,
I knew this was going to come to a head-
But I believe there's more to come...
http://m.weeklystandard.com/blogs/petraeus-throws-obama-under-bus_657896.html
Jill

He didn't like the situation, obviously:

On Oct 26, 2012, at 6:53 PM, "Petraeus, David H Former COMISAF"
<david.h.petraeus@afghan.swa.army.mil> wrote:
Jill,
Thx, ridiculous....
....
Dave

I tried to be subtle, but I was warning him to take control of his career before it was ripped away from him:

From: Jill and Scott shared email
Sent: Friday, October 26, 2012 7:00 PM

To: Petraeus, David H Former COMISAF

Subject: Re: RE:
        Dave,

A lot you should be aware of....I think you should take the job at Princeton
Jill

He tried to respond with humor:

On Oct 26, 2012, at 7:06 PM, "Petraeus, David H Former COMISAF" <david.h.petraeus@afghan.swa.army.mil> wrote:
Jill,
Will be glad when 6 Nov gets here!
....
Dave

Again, I tried to nudge him:

From: Jill and Scott shared email
Sent: Friday, October 26, 2012 7:08 PM
To: Petraeus, David H Former COMISAF
Subject: Re: RE:
Dave,
That's what everyone is waiting for...
(read between the lines)
Jill

His next response let me know that he understood what I was trying to convey, but he wasn't budging:

On Oct 26, 2012, at 7:11 PM, "Petraeus, David H Former COMISAF" <david.h.petraeus@afghan.swa.army.mil> wrote:

Jill,
Say it ain't so!
....
Dave

From: Jill and Scott shared email
Sent: Friday, October 26, 2012 7:15 PM

To: Petraeus, David H Former COMISAF

Subject: Re: RE:
    Dave,
    We need to speak.......Unless you already know everything?
    I'm your friend, and really care about you -more than you know,
or appreciate.
    JILL

This response left me with chills; I was very much in the dark:

**On Oct 26, 2012, at 7:30 PM, "Petraeus, David H Former COMISAF"
<david.h.petraeus@afghan.swa.army.mil> wrote:**
    Jill,
    No worries; and best not to talk to each other ....thanks!

That very same day, agents arrived at CIA headquarters to interview the director. During his interview Petraeus admitted to the affair. A couple days later Paula Broadwell was interviewed. She was found with classified documents (which she stated Petraeus had NOT given her), and Broadwell, too, admitted to the affair.

Also on that day, less than two weeks before my name was maliciously leaked to the press, I had a text exchange with Fred Humphries. Fred clearly knew what was coming — he'd been right all along. So I texted him the same story I had forwarded to Petraeus, since it supported Fred's eerie warning.

But what I didn't understand about his response was its disturbing warning now directed to ME:

October 26, 2012
JK: http://m.weeklystandard.com/blogs/petraeus-throws-obama-under-bus_657896.html FYI in today's news This whole thing will become a political play of events
FH: Don't think you're immune from looking at the underside of a bus either. You don't know all the pieces.

The very next day, although I was not aware of his interview and didn't know what he had divulged, the writing was on the wall. I emailed Petraeus:

> **From: Jill and Scott Kelley shared email**
> **To: Petraeus, David H Former COMISAF**
> **<david.h.petraeus@afghan.swa.army.mil>;**
> **Subject: Re: RE: RE: RE: RE:**
> **Sent: Sat, Oct 27, 2012 4:43:45 PM**
> **David, remember the surreal story with Charlie Crist -with all the secret senior level meeting going on around him?**
> **It was political horror movie.**
> **So, what You have been told....and 'think' you know -is NOT correct!**

I was trying to be discreet and cryptic, since I figured that communications might still be monitored. I was referring to a situation I'd been part of personally, and that I had relayed to Petraeus.

In 2010, I attended a meeting where senior Florida Republicans decided to throw all of their weight behind Marco Rubio for senator. Crist, a "shoe-in," was subsequently ousted from his Senate seat. (He later switched to Democratic Party.) In mentioning this meeting we had once discussed, I was attempting to tell Petraeus that people were also having secret meetings without him — the director of the CIA — and were likely conspiring to oust him.

Chapter 15: The Ill-Fated Friday

Most people watched the election wondering if Obama would win re-election. A few people "in the know" were waiting for the other shoe to drop. As it turned out, less than 72 hours later, everything came crashing down. The ill-fated Friday would be November 9th, 2012.

By now, I was slowly, very slowly, beginning to believe that everything that Fred Humphries had suspected and warned me about was coming true. But why was General Allen part of Fred's warning call? Allen, like other CENTCOM generals, was a target of Broadwell's stalking.

Bizarrely, the FBI chose Election Day as the day to call up General Allen requesting an interview "for National Security reasons." The FBI met Allen in his Pentagon offices. A few weeks later, it was repeated to me that Allen complained that none of the questions had been about the deplorable stalker, Paula Broadwell, who targeted high-profile world leaders. He also complained that the agency never addressed the breach to our national security, and didn't even address the issue of Director David Petraeus being compromised. All of these illicit acts had been known to the FBI in mid-June, five months earlier. Yet the FBI's interview of General Allen focused on whether he or any other general ever could have had an affair with me. The investigation had clearly turned to very different targets.

By this point, it was clear that none of what was going on was about Broadwell the cyberstalker. It was about destroying the credibility, privacy, and integrity of all of the ancillary witnesses — people who knew the real acts, the true timeline, and the actual cover-ups — and destroying the political futures of anyone who might be a threat.

It has been reported that the evening of the election, the FBI briefed National Intelligence Director James R. Clapper about the fact that the CIA was compromised. Allegedly, that's also the evening when President Obama first found out.

The Tuesday election seemed to embolden Paula Broadwell. On the eve Petraeus' unexpected resignation, Broadwell, I suspected, continued her relentless vigilante campaign and contacted more ambassadors to sully my reputation in efforts to make them too frightened to communicate with me. I realized as long as I communicated with Petraeus, this assault on me was never going to be over.

> **From: Jill and Scott Kelley shared email**
> **Sent: Thursday, November 08, 2012 9:37 PM**
> **To: Petraeus, David H Former COMISAF**
> **Subject:**
>
> **David,**
> **You told me you this was over??????**
>
> **She just contacted more DC Ambassadors!**
>
> **Paula is ruining my marriage, my reputation.....and now my life!!!**

On that ill-fated day, Petraeus responded:

> **On Nov 9, 2012, at 5:52 AM, "Petraeus, David H Former COMISAF"**
> **<david.h.petraeus@afghan.swa.army.mil> wrote:**
> **Very sorry, Jill.**
> **.... just told her to cease/desist.**

It was an interesting choice of words. Replaying them later, I noticed the word "had." Petraeus "had" cut off communications. Or, more precisely, maybe he "had to" cut off communications, "or else" his resignation was in the bag.

At 5:52 a.m. on November 9, before the break of dawn, Director Petraeus informed me of his life-changing words: He had finally ordered Broadwell to cease and desist. My mind boggles at the thought of it all. General Petraeus was still hoping to contain the situation and expected Broadwell, an Army captain, to follow his "orders." What happened that had forced his historic decision to unexpectedly resign that day?

Coincidentally, that same day was actually Paula Broadwell's fortieth birthday. Sources tell me that she had expected Petraeus to attend her birthday party. Apparently, the guest list contained people she wanted to be seen with, including many reporters. The unrepentant mistress probably thought that this was going to be the day of her validation, the day she would finally be publicly recognized by CIA Director Petraeus, and formally acknowledged, and thanked for her peculiar brand of vigilante justice. Instead, the birthday present from her boyfriend was a sterile warning to "cease and desist."

Approximately eight hours later, Director Petraeus announced his resignation to the world.

That same fateful day, the FBI needed to react to Petraeus' abrupt resignation. Agent Malone sped to MacDill Air Force Base to request/demand that General Mattis hand over his email communications with me. General Mattis wanted to know why. The upstart Agent Malone proceeded to smartly suggest that I was a "femme fatale" and explained that the FBI was investigating, looking for evidence of an affair — the very suggestion that had so repulsed General Allen. General Mattis was offended on my behalf. After rebuffing his ridiculous accusations, General Mattis unceremoniously kicked Malone off the base.

I suppose that General Mattis anticipated what was about to happen; soon thereafter Admiral Harward arrived at my house on Sunday, November 11. That's why you see Harward, in uniform, in the middle of a child's seventh birthday party! Mattis, a true leader, impervious to the pressure of politics, wanted to have his command's physical and visible show of support of his honorary ambassador, in case anything went haywire.

(Licensed from Getty Images)

Agent Malone had a lot of "Turn-the-Investigation-On-the-Witnesses" on his to-do list. He also contacted my husband on November 9, leaving him a voicemail saying he wanted to meet with Scott for an interview. Suddenly the FBI was very interested in following protocol, which requires a victim statement (something it should have done when it identified the stalker six months previously). But in practical terms there was no rush to get a statement: The FBI had just leaked to national television that no charges were to be brought against Broadwell. It had announced this decision without that mandatory statement. The bureau didn't cross its T's and dot its I's before that announcement. Tsk, tsk.

This fire-drill Friday was a hapless fluke, even for the director himself. In fact, Petraeus had no intentions to resign that soon. He had just traveled to four countries in less than a week in preparation for the following week's meetings! Most people who are planning to resign take it a bit easier.

From: "Petraeus, David H Former COMISAF"
<david.h.petraeus@afghan.swa.army.mil>
Date: November 1, 2012 at 11:19:13 AM EDT
To: Jill and Scott Kelley shared email
Subject: RE:

....Just left Tripoli.

He was making so many stops you'd think he was a pop-star on a music tour:

From: "Petraeus, David H Former COMISAF"
<david.h.petraeus@afghan.swa.army.mil>
Date: November 4, 2012 at 10:12:00 AM EST
To: Jill and Scott Kelley shared email
Subject: RE:

Left Doha this morning....

He was all over the place, in multiple cities in the same day:

From: "Petraeus, David H Former COMISAF"
<david.h.petraeus@afghan.swa.army.mil>
Date: November 5, 2012 at 11:08:27 AM EST
To: Jill and Scott Kelley shared email
Subject: RE:

.... hard at it in the ME...

And he really didn't get any downtime.

From: "Petraeus, David H Former COMISAF"
<david.h.petraeus@afghan.swa.army.mil>
Date: November 5, 2012 at 3:30:19 PM EST
To: Jill and Scott Kelley shared email
Subject: RE: RE: RE:

Just left … Dead Sea resort... But never even got into the water......

He was also set to testify to Congress about Benghazi the following week and had to prepare for his testimony with details and more information that he was gathering on the ground. Again, that's not typical behavior for a person about to resign in less than 72 hours.

Around 2 p.m. on that Friday, November 9, 2012, General Petraeus issued a press release about his shocking resignation.

As Fred Humphries had prophesied in July, General Allen's destruction was now only hours away.

Chapter 16: The Feeding Frenzy

The 24-hour news cycle is a machine. When the news machine seized on the Petraeus/Broadwell sex scandal, it nearly overloaded the system. What a scoop! But what is lost in this machine? Humanity. The media transformed all of the ancillary characters in this drama into targets. People's lives and careers were reduced to salacious headlines and sentence fragments scrolling across the bottom of the TV screen. Paula Broadwell cemented her name in infamy, and Petraeus moved from champ to chump, from hero to humbled.

Finally, on November 9 the truth was out. I was more sad than shocked. The knowledge that David had had an affair with Paula Broadwell explained so many mysteries around the whole stalking business — foremost among them why David had been so reluctant to seek out the truth and do something about the stalker. It crossed my mind, of course, that he had suspected Broadwell was behind the emails as early as July 22 (the day of our childish bike race), but I didn't want to make his life more difficult by confronting him.

In my mind his resignation was simply tragic. As a general, Petraeus had been one of the most admired leaders of our times. As director of the CIA, his stature was unquestioned. The rumors about a potential presidential candidacy, perhaps in 2016, had only grown stronger. A lifetime of service had led him to this humiliating moment. It was a tragic ending. But even in the midst of the storm, I had to admire David: He accepted his disgrace with grace.

I believe that Director Petraeus tried his best to manage the unraveling situation as well as he could. Until the end, he thought he could keep his job and his dignity. But, as he told me, with Paula's threats escalating, he'd had no choice but to reveal the truth of his affair. My first response was to be sorry for David, who obviously had been caught up in a moment of weakness that now threatened to destroy his iconic career.

When he spoke those words to me on the phone that day — "She can't compromise me anymore" — I felt the full force of his misery and how deeply trapped he'd been feeling. Those of us who loved the Petraeus family tried our best to reassure them and buck them up.

Later that day Kathy Allen, a dear and caring friend, and wife of General Allen, wrote:

> On Nov 9, 2012, at 11:20 PM, Kathy Allen AOL wrote:
> Jill, …. My heart is so heavy for them …. a SICK person …. I actually find this whole thing scary. I wonder what she thinks she has to gain ….
> I want you to know I feel your pain, …. You have been like a family member to them -- …. This is going to be tough. ….
> I'm keeping you in my prayers to comfort and reassure you, Sweetie.
> Love you,
> Kathy

As the clock ticked toward midnight on Friday, I was restless and unable to sleep. I replied to Kathy:

> In a message dated 11/9/2012 11:56:57 P.M. EST
> Jill and Scott Kelley shared email account writes:
> Thank you Kathy!
> Your love and support means the world to me. We've been in touch, and they're hurting. Hopefully, the media doesn't learn any more. I pray for everyone hurt by this. My husband tries to put things in perspective by reminding me that "no one has cancer!" But nonetheless, I can't think or sleep! So sad.

Kathy was having trouble sleeping as well. At dawn she wrote:

> On Nov 10, 2012, at 6:22 AM, Kathy Allen AOL wrote:
> Jill, …. He is a man of great pride, and he has a reason to be proud. …. I believe she was so jealous of his friendship with you. ….We're dealing with an unbalanced person. ….
> Love you,
> Kathy

At that point I was feeling generous about my own emotions, even considering that all the trouble raining down on me was directly the result of this affair. David and Holly Petraeus were closer than family to us, and Scott and I wanted to support them in any way we could. Unfortunately, soon we would be faced with unexpected challenges of our own.

Petraeus was busy with personal damage control, but by Saturday I saw that I would have to worry about it too. David and I emailed throughout the day as I became increasingly resigned to the fact that I might be sucked into this messed-up story. People in the government were leaking like sieves, and once reporters seized on the fact that the uncovering of David's affair originated with an investigation into a series of stalking emails, they naturally wanted to know who was the stalker's target.

The press didn't have my name yet, but I should have believed Fred when he warned me about "looking at the underside of a bus," since he knew how the FBI had abused me over the course of this investigation. It was beginning to slowly but surely come out in the Saturday headlines: Reuters: FBI probe of Petraeus began with "suspicious emails." Washington Post: "FBI probe of Petraeus triggered by e-mail threats from biographer, officials say." ABC News: FBI Probe Into Inbox of Paula Broadwell Uncovers 'Human Drama' — and so on. How long would it take for reporters to find me?

My lawyer reached out to David Petraeus, on my behalf.

Begin forwarded message:

From: "Lowell, Abbe D."
Date: November 10, 2012, 5:57:21 PM EST
To: "'david.h.petraeus@afghan.swa.army.mil'"
<david.h.petraeus@afghan.swa.army.mil>
Cc: Jill and Scott Kelley shared email account
Subject: Telephone Call

General,

….The way that the media might stop sniffing around and out Jill in that position is if you were to make a brief statement saying this is about one event you did and they ought to leave your family AND friends alone. ….

I can be reached in reply to this email or my ## below.

Abbe Lowell

I, too, reached out to David:

From: Jill and Scott Kelley shared email account

Sent: Saturday, November 10, 2012 6:40 PM

To: Petraeus, David H Former COMISAF; Abbe D. Lowell
Subject:

David,
As you see all over the news, they're looking for the mystery lady.

Every news station is asking "Who is she? What's her relationship
with the Director that caused Paula Broadwell to do threaten her and
other US Leaders -which inadvertently exposed his affair.
With that said, I'm hours away of having every news station on my
front lawn.

However, I'm considering doing something I never ever thought I was
brave enough to do...exactly what you did:
Have my attorney get ahead of this, with a statement -in efforts to stop
any speculation that You had other affairs...and to clarify that we are
simply friends of the family.

With that said, my attorney, Abby, asked to speak to you.
(email below)
Can you communicate with him, since I would like to be on the same
page, and putting this speculation and accusation to an end.
I look forward to hearing from you -and hope you're hanging tough.
Sincerely,
Jill

David didn't want to go on camera, but he suggested that my lawyer do what he had done: Come forward and beat any rumors or speculation. He believed telling the story first would kill any false allegations or accusations leaked by the government. He also suggested that I explain to the media that "we were family friends from the past who went out to dinner a lot and did things together, as that was what caused the jealousy." I believed him, since this was the same exact story he'd told me at The Prime Rib, the evening he revealed the stalker's identity and remorsefully explained why someone I had never met before was terrorizing my family.

On Nov 10, 2012, at 7:44 PM, "Petraeus, David H Former COMISAF" <david.h.petraeus@afghan.swa.army.mil> wrote:

I'm not going to make any comment, Jill. Let him go ahead. (Might note we're family friends …., as that was what caused the jealousy.)

Trying to hang tough, having screwed things up royally….Going to continue to be a feeding frenzy.

…. Best – Dave

My lawyer was also against coming forward. He told me it would be unnecessary to speak to the press since the Privacy Act bars the government from leaking the name of a victim. The Privacy Act protects the name and any personal information gained about a victim, or witness, of a crime so that law-abiding citizens have legal guarantees and protections and will feel safe reporting a crime.

Little did I know that Petraeus had already tried to mitigate the investigation on Broadwell during his FBI interview a few weeks before. I later learned from reporters that Petraeus was advised that if he misrepresented my relationship with him, his mistress would be spared from jail time. He probably thought that if he played along with the narrative, everything would work out for her. Apparently, it worked — but only for her.

I say this because it has been asserted through government leaks that I inappropriately touched Petraeus. Let me be clear: I never groped CIA Director General David Petraeus. That's absurd. It did not happen. And if it did, WHY would I go to the FBI if I were having an affair with the director of the CIA? That's even more absurd.

For the sake of argument, however, let's pretend that happened. What's the director of the CIA to do? Solution A: The director of the CIA should go to a top advisor for guidance to extricate himself from a difficult situation, such as canceling all future meetings with that person to ensure that nothing further can happen. Solution B: The director of the CIA thinks it's best to ask for rational advice from his on-again, off-again mistress?

That lie clearly backfired on me — and him.

What's mystifying was his urge to tell her I had touched him to make her jealous. That was just preposterous. And what's even more baffling is why an ex-girlfriend would cause so much damage and detriment because of jealousy. Let me repeat: I did not grope Petraeus, and I'm so embarrassed to even have to repeat in my memoir the vulgar words that were reported.

Needless to say, I was blinded. I didn't understand the connection before, but now I do. As promised, Paula never did get any jail time. All her veiled threats and predictions of doom became reality, and she walked away from the carnage.

From: Jill and Scott Kelley shared email account
Sent: Saturday, November 10, 2012 8:39 PM

To: Petraeus, David H Former COMISAF

Subject: Re: RE:

sigh
Hanging tough isn't the term I'd use to describe this nightmare, alas - but we'll get through this, David!

How is Holly doing?
I'm worried about her. I already sent your kids an email telling them to support you, since you need their love, support and forgiveness

My lawyer just decided not to come forward to the media, for a number if reasons....
however I "know" we'll be fighting speculation all over the news once I'm identified
(Ughhhh ... "everything" I ever feared in life exposure -is now making the person every news station is looking for

Can't believe how surreal this all is...
I told my girls that they may see me on TV....to not to believe anything: and not to be scared if the News and cameras come knocking on our door.
(now they'll understand my phobia of media -unfortunately I didn't want them to learn this way)

As for the FBI interview today.....
No. My lawyer agrees with me to not give a statement. So I didn't
They wanted to know "how I felt" when I was receiving the harassing emails/threats of Paula extorting and blackmailing me when she threatened "if I continue to communicate with US Leaders, 4 star Generals, and Ambassadors....then she was going to go to the media

and make national headlines that will embarrass our leaders and
their spouses."
(as you know, I was so scared someone was trying to hurt you)
But as I said, we didn't give any statements today.
(but I know they'll be back)
 Do you have an adviser that my lawyer can communicate with?
I'd like to make sure he knows what our plan of action is -since we're
anticipating the worse is yet to come

We'll get through this, Sadiki....
Never forget, true friends are there for good -and bad.

_____

Sadiki means my friend in old Arabic. David was remorseful,
but determined that a "hang tough" attitude would win the day:

On Nov 10, 2012, at 8:59 PM, "Petraeus, David H Former COMISAF"
<david.h.petraeus@afghan.swa.army.mil> wrote:

…. I sure made a hash of things. And Anne and I talked today. Just
lying low ….Gonna be tough, but we'll get through it. Hang tough
there…

I wanted David to give me something substantive:

From: Jill and Scott Kelley shared email account
Sent: Saturday, November 10, 2012 9:04 PM
To: Petraeus, David H Former COMISAF
Subject: Re: RE: RE:

What did you tell them about Me?

His response brought forth more questions than it answered:

On Nov 10, 2012, at 9:37 PM, "Petraeus, David H Former COMISAF"
<david.h.petraeus@afghan.swa.army.mil> wrote:

What I told you... Minimizing

....

I also wanted to know if Holly had been read in to the drama:

From: Jill and Scott Kelley shared email account
Sent: Saturday, November 10, 2012 9:39 PM
To: Petraeus, David H Former COMISAF
Subject: Re: RE: RE: RE:

Does Holly know Paula was coming after me? Etc?
I hate for her to think I hid anything from her....

On this point, David's response was quick and painless.

On Nov 10, 2012, at 9:44 PM, "Petraeus, David H Former COMISAF"
<david.h.petraeus@afghan.swa.army.mil> wrote:

No worries
....

I still longed for the past, before things had become complicated by his affair:

From: Jill and Scott Kelley shared email account
Date: November 10, 2012 at 10:08:57 PM EST
To: "Petraeus, David H Former COMISAF"
<david.h.petraeus@afghan.swa.army.mil>
Subject: Re: RE: RE: RE: RE: RE:

Thank God!
When I came to the assumption that I had to stop speaking to you -to
stop being a target/ or making you a target of the stalker- I actually
thought about how much I would miss your family and our family
together.
(But thought it would be the selfless thing to do- for your safety)

Kathy Allen continued to send lovely and supportive emails to me. She and John were together, but she stepped away to encourage me:

> On Nov 10, 2012, at 10:09 PM, Kathy Allen AOL wrote:
> Jill, I'm following the breaking stories about Dave. Please, please, don't let this bring you too much pain. You haven't done ANYTHING wrong. You've just been the very best friend someone can be.
> ....
> Love you,
> Kathy

We spoke on the phone once, and late that night, her family asleep, Kathy sent a longer missive:

> On Nov 11, 2012, at 4:50 AM, Kathy Allen AOL wrote:
> Jill, I want you to assume that they will "find you" ... Tell them that your whole families have spent Christmas together, and whatever other occasions you think of. .... Jill, one thing I'm a little bit worried about is someone in the media offering Paula a large sum of ... I really believe there is something wrong with her Jill. ... I think she has to prove something. ...
> ... I NEVER thought it was you, I just worried about how hurt you would feel for the family.
> I knew you'd be in tremendous pain over what they were going through. ... I will never lose my sense of all the good Dave Petraeus has done for this country. This is a man whose service to his country has made up his whole life. I can't and won't believe that this woman cancels everything out.

****

The next day all my fears came to pass. On Sunday, November 11, two days after David's resignation, and despite my lingering shock from that event, I had to host a party for my daughter Caroline's seventh birthday on the front lawn. Since very few of the guests knew of my ties to David Petraeus, I had to pretend that nothing was wrong in order to be the great hostess for seventy kids and their parents frolicking in the warm sun. It was a perfect day, with the blue water of Hillsborough Bay across the road shimmering in the light. It was one of those idyllic days so common in Tampa, which made it helpful for me to focus on the joyous celebration that my daughter had anticipated.

My cellphone beeped and I answered it mindlessly as I walked across the lawn. The caller identified herself as a reporter from a network, who claimed to be standing in a hotel lobby downtown. "Jill Kelley … can we speak about this Petraeus matter?" she asked sweetly. "Are you the woman who —?" I hung up before she could finish her sentence, my heart pounding. How the hell did she know my number? And how had she learned my name?

No sooner had I shut off my phone than there was a storm of activity on the streets surrounding my house. For an instant I thought I was watching a car-chase scene from a movie. Cars and vans and TV trucks careened toward my house, screeching to a halt in front and along the side streets. People with microphones and gear spilled out onto the pavement and inched forward onto the lawn. They were all shouting questions at me, as my neighbors and friends looked on in horror. "What's going on here?" demanded one of the parents.

"I'm sorry, I'm sorry," I cried. "I have to go inside while we start wrapping up the party." I pushed toward the side door and into the house. Balloons and party favors fluttered on the lawn as a stampede of reporters held their ground, cameras clicking and microphones poised.

> **From: Jill and Scott Kelley shared email account**
> **Date: November 11, 2012 at 3:34:05 PM EST**
> **To: David Petraeus <david.h.petraeus@afghan.swa.army.mil>**
>
> **Oh my God, it's Caroline's Birthday party and I have 70 kids on my front lawn and.....100 News vans JUST pulled up!!!**
>
> **God help me...**

It was shocking and awful, but in one sense I had been completely prepared for it. "I see the media storm has now engulfed you, too. So sorry," Holly wrote.

Who was the source? The press quoted "a senior military official."

After shutting down the party and fleeing into the house, away from the prying eyes of the cameras, I poured out my exasperation to Holly Petraeus.

From: Jill and Scott Kelley shared email
To: Holly Petraeus (Holly and David shared email)
Cc:
Sent: Sun, Nov 11, 2012 5:26 pm
Subject: Re:

It's horrible they're calling me, my parents, and siblings.....
AND just crashed Caroline's 7th Birthday party on my front lawn!
.... How can I be "the other women"?
What [is] he [like] Tiger Woods!?

And to say:
... I knew he had a mistress and was "competing for his affection!" Hah!
I found out about the affair on Nat'l TV -the last to know ....

Needless to say THIS is why I never desired any public attention

We just escaped the Birthday party out the back door, and en route to Capitol Grille!
This is surreal....

By now I was all over the news. Sitting at The Capital Grille, I looked up and saw my face for the first time plastered on every news channel. I couldn't swallow a bite at dinner. I looked down at my phone:

On Nov 11, 2012, at 5:17 PM, Holly Petraeus (Holly and David shared email) wrote:

I see the media storm has now engulfed you, too. So sorry
H.

Late in the day, after so much begging to my lawyer, he finally issued a brief statement: "We and our family have been friends with General Petraeus and his family for over five years. We respect his and his family's privacy and want the same for us and our three children."

The following days were a nightmare, with the media camped outside waiting for my every move. As anyone who has been under the scrutiny of the media can tell you, it's a deeply disturbing and even frightening experience. With children involved it was even worse. Our whole family was under siege.

How do you reconcile your disappointment over a person's failings with your feelings of genuine fondness for a dear friend? I was hurt and yet still deeply conflicted about David's actions, since I felt genuine affection for the Petraeuses. Those feelings were reinforced by the knowledge of all that they had meant to me and my family, all the memories of the joyous holiday get-togethers, exuberant dinners, and the ease and trust we had with one another. And so, despite my disappointment, I tried to stifle my emotions and be supportive. But in the coming days, my life was unraveling very fast.

From: Jill and Scott Kelley shared account
To: Holly Petraeus AOL email address email
Cc:
Date: Mon, 12 Nov 2012 19:07:17 -0500
Subject: Update
Holly
I hope you, Dave and the family are hanging in there. We're trying to as well- as the kids are hiding at Jill sister's home -the paparazzi have doubled in size since yesterday.

I spoke to our attorney today, Abbe Lowell, and he asked if you could have your family adviser contact him, since he thinks Paula's attorney will be coming out hard against David and us...and he wants your advisor to have a heads up of our our plans-

Abbe's contact is
Cell +1 (202) 841-XXXX
Email

Thanks and stay strong
Love
Scott
Scott T. Kelley, MD FACS

His response was unbelievable:

On Nov 12, 2012, at 8:53 PM, David Petraeus wrote:

.... We think we'll wait to see what happens. Don't have $ to hire a lawyer and don't see a need to at this juncture. (And not asking for a subsidy!) Nothing criminal of which I'm aware. And we've not been feeding the stories. All best/thanks again - Dave

I called and offered Holly and David help with legal fees, but they respectfully declined, believing a lawyer wouldn't be necessary since "no crime was committed."

From: Jill and Scott Kelley shared account
Subject: Re: Update
Date: November 12, 2012 at 9:47:33 PM EST
To: David Petraeus Gmail
Cc: Holly Petraeus AOL email address

I understand. Thanks for the info- you and Hol, pls hang in there.

Scott

By now, our concerns weren't only about being available to emotionally and financially support the Petraeus family through its heartbreaking scandal. Their scandal quietly stepped aside as our family was now cast into an evil net webbed by leaks and lies. We now found ourselves asking for help. Scott wrote an email to Holly:

From: Scott Kelley MD personal email
To: Holly Petraeus
Sent: Fri, Nov 16, 2012 1:36 pm
Subject: Update

Holly

I suspect you have witnessed the circus that has become our lives. Every fact, every detail out there like an open book- with just enough shred of truth to cover the lies and distortions.

Our family, our finances, Natalie's divorce- it reads like a bad movie. My whole life I have tried to be private, unassuming- I just wanted to be a great surgeon, dad and husband.

The media wants to know "who the Kelley's are"

-Instead of wondering why we were friends, they assume social climbers
-Instead of asking me about the thousands of cancer patients I've saved - they asked about the one that died
-Instead of asking about the decade of service that Jill gave to our troops, or all the homeless she fed -they have some (opportunist) freak saying she wanted millions from a deal in Korea

They talk about all the debt we have but fail to mention the fact that it was an isolated investment from a commercial real-estate property, caused by a fraudulent tenant we evicted right when the real estate market collapsed.
The debts are also associated with that. And it's pending litigation.

They talk about our home in foreclosure- instead of revealing that we were advised to stop paying and put the money in escrow, in order to modify our mortgage since it is 'under water'

Everything I have worked to achieve has crumbled- I am the butt of jokes on CNN because Jill involved the FBI after John Allen and I (among others) received these threatening emails (ironically it was Allen's recommendation to report it)

I believed at the time that not taking the threats seriously would put your and my family at risk.

....

I wake up and go to bed with over 125 paparazzi filming me and my children.
....

At some point soon Holly, I need David to state to the press that ... our reputation and integrity have been unfairly attacked.

I am very concerned that my hospital will never keep me with this irresponsible and inaccurate press. This scandal already killed Jill and I....I don't want it to starve our children.

I'm still dumbfounded by how our life has been destroyed after David's announcement. Please ask him to vouch for our honor.

Scott T. Kelley, MD FACS

From: Holly Petraeus
Subject: Re: Update
Date: November 16, 2012 at 10:10:43 PM EST
To: Scott Kelley MD Personal email

Dear Scott, …. we have been so saddened to see the cruel way you've been treated.
Let us look at what we might be able to do.
H.

One media outlet called me "the other other woman," and still another "the mystery vixen in the Petraeus scandal."

Not one referred to me as a victim, or told the story from my point of view. Whoever was leaking to the press seemed intent on creating a side-show by casting me in the worst possible light.

In fact, the White House, the Pentagon and U.S. State Department held many press conferences that created more fodder for the press, at my innocent family's expense. These multiple press conferences were nothing more than an unwarranted attack.

The reckless side-shows were designed to paint me as a phony of some sort, and distract the American public from the fallout of other people's bad actions. Then, to add insult to injury, the U.S. State Department made repeated statements that I "had no formal affiliation with the State Department." That was not only disingenuous, but it also implied that I was a liar. Despite their ulterior agendas, I believe government officials' public smears made me so radioactive that Korea had no choice but to revoke my prestigious honorary diplomatic appointment. The honorary consular title was not an invention; nor was it a trifle. The civilian corps of honorary consuls serves a necessary role for the State Department. I was required to submit to a State Department security clearance and approval process; I was issued an official identification State Department identification number; received a State Department-approved Florida license plate noting my diplomatic status; and received instructions and other communications on State Department procedures applicable to my official duties.

Not only did the American public believe the scandalous claims made in these preposterous press conferences, I later found out I was even the subject of several of those famous emails Sidney Blumenthal wrote to Secretary of State Hillary Clinton. On

November 15, 2012 Blumenthal, who obviously had no idea who I was, wrote:

> **From: Sidney Blumenthal**
> **Sent: Thursday, November 15, 2012 9:57 AM**
> **Subject: H: whole lot of things. Sid**
> **See below. Projection, madness, revenge--you pick the Shakespeare plot. .... Not to mention the Dittohead FBI agent. ....Peter .... witnessed the financially and personally sketchy Jill Kelley's appalling social envelopment of virtually the entire social life of the base, coopting the generals, admirals and their wives with herself at the center as queen bee. So who the hell is she? South Korean honorary consul? Huh? Even if she is just an ambitious dope (or in another jargon, unwitting asset of someone or some power), the scene is squalid. ....**

Later, he followed up with:

> **"Omigod – there's a new twist. You wont believe who tipped off the FBI .... you're going to like this."**
> **(quoted from the Guardian [http://www.theguardian.com/us-news/2016/jan/08/sidney-blumenthal-clinton-adviser-hurricane-isaac-obama-re-election-benghazi])**

It's probably just as well I didn't know about these emails until years later, when Clinton's emails were made public as part of a Freedom of Information Act request. Blumenthal's gratuitous gossip mongering had nothing to do with matters of State. I am embarrassed for him, as much if not more than I am by his description of me. And he was just plain wrong in labeling Fred Humphries a "Dittohead." Fred Humphries is apolitical, who doesn't listen to political talk radio.

In the days, weeks, months and years since my name was leaked to the media, I have desperately wanted to set the record straight, to defend myself. I had many arguments with my lawyer about this. He was firm: "Say nothing. Keep your lips closed," he said. "Pretend nothing can get out." I had no choice but to trust him.

The Monday after my name was leaked, I walked outside to go pick up my kids from school, and my lips were pressed tight, as if to remind myself to not say anything to anyone. The snapshot of me in a yellow dress with my mouth sealed became the most viral image of me. To this day, if you Google me, there's that damn picture, where I look like I was throwing up in my mouth.

That day, I kept telling my attorney "I didn't do anything wrong" — I said it over and over again. "Why can't I speak?" But my attorney insisted that when you don't speak, the media go away. Thinking it would be hours away from being over, I stayed silent. Months later, watching two journalists discussing the matter on television, I was jolted when one of them said, "If she had only spoken to the media, it would have gone easier for her. When a subject doesn't talk, we assume she has something to hide." So much for silence. I can't tell you enough how much I regret listening and staying quiet.

The media hysteria was relentless as a result of the flagrant government leaks. I went from being a private person with no history on Facebook, Myspace, Twitter or any social media site — basically a ghost on the Internet — to trending online. I was the focus of every cable news show in the U.S. and on the front pages of every national and international newspaper. Billions of people across the globe saw me wrongly portrayed, with headlines referring to the "femme fatale socialite" ... "the other other woman" ... "the mystery vixen" ... "20,000-30,000 emails," etc. Notice they were all sexist leaks to reinforce their invention that I had an affair? It was, as Petraeus had warned, a feeding frenzy.

He was indeed right about the frenzy, but wrong in his latest emails promising me that if I stayed silent it would go away. The sham grew with size and speed. I was even satirized on "Saturday Night Live." My husband and I were in bed trying to relax and watch something that could make us forget and laugh for a bit. We clicked on SNL only to see, to our horror, a full spoof about me. I had purposefully wanted to be under the radar in order to maximize my efficacy in the diplomatic world; now I was headline news. It was all too surreal.

Chapter 17: The Big Dog

How do you distract the American public from a scandal that puts national security in question? What do you do to draw fire away from the FBI improprieties? Perhaps reminiscing about the good old times in the J. Edgar Hoover-style FBI, the bureau worked with "Big Dog" at the Pentagon to gin up a completely fabricated story designed to destroy political rivals. It worked, and it even earned the "Big Dog" a Cabinet seat. (Under advisement of counsel, I'm withholding the name of the "Big Dog.")

Minutes after Petraeus resigned on November 9, there was a mad scramble to do damage control to cover up the FBI wrongdoings and delays. People were asking inconvenient questions about who and what else was being investigated.

It was reported that a "Big Dog" at the Pentagon received a phone call from the FBI soon after David Petraeus resigned on November 9. Someone pretty high up in the FBI must have been on the other end of that phone call. Personally, I suspect the caller was Deputy Director Sean Joyce. According to a Tampa Tribune interview, the Big Dog was informed that the FBI had years of emails from Jill Kelley to General Allen, clarifying that Jill Kelley was the "victim who reported the crime."

The FBI official suggested that the Big Dog "check out" emails between General John Allen and me. The Big Dog admitted to reviewing all of the correspondence between us (including emails from other personal accounts) over a 24-hour period.

After the Big Dog received that tantalizing offer to search through my personal email trove, the Big Dog, a person well-informed about the Constitution, should have declined to review my emails for multiple reasons. I was a civilian, not a Marine or soldier. Therefore, he had no rights over my email property, since I was a law-abiding private citizen. He was informed that I was the victim who had reported the crime (everyone knows victims have rights). Moreover, the Big Dog could have read the emails General Allen had sent to me; he should have requested only John Allen's emails to Jill Kelley. Had he done it that way, it would have at least been technically correct. In short, there were many, many reasons he should have declined to review my emails to the general. Moreover, had the Big Dog had better judgment and asked General Allen for his emails, there would have been another possible opportunity to avert the destruction of General Allen's career ... but the Big Dog chose not to proceed in that reasonable manner.

There are also serious problems with veracity and timing. The Big Dog knew that General Allen's FBI interview about his emails had already occurred three days before. General Allen's interview had been given under oath. Why wasn't a highly respected four-star general believed? Even after receiving my email trove, the Big Dog could have handled things differently. The Big Dog could have picked up the phone or walked a few doors down into General Allen's office and had a discussion to clear things up. But he didn't do that. Instead, he pored through and read years of my emails — essentially looking for an extramarital affair. (This was the same deplorable and sexist treatment that I was afforded by the FBI.)

But the story doesn't end there. It had just begun. Someone, secretly and insidiously, disclosed career-ending rumors about John Allen's emails. It was a libelous suggestion of a "sexual relationship" with the demonstrative claim of "30,000 emails" exchanged with Jill Kelley, "the other-other woman." These disgraceful disclosures were part of a methodically orchestrated press plan to distract the world from asking questions related to the actions that led to Petraeus' abrupt resignation, whether the Congress and president had been briefed on national security implications, and the length and breadth of the FBI investigation.

And why was the focus on Allen's personal emails, while Broadwell, a major the Army Reserve, had compromised the director of the CIA?

Reading the context of the emails they used to destroy General Allen could break your heart for a great Marine who served his country proud. Keep in mind, he was burdened by the ongoing war on terror, and he had just commiserated with a family friend to unwind. Here's the actual email exchange, which followed after I asked how he was doing. After running a war in a country where alcohol was forbidden, General Allen was looking forward to a time again when he could chill out with a glass of Riesling, as in former times.

From: Jill and Scott Kelley shared email
Sent: Tuesday, July 10, 2012 9:45 PM
To: Allen, John R Gen USMC COMISAF
Subject: Re: (U) Re:

Please be careful. You know I always worry about you.

His emails were heartbreaking:

On Jul 10, 2012, at 1:17 PM, "Allen, John R Gen USMC COMISAF"
<john.allen@afghan.swa.army.mil> wrote:

UNCLASSIFIED

... I wish we could protect the troops. I put six more on the plane
....

His words moved me to action, in my limited way.

From: Jill and Scott Kelley shared email
Sent: Tuesday, July 10, 2012 9:54 PM
To: Allen, John R Gen USMC COMISAF
Subject: Re: (U) Re:

Heartbreaking. So sad. I'm sorry.

I asked Harward to take me to see the wounded warriors in Bethesda
on
Monday. He's working on it.

I hope I can raise their spirits and show them my undying support.

Unsurprisingly, General Allen thought that volunteering with Vets is meaningful for both parties:

On Jul 10, 2012, at 1:34 PM, "Allen, John R Gen USMC COMISAF" <john.allen@afghan.swa.army.mil> wrote:

UNCLASSIFIED

Actually, I believe you'd be fantastic at that. Thank you in advance. Don't hesitate to ask them how they were hit. It actually helps them learn to cope with the their trauma ... physical and mental.

The six troops we sent back yesterday were a group of seven. Their vehicle was torn apart by a massive IED that killed six of them instantly. A seventh soldier survived ... God knows how. His portion of the
vehicle was massively crushed. …. he was also the sole survivor of an IED strike on his
vehicle in Iraq, which killed the other four troops in his Up-armored HMMWV (UAH).

It was a truly sad story. I responded:

From: Jill and Scott Kelley shared email
Sent: Tuesday, July 10, 2012 10:08 PM
To: Allen, John R Gen USMC COMISAF
Subject: Re: (U) Re:

Unbelievable. If that doesn't make you say your prayers at night, what Would?

I pray you stay safe, John
Please be careful.

This is where he shares a very human moment. All he wants is to kick back with a nice glass of wine, rather than ruminating on the death and dismemberment of his troops.

From: "Allen, John R Gen USMC COMISAF"
<john.allen@afghan.swa.army.mil>
Subject: RE: (U) Re:
Date: July 10, 2012 at 1:48:53 PM EDT
To: Jill and Scott Kelley shared email account

UNCLASSIFIED

Always careful. Saving myself for a glass of Riesling in Tampa ….

Before bringing in the inspector general to seek the truth, I believe this politically appointed senior defense official acted like judge, jury, and executioner of General Allen. On November 11, in the midst of the media frenzy about Petraeus' politically delayed investigation into the stalking/national security breaches, a small cadre of people trumped up bogus accusations of a new sex scandal.

In September 2015 The Associated Press reported: "Pentagon officials acknowledged in depositions that they developed a 'press plan' with members of an unspecified delegation from the White House in November 2012 to tell reporters that emails between Allen and Jill Kelley were "potentially inappropriate"[2] and to suggest that the two had a sexual relationship.

The outcome of this "press plan" was to report to the American public a (bogus) sex scandal: to fan the flames of the scandal, the media equated our emails to "phone sex."[3]

But consider this farce: A scandal was orchestrated by a politically motivated delegation. Someone in the Department of Defense wrongly characterized them to other officials, including Philippe Reines, the deputy assistant to Secretary of State Hillary Clinton.

Eventually, the inspector general's findings concluded to the contrary. Ultimately, they determined there had been no wrongdoing or inappropriate emails — and certainly not an extramarital affair. In a 2013 Tampa Tribune article, on the record, a former Pentagon

---

[2]http://bigstory.ap.org/article/3dfbd494240d4d21bb3b3db85bd f914a/reporters-face-subpoenas-case-over-cia-chief-resignation

[3]http://www.foxnews.com/politics/2012/11/13/top-us-commander-in-afghanistan-gen-john-allen-under-investigation-for-alleged.html

official admitted that — even in the moment — they had known the emails did not in any way support an accusation of an affair: "There was nothing like 'oh we had a great time last night.'" That same article characterized Allen's decision to retire as "a loss for this nation."

I now believe that this interview was designed to avoid a congressional investigation. Representative Jackie Speier of California called on Defense Secretary Chuck Hagel to reopen the email investigation and make it public — something that would have revealed the extent of the Big Dog's role.

****

By now, as you've read this chapter, you may be wondering where the moniker "Big Dog" comes from; here's the story.

In June 2013, I filed my lawsuit against the government for snooping into my personal emails and leaking them to news outlets with false and defamatory allegations of extramarital affairs with the generals. Soon thereafter, someone put in a very, very strange call to my lawyers. I was told that two different operators on the receiving end announced the instruction to hold the line and a gentleman will introduce himself. It is my understanding that the double-connection "two-hop" call is used as a precaution so that a phone call can't be traced. The person on the line referred to himself multiple times in this conversation as a "Big Dog." He first reminisced with my lawyer about his Clinton White House days and then thanked him for his service to "the Party." The conversation went south when the Big Dog became stern in reminding my lawyer where his loyalty should lie (indicating that the lawyer's loyalties should be with the Democratic Party, not his client). With this logic, he tried to convince my lawyer that he'd ruin any political career in the White House if he, the Big Dog, were named in the lawsuit or deposed. My lawyer questioned if this was a threat. Supposedly, the Big Dog changed his tone to conciliatory instead, saying something like since he was "a Big Dog" he could make sure that my lawyer was appointed to the role of deputy attorney general under Eric Holder if we did not depose or name him as a witness in the lawsuit. When my lawyer became increasingly uncomfortable with what appeared to be a threat (or bribe), he conferenced in another attorney, hoping to change Big

Dog's tone. When the other lawyer joined the discussion, the Big Dog began to chronologically account what had taken place between an initial phone call he had received from a senior FBI official soon after Petraeus resigned and the occasion of my name being maliciously leaked on November 11 — events immediately used to create a (new, bogus) sex scandal with General John Allen. During this bizarre call, the Big Dog (allegedly) threw former Pentagon spokesman George Little under the bus, suggesting Little had leaked my name with the false accusations, and that Defense Secretary Leon Panetta had had some involvement, calling in reporters to have an off-the-record meeting. Instead of Panetta giving General Allen the respect of telling him he was under investigation for an (invented) affair, Allen learned of the investigation by watching national television as he sat with his wife. (This, incidentally, was the same way Scott and I found out about the bogus accusations.)

Even though it was a sham scandal, it became a real catastrophe, with countless headlines, untraceable leaks, and outrageous lies.

So what was this all about, anyway? Obviously, General Allen was attacked in order to stop him from testifying about the progress of the war to Congress. The allegations of an affair cast doubt on anything he might say if he were to testify, and the timing of the allegations prompted General Allen to resign.

Meanwhile, the maneuver very effectively redirected the media. After this sham campaign was executed, the media stopped asking the more important questions: Why was Congress not informed that the FBI had known for approximately six months before the election that the director of the CIA was compromised? Why was the compromise allowed to continue? Did the White House know that the director was compromised before the election but choose not to do anything about it in order to keep re-election momentum? Why did the president deny national security implications when Petraeus himself made a plea deal in response to these implications?

As Representative Peter King, the Chairman of the Committee on Homeland Security, said about the timelines: "It just doesn't add up."

The timeline has always nagged at me. It was impossible to know if the revelations about Petraeus and Broadwell would have affected the election had they been made public earlier. Perhaps it would have (as the Clinton/Blumenthal emails suggest) — not so much because of the affair, but because of national security concerns.

Despite the wrongs my family endured at the hands of a stalker, and the FBI, I voted to re-elect President Obama. That said, I think it's unconscionable and un-American that citizens were duped and innocent reputations and careers were destroyed. And if it's true that Obama really didn't know until after the re-election … well … that's just scary.

Chapter 18: Ruination/Ruined Nation

As you know by now, I gravely regret having gone to the FBI to protect my family. Unbeknownst to me, the bureau turned the investigation on us, believing that I may have had an affair. The series of sexist leaks, which resulted in my name being splashed across the media landscape, created an unbelievable frenzy in the press. The fabricated sex scandal and libelous claims caused irreparable damage to my career and reputation.
I am collateral damage. I went from mom to meme, from patriot to pariah. I cannot unread what was written, nor unhear what was said. Meanwhile, the country lost the indefatigable and unassailable leadership of COMISAF General Allen.

General Allen and I found out about these outrageous claims of our supposed affair from national television. In both cases, our spouses were sitting next to us. To this day, I'm utterly amazed that people got on conference calls and callously planned my fate without any respect for the truth. The only thing I can do is relay my story and hope that the justice system will hold these people accountable in court. The damage cannot be undone, but I hope that the unwarranted pain that my family and General Allen's family endured will never happen to another innocent family again.

It's wrong that the esteemed General John Allen was caught up in a bogus scandal designed to tarnish a stellar career solely because he and I emailed each other. Keep in mind that General Allen urged me to go to the FBI in the first place. He would not have suggested this were we having an affair.

On the contrary, my emails with Allen were timely and platonic. In one email exchange, I was corresponding with an Afghan contact on his behalf.

I wrote to my contact, copied and pasted the dialogue that was sent.

From: Jill and Scott Kelley shared email
Sent: Friday, August 17, 2012 7:26 PM
To: Allen, John R Gen USMC COMISAF
Subject: Re: (U//FOUO)

That's atrocious. These ongoing murders by the Afghan forces make me
sick to my stomach.
These brave soldiers are in my prayers.
Please John..... please be careful.

And yes, I'm fully aware of BOTH Ministers being fired.
As you can read (below) I accepted the invitation to meet him (them)

I realize that the Parliament made the vote. But wanted Him to believe

I gave him the benefit of the doubt.
He does seem to NOT support the wrongdoings -especially because he's
very modern and westernized -and would like to see Afghanistan as a
secular nation

Thankfully, he's very outspoken and influential, hence could be a
great conduit for my voice & cause.

Would you like me to ask him for anything else?

General Allen responded with good suggestions and praise:

On Aug 17, 2012, at 11:48 AM, "Allen, John R Gen USMC
COMISAF"
<john.allen@afghan.swa.army.mil> wrote:

UNCLASSIFIED

Your message is simple and understandable. Stay on it that track.
....
Nonetheless, well done to you. He's feeling some heat from you and
that's good.

Thank you for your help.

I was happy to be helping:

From: Jill and Scott Kelley shared email
Sent: Friday, August 17, 2012 8:37 PM
To: Allen, John R Gen USMC COMISAF
Subject: Re: (U//FOUO)

Please never thank me John.......if I could use my powers for good -
then
I'm doing what God intended.

I'm sorry that you're fighting this uphill battle. It seems that every
step you take, someone tries to trip you two steps behind...
(and it's these political players that are pulling the carpet from under
you)

But, with chaos comes opportunity.
I'm here for you.

At that time, General Allen was planning his trips to return home. And his email was very prescient. After giving me a preview of his itinerary, he wrote the following statement, which foreshadowed events. In actuality, Allen's emails were being read by political enemies who would stop at nothing (including subverting his testimony) to ensure the election of their preferred candidate.

General Allen had no idea how true his words were:

On Aug 19, 2012, at 9:53 AM, "Allen, John R Gen USMC COMISAF"
<john.allen@afghan.swa.army.mil> wrote:

UNCLASSIFIED

...Showing up in Washington this close to the election is high risk. If it
became public
knowledge I were in DC the Congress might summon me to the Hill
....

Shortly after the trumped-up scandal broke, Defense Secretary Leon Panetta announced that General Allen's nomination for the post of Supreme Allied Commander would be delayed indefinitely while the FBI further "investigated" his "inappropriate" relationship with me. General Allen lost out on an opportunity of a lifetime, the capstone to a glorious career, because of political spinmasters who needed to distract from a more serious scandal. General Allen was too honorable, too well-respected. His credibility and integrity had to be challenged. Had he testified to Congress about the truth — the truth of the timeline, the truth of the improper investigation, the truth about the National Security threat — had he testified, he would have been believed. That couldn't happen. The dirty-dealing politicos needed to "take out the trash before the whole house started to smell." So they trashed one of the most honorable, honored, respected patriots in American history. And they used lies about me to do it. It was — it is — deplorable.

Three years after the scandal that ended Petraeus' career as director of the CIA, the false portrayals of General Allen, FBI Agent Humphries and me are still out there. Not many media outlets tried to set the record straight. Why should they? They trusted the leaks by "unnamed government officials." Just as I trusted the government with my privacy, the media (and American public) trusted government officials who supplied those false leaks.

The most painful aspect was the falsity of the takedown. I hadn't had an affair. I hadn't been a stalker. I wasn't a femme fatale or even a socialite. But false narratives about my private emails, released into the craven media maw without my permission or knowledge, were a red bouncing ball begging for attention. The public imagination was tweaked with the lascivious hints of sexual impropriety in clever headlines and eyebrow-raising cable news discussions.

I did nothing to deserve these smears on my good name — smears that devastated my family, caused me to lose everything I had worked so hard to earn and left my reputation in shambles.

Distorted and perverted depictions of my emails, which were private, were spilling out into the news for all to devour. I challenge anyone to think of how it would feel to have one's every private thought and every teasing chat with a friend made public. I was forced to confront a horrible realization: Political appointees within the FBI used the resources of the agency to inappropriately gain access to my emails, then leaked fabricated and distorted descriptions of those private emails to the media.

For a long time I obediently kept my head down and didn't speak to the press. I felt, perhaps naively, that the truth would come out. It never did. After a time the media spotlight turned away from me, but it left my life in shambles. My diplomatic role as honorary consul was revoked. My reputation, my standing in the community and my business relationships were obliterated. My diplomatic connections were severed. My longtime access to the MacDill Air Force Base was revoked, in spite of a decade of voluntary service. My husband's medical practice has suffered. Worst of all, my character, my sense of honor and integrity, was damaged.

CONSULATE GENERAL OF THE REPUBLIC OF KOREA
SUITE 2100, INTERNATIONAL TOWER
229 PEACHTREE STREET
ATLANTA, GEORGIA 30303

PHONE (404) 525-1611
FAX (404) 521-3169

Ms. Jill Kelley

November 27, 2012

Dear Ms. Kelley,

On behalf of the Minister of Foreign Affairs and Trade of the Republic of Korea, I regret to inform you that my government has decided to revoke the title and duty of Honorary Consul in Tampa. This letter serves as notification of the immediate revocation.

In spite of these circumstances, I look forward to your continued support in promoting friendship and understanding between our two countries.

I wish you and your family all the best.

Sincerely,

Kim, He Beom
Consul General

Chapter 19: Putting Humpty Dumpty Back Together Again

Now that some time has passed, I have some perspective on our pain. My family and I were crushed in the immediate aftermath of Petraeus' revelations and resignation, followed by the media blitz, which produced the horrors of undeserved infamy. The average American consumer of the media simply can't fathom what it feels like to lose one's privacy in the way that my family and I have lost ours. Not only is it illegal, it is irreparable.

Scott and I entered 2013 still feeling devastated and trying to find our footing in the "new normal" of our lives. One day Scott wrote this note to himself after he once again walked through the hospital halls, surrounded by TVs playing coverage of me.

I will not let this adversity define me.
I will not let it break me.
I will not let it ruin me or my family.
It is how we act during these times of extreme challenge and adversity that shows our true character.

Scott was right — our problems seemed small and insignificant compared with those of his patients. But I also felt entangled and had to figure out how to get loose of it so I could resume my life. I thought it was time to break the silence. The press was filling a vacuum that existed because we said nothing. It was time to change that. In January I decided to give a single interview to Howard Kurtz for the Daily Beast. Kurtz was a highly regarded journalist who had spent nearly thirty years at The Washington Post and hosted CNN's "Reliable Sources" before joining the online publication.

During a two-hour interview with Kurtz in Washington, I told the story of what had really happened and described the toll it had taken on my family. I avoided any direct criticism of Paula, only saying how absurd it was that the press characterized us as romantic rivals. I was not romantically involved with David — and I was certainly not a rival to Paula, having never met her and knowing little about her. Of the media frenzy I told Kurtz: "As much as I appreciate that they want to be the first one to come out with a headline, regardless of whether they did any fact-checking, they have to consider the impact they have on our life and our children's lives. Just because it's repeated doesn't make it true. It was living a nightmare."

It was my first and only press interview. However, Scott and I also decided to bite the bullet and pen an op-ed for The Washington Post. Our aim was to highlight the need for stronger privacy protections. It shocked us to learn that the Electronic Communications Privacy Act had been enacted in 1986, before the Internet even existed, and was hopelessly outdated.

Our experience of having our privacy invaded and our lives turned upside down by authorities leaking our names and the existence of private electronic correspondence highlights the need for measures that ensure citizens retain their privacy when they seek assistance and protection from law enforcement and that the names of those who report a crime are not made public.

Our story stands as a cautionary tale. We have experienced how careless handling of our information by law enforcement and irresponsible news headlines endanger citizens' privacy. We know our lives will never be the same, and we want to prevent others from having their privacy invaded merely for reporting abusive, potentially criminal, behavior. That is why we believe Congress must consider how the rights that we carefully safeguard in other forms deserve equal protection in this age of digital communication.

I shouldn't have been surprised that the countless comments to the online edition our op-ed largely piled on, expressing a startling level of vitriol, although some came to our defense. "Ironically, all these hateful posts about the Kelleys merely serve to prove their point," wrote one — a sentiment with which I heartily agreed. Another addressed the attackers, writing, "I hope this never happens to you or your family. Your lack of empathy and thoughtfulness reveals a shallowness unable to comprehend what happened here or why."

But that was our point — with everyone's electronic communications apparently being collected, it could happen to anyone.

****

I thought that David owed me at least a small gesture of support, since none of this would have happened if it were not for his relationship with Paula. In February 2013 I wrote to him:

> **David,**
> As you may have noted in the past 3 month...every outrageous headline and article printed (and continues to be printed) is because I was silent.
> That plan works very well for someone like you--a public figure with a long reputation with the media; and works most especially for Paula--someone that can only incriminate herself by speaking. But it's clearly a disservice to me!
> When they tried to answer "Who is Jill Kelley" and turned up with nothing.....no Facebook, Google, MySpace—nothing--they instead just "created" me. (not sure how I became the "subject" of this scandal, and Paula was only the object)
> Unfortunately, I was too considerate to ask you to attest to our honor in November--thinking it would go away--so the media found a few jealous people that had an ax to grind...and even some people that claimed they knew me.
> These liars along with the irresponsible media that never did any fact-checking filled my vacuum with outrageous allegations, accusations and misrepresentations in efforts to strife our integrity.
> So to reply to your advice, staying silent didn't work for me before so I know it won't work again.
> I know we'll never totally recover from the irreversible damage that was done by Paula, so I do not think it's asking too much to make one statement to help preserve what we worked so hard our entire lives to earn--since it was wrongfully taken away by your affair.
> I did so much to protect you behind the scenes so that your future didn't end up as bad as it could've been.... But please reconsider so I have a future as well.

David's response was cool — and not particularly helpful.

> .... rest assured that Holly and I feel very, very badly for you and Scott and your family ...The press treatment has been unfair and outrageous. Having said that, however, I firmly believe that you are not going to get a fair shake if you go public and that all such overtures will do is remind everyone of the controversy, ...
> I am not engaging with the press at all at present .... I will resurface in a month or two and then gradually embark on various activities that will comprise the future portfolio. Over time, I will have

an opportunity to say nice things about you and Scott and your contributions to the coalition effort, etc. And I'll take advantage of those opportunities. Sadly, however, I do not expect those comments or statements from anyone to be sufficient to undo the damage that has been done. ... my strong advice is to lie low, try to be low profile,
...
All best --

I wasn't prepared to let it go. It continues to disturb me to see our honor and integrity continuously attacked with false accusations and allegations.

David wasn't budging. He had his own strategy, and I know he decided, probably on the advice of his lawyer, not to say anything publicly about me. He repeated his mantra: "Best course is just to lie low." He said he was avoiding photos, not going to restaurants and, most of all, not giving interviews. And that was that.

I could sympathize with David. What initially received little coverage was the possibility that Broadwell had access to highly classified information. There was going to be more to this story, and David knew it.

The day after Valentine's Day 2013, we had an interesting email exchange about his "low profile" strategy.

On Feb 15, 2013 6:52 AM,
Jill and Scott Kelley shared email account wrote:

I noticed [that you are staying low profile]...
But I only gave one interview (Daily Beast a month ago).....because they're attacking me, not you

People claim I gave more than one interview.....it's the same circus that continues to print -as ALL the outrageous headlines and bogus articles that runs -whether I speak or not
Do you have any advice?
(not really used to this)

Again, his response was milquetoast advice to not comment and not attend high profile events. I wanted to break through his narrative.

On Fri, Feb 15, 2013 at 7:59 AM,
Jill and Scott Kelley shared email account wrote:
No it's not fun. Actually quite disturbing to see our honor and
integrity continuously attacked with "false" accusations, and
allegations.

We've never hurt anyone in our life -never even did a crime or smoked
a cigarette!
In fact, could've done anything in life, but decided to dedicated our
lives to helping make other's lives better....
I've never seen anything like this in my life!
Wish any of these phony stories was true -than I could justify it.
(still can't believe I lost my Consul General because of the out right
"lies" being printed over and over -without any responsibility or
accountability)

[Broadwell] ruined our life - and walked away unscathed. I'm
dumbfounded.

I truly prefer not to do another interview to correct the record about
our the false stories that attack our honor and integrity......but beg you
(or your spokesperson) to release a brief statement in support of the
Kelley's integrity.

I'm worried that these bogus stories (being repeated over and over) is
going to make Scott lose his job.

I need your help David....and all the journalist will only do it -but they
want it exchange for the story about the scandal.
(I don't want that anymore than any of us)
Please help. It would mean the world to me.

Petraeus, shaken but not particularly humbled or sympathetic,
simply referred to Broadwell as a "catalyst" rather than perpetrator:

On Feb 15, 2013, at 3:16 PM,
David Petraeus personal Gmail account wrote:
I will not engage the press on virtually anything.... the catalyst did not
walk away unscathed, I'm sure you recognize, anything but. Hang
tough, lie low, focus on family, and keep your head down...

I was not amused by his response. This is when I knew,
beyond a shadow of a doubt, that he was not going to move to help
me.

But the fallout continued with the resignation of John Allen in February. Although a subsequent investigation into our emails concluded that there was nothing untoward about any of them — which, of course, was the case — it was enough to sidetrack John's career and force him into a premature retirement. Like me, he was collateral damage in a scandal that had not involved him. With a heavy heart, I broke my silence to release this comment on John's retirement:

> "General Allen is an epic military leader, a great patriot and a tremendous human being. With her unconditional support for her husband's mission to the world, Kathy Allen is every bit the American hero that he is. His spotless record was unnecessarily tarnished by baseless accusations perpetuated from a media sideshow. This absurd witch hunt has haunted both of our families with shameless innuendo for no other reason than to feed an insatiable need for scandal. We should not allow any part of this nonsense to mar the memory of 38 incredible years he dedicated to our nation."

In spite of being cleared completely, John still had to face public humiliation and recrimination. He was worried about the effect on Kathy, who suffered ill health with an autoimmune disorder, and finally decided that resignation was his only viable option. His statement upon resigning was directed at Kathy and his love for her, something I had seen expressed on so many occasions. "My primary concern is for the health of my wife, who has sacrificed so much for so long," he said in a written statement. "For more than 35 years, my beloved Kathy has devotedly stood beside me and enabled me to serve my country. It is profoundly sobering to consider how much of that time I have spent away from her and our two precious daughters. It is now my turn to stand beside them, to be there for them when they need me most."

Newsweek published a story that month, "The Tragedy of John Allen & the Petraeus Scandal," that would have made any reader experience deep regret at the loss of Allen.

In May John and Kathy agreed to a television interview by ABC reporter Martha Raddatz. John spoke frankly about the swirl of publicity that consumed them once our emails were out in the press.

"Every phone call was pretty grim. And they were getting worse by the minute. ... For many years, I had told Kathy, as we had dealt with these issues, that the day that this becomes too big, I will drop my letter the next day. ... And I finally made the decision it was time to go home."

Sitting beside her husband, Kathy expressed her dismay that so much was made of the emails — especially considering that they had been read by our spouses. Remember, Scott and I shared an email address and I never hid anything from him. As Kathy said, "When someone shares an email with her husband, you know, I thought, 'Is somebody thinking this is a little odd that, you know, they're taking this so seriously?'" Nevertheless, she worried about the stress on her husband. "I don't know how he can run a war and then have this added pressure."

It was just a shame. Despite General Allen's having testified to the FBI (under oath) that no sexual affair or inappropriate relationship existed between him and me, his illustrious career was tarnished by the fabricated scandal orchestrated by political appointees. He had been prescient. He didn't want us "to be misunderstood by the people now monitoring [his] account," yet they seized on the opportunity, purposefully misunderstood, misrepresented, mischaracterized and leaked this false story.

In March General Jim Mattis also announced his retirement. There was a wonderful tribute to him in the Marine Times titled "The man. The myths. Mattis." It was a glowing piece that perfectly captured Jim's irreverence and commitment, both on the battlefield and on the homefront. He was unquestionably one of the most beloved generals of our era.

One night when Scott and I were out to dinner, a young former Marine came up to me and thanked me for my support to Central Command over the past decade. He then immediately followed his association to me by telling me that he was part of Jim's security detail in Afghanistan. He said, "I'm not enlisted any longer, Mrs. Kelley, but I would still take a bullet for General Mattis! He's one of the most honorable men I ever met."

Scott and I were invited to attend the change of command ceremony at MacDill — I'm sure at Jim's request — but we decided not to attend. His invitation came as Mattis read and responded to one of my op-ed pieces:

From: "Mattis, James N Gen MIL USMC USCENTCOM CCCC-CCCC" <james.mattis@centcom.mil>
Date: January 23, 2013, 2:27:05 PM EST
To: Jill and Scott Kelley shared email "Harward, Robert S VADM MIL USN USCENTCOM CCDC-DCDR"
Subject: RE:

Thanks, Jill. My best to you and Scott always. I just pulled up your very well written article—you wrote powerfully and persuasively. I am unapologetic about our friendship and will remain forever proud to say that I know you both and admire you.

[A] mendacious REDACT is not something for our country to be proud of; we need a responsible REDACT, not a breathless, hysterical REDACT that makes sport of destroying reputations.

.... you wonderful folks are on the invitation list for the 22 March Change of Command in the hanger....

, Jim

The last thing we wanted was to distract attention from this American hero in his final moment. I gave a heartfelt statement to the media:

> "We are extremely humbled by General Mattis' gracious invitation to attend his ceremony in honor of his exemplary years of service to our nation. Today's Change of Command will be a well-deserved tribute to General Mattis' legacy, and a reflection of his incredible character and integrity.
>
> General Mattis is one of our country's greatest leaders, and I am proud that our men and women have been led by such an extraordinary leader, and magnificent human being. ...I would like to thank General Mattis for the decades of his selfless service, and congratulate General Austin as our newest commander at Central Command."

I was stung by the realization that while I continued to suffer the repercussions of the scandal, Generals John Allen and Jim Mattis had their noble careers shaken to the core.

****

Much of what happened to me was a cynical sideshow of the type that only Washington is capable of choreographing, or Hollywood is capable of writing. One example of the ongoing narratives is the connection between the Petraeus scandal and the tragedy in Benghazi, Libya, that resulted in the deaths of four Americans, including the U.S. ambassador to Libya.

Benghazi was, and is important, but it didn't weigh on Petraeus as much as the FBI investigation (the domino effect of Broadwell improperly accessing his official government emails) weighed on him. It is not a surprise that the CIA and State Department were not communicating effectively or efficiently at the time of Benghazi. I was told that many people knew that Petraeus was compromised, and, as a result, meetings were happening "around" him- without the Director of the CIA. Within a few days of Benghazi, David and I spoke about it. He expressed some issues facing Benghazi right after the attack, then followed up with an email that described his view of the work effort that Benghazi debacle represented.

From: "Petraeus, David H Former COMISAF"
<david.h.petraeus@afghan.swa.army.mil>

To: Jill and Scott Kelley shared email
Sent: Wednesday, September 12, 2012 6:43 PM
Subject: RE:

Enjoy, Jill. Tough/long night last night.... Touch wood on days ahead... Hard work ongoing to assess, anticipate, monitor, and prepare....

From: "Petraeus, David H Former COMISAF"
<david.h.petraeus@afghan.swa.army.mil>
Date: September 14, 2012 at 5:54:06 AM EDT
To: Jill and Scott Kelley shared email
Subject: RE:

Heading to Cap Hill shortly. Tense day ahead in the CC AOR
[Central Command Area of Responsibility] ....

Later, when Petraeus and I saw the way that Benghazi was being spun, we understood that Benghazi was going to be a major issue for Petraeus' career.

> From: Jill and Scott Kelley shared email account
> Sent: Friday, November 02, 2012 12:00 PM
> To: Petraeus, David H Former COMISAF
> Subject:
>
> Did you see the cover of the Wall Street Journal?
> Unreal.
>
> When ever does intelligence agencies of other counties ever disclose "classified" information -- in efforts to serve the ulterior motives of a reporter?
>
> Needless to say, this was purely tragedy --but any information, criticism or actions to throw You under the bus......won't bring back the lives of these men.
>
> This is only going to get bigger, uglier and out of control....
> I'm afraid for you, Sadiki.
>
> You selflessly served your country your entire life- and now this? Can you put a stop to this with your agency's "entitlement" to stay discreet?

Petraeus referred me to a New York Times article to explain the initial Benghazi fallout. He also explained how he attended the funeral of someone who had worked for the CIA. I responded with another article that was speculating about Petraeus' resignation:

> From: Jill and Scott Kelley shared email
> Date: November 2, 2012 at 6:15:05 PM EDT
> To: David Petraeus <david.h.petraeus@afghan.swa.army.mil>
>
> Check out this "wired" article...
> I understand, there's an agenda -whoever it may serve?
> It's not the first article to mention you resigning.

Do you want to resign?
You know I support whatever choice you make - and I mean it when I say "the Malik could do anything!!!!"

http://www.wired.com/dangerroom/2012/11/petraeus-benghazi/

Less than a week after his resignation was announced, David was scheduled to testify on Capitol Hill. He was asked why the CIA's talking points about the tragedy had been changed to minimize assertions that it had been the result of a terrorist attack, a fact that would soon be confirmed without caveat.

In fact, the whole Benghazi thing has been quicksand for Petraeus. I feel as though the government wanted to keep Petraeus in line with the new —changed — talking points. They must have used the threat of disclosing the affair as a way to accomplish this. This is reminiscent of how Martin Luther King was forced by the FBI as it spied into his extramarital affair to remain silent while it attempted to blackmail him into committing suicide, with the threat of corrupt political officials revealing the affair to the American public. History repeats itself.

On Sat, May 11, 2013 at 4:19 PM, Jill Kelley wrote:
I'm hearing they're trying to blame you for Benghazi (since the testimony of the whistleblower) based of Paula's speech about the attack on the embassy because of the terrorist held in the annex....
I'm so concerned her statement will incriminate you -since this blame game has become so political.

For his part, Petraeus dodged all references to Benghazi that I had included in emails. He didn't want to talk to the press and was concerned about someone leaking emails of his talking points to the Weekly Standard.

From: Jill and Scott Kelley shared email
Date: May 11, 2013, 7:47:43 PM EDT
To: David Petraeus personal email
Subject: Re:

Ugh. Unreal. But maybe that leak was a good thing for you! Fingers crossed.

But I agree that you shouldn't talk to any press.

However, I'm concerned that since this got so contested, that the adm. may make you go back on the hot seat to save face of others -in efforts to keep them in power, since you're out.

Unfortunately the recent connection that was made about your Nov testimony and her conflicting Denver speech was not what you needed in this political blame game. I was concerned that she got it from reading your emails, and you didn't put one-and-one together, therefore I do not want anyone to use her speech to throw you under the bus.

Chapter 20: From Ashes to Advocate

As things have become more salient, I become more indignant as I paved my road in advocacy and activism through journalism. There are many aspects of my story worth analyzing. Perhaps this is another example of undermining an outspoken female. It is also an iconic case study about privacy concerns on the Internet.

Like most Americans, I am comfortable with email and texting. I rely heavily on technology as a means of communication and self-expression. I am authentic and present in my correspondence (with both men and women) not stilted, sterile, or androgynous. I am a modern feminist who believes that I can still be feminine in my professional life. I'm comfortable wearing a canary-yellow dress with high heels while making a difference in the world.

The zealous government officials involved in this debacle couldn't grasp that a woman could have close, platonic, professional, and personal relationships with men. This mentality infected every indefensible government action during the investigation of the crime that I reported to the FBI. The investigation, driven by sexist speculation and bigotry-based gender-rights violations, wrongly shamed me. It is my strong opinion that, if my husband had reported the crime, this would never have happened.

The diminishment and objectification invaded all of the media coverage, based on sexist leaks from unnamed government officials. The barefaced innuendo was excruciating. I saw it as nothing less than a pitiful example of an anachronistic culture where ambitious, attractive, vivacious, and intelligent women are shamefully reduced to nothing more than a badge of infamy. Why are women publicly humbled when we dare to lean in to leadership roles?

I am a fourth-wave feminist. As a now forty-year-old woman, I am standing on the shoulders of giants who made those sacrifices and broke through the glass ceiling. I embrace my gender, own my feminism, and call out everyone who tries to undermine me as a strong woman.

I think it's a disgrace that government officials were so fueled by misogyny and sexism that they went desperately snooping through my emails to try to locate an affair. Ironically, at least one of the hypocrites who accused me was simply projecting; perhaps the presumptuous government officials were also engaging in vice-laden activities that filled their foul imaginations.

In my case, this chauvinism and bigotry combined with ageism and generational misunderstanding. The diplomatic environment that I entered a decade ago was a male-dominated, fully saturated market. Like many Generation X females, I knew there was no clearly defined path where a young, bright female could reasonably assume that conventional career advancement would be fair. I felt the need to pave my own road: So I paid my dues and volunteered tirelessly at CENTCOM without any pay or official title. Over the course of many years, I earned respect for my proven capabilities, and garnered more and more recognition from top military and diplomatic leaders.

In my role as honorary ambassador to CENTCOM's coalition, I was a symbolic bridge to female leaders of Middle Eastern countries, CENTCOM's area of responsibility. I speak their language — literally and metaphorically. I understand the ideology, culture, and values. I'm proud of the diplomatic dialogue that was established. Unfortunately, that progress, along with my skill set, has been thrown away because of our sexist government officials.

I often find myself thinking about my daughters. It troubles me that they're growing up in a world where every word and action can subject them to extreme sexist scrutiny. I don't want them to live in fear — to be people who keep their heads down and don't pursue their interests and passions because of what bigots might think or say. I want my daughters to be strong, outspoken women who fully embrace every opportunity. The next generation of talented women deserves better. I am fighting for a brighter tomorrow.

****

Eventually, I decided to reclaim my narrative. I saw that I had a choice about my own life. I could use my renown for public advocacy — to bring awareness to the problem so make this never happen again to another innocent family again. How could I do that? I began to focus more on the ever-changing issue of privacy and data protection.

It might surprise people to know that before November 2012, I was virtually unknown to the public. I did not seek the limelight, never used Facebook or other social media, and wasn't interested in publicity. Yes, I had social skills, but I was basically a private person — as was Scott. We were nose-to-the-grindstone people, a tight-knit family that still shared the single email address we'd created when we lived in Philadelphia.

In November 2012, our peaceful life was upended when the government leaked my name from the investigative files of an anonymous cyberstalking crime my husband and I had reported to the FBI. Despite the government's promise to look at only the stalker's threatening email sent to my husband's email address, agents secretly pored through years of my electronic communications in a completely separate account. Then, without regard to our privacy and the law that protected it, the government publicly leaked and selectively distorted details of my emails to the world.

I learned along with the rest of the world that my emails were read. There was no "public interest" in rooting through my emails. We were improperly targeted twice — first by a stalker, and then by a government that abused its own limits on personal privacy.

On June 3, 2013, I filed a lawsuit against the FBI, the Defense Department and others in the federal government asserting that my right to privacy had been infringed upon — the very right that Agent Malone had repeatedly assured me I had. As a crime victim, my privacy was sacrosanct.

In my complaint I asserted that the government and its agents had willfully, and maliciously violated Scott's and my constitutional and statutory privacy rights. As private citizens who sought the assistance of federal law enforcement by reporting evidence of possible criminal activity, we were supposed to be protected. However, rather than protecting our privacy interests, by their actions they thrust us into the public eye in the midst of one of the most widely reported sex scandals in the United States government. Not only did they fail to keep our identities and emails private, they deliberately leaked information in what could only be characterized as a "blame the victim" campaign.

The issue for me boiled down to government snooping through my private electronic communications. And for whatever possible agendas (abusive officials, or a presidential election, etc), my name and especially my private emails should never have been made public. Somewhere down the line, I stopped being a person who was worthy of equal rights and protections. Thinking of those who might find themselves in a similar situation, I decided that even if I could not advocate for my own name, I could advocate for all Americans.

My lawsuit tries to establish what had happened: I reported a crime. And I expected the anonymity and protection consistent with every victim's rights.

I want to believe the statements made by Attorney General Eric Holder: "Our core mission is to pursue justice for criminal acts, and that pursuit includes justice for the victims of and witnesses to crime. Every day, Department personnel encounter individuals harmed by crime or who witnessed others being harmed by crime. How we treat those individuals has a huge impact on their confidence in the criminal justice system and their ability to heal and recover from crime." If the Justice Department practiced this policy, what happened to me could have been avoided.

Several privacy experts publicly agreed that, regardless of the specific details of who I was, or whatever anyone thought of me, the government's actions crossed the line. Privacy Professor Dan Metcalfe told Fortune magazine that Secretary Panetta's comments alone about the emails John and I exchanged probably constituted a Privacy Act violation. "This is not how federal law enforcement investigations should work," said Metcalfe. "Would-be tipsters may now ask themselves, 'Do I want to end up like Jill Kelley?'"

When President Obama nominated Judge Merrick Garland for the U.S. Supreme Court, Judge Garland spoke of the essential trust between witnesses and the judicial system. Though he speaks of witnesses, this applies to anyone else who cares to preserve their privacy.

> "It was the sense of responsibility to serve a community, instilled by my parents, that led me to leave my law firm to become a line prosecutor in 1989. There, one of my first assignments was to assist in the prosecution of a violent gang that had come down to the District from New York, took over a public housing project and terrorized the residents. **The hardest job we faced was persuading mothers and**

grandmothers that if they testified, we would be able to keep them safe and convict the gang members. We succeeded only by convincing witnesses and victims that they could trust that the rule of law would prevail."

– Judge Merrick Garland speech after being nominated for the U.S. Supreme Court, March 16, 2016 (emphasis added)

The damages were clear: I was held out as an object of ridicule, scorn, and derision, costing me my diplomatic positions and transforming my reputation from that of a respected business and community leader and energetic advocate of the military, to, in the words of one press report, a "vixen."

The Department of Justice responded promptly to our lawsuit, arguing that while it did not deny that the government leaked adverse information about us, or that we were damaged, the Privacy Act protections did not apply to the department. "The FBI has exempted its Central Records System, which contains investigative, personnel, applicant, administrative, and general files from protection under the Privacy Act" was the official response.

Well, that was shocking and would be news to most Americans. As my lawyer stated to a reporter:

> "The Government did the wrong thing. They adopted a 'blame the victim' approach that prompted Government agencies to dig through the Kelley's private email accounts and then unfairly dragged the Kelley's through the mud. If this egregious violation of privacy and email overreaching can happen to an honorable couple like the Kelleys, it can happen to any law abiding citizen. The Kelley's legal complaint seeks an apology and justice for themselves and their family. They also hope their lawsuit can help prevent other innocent citizens from experiencing this same electronic overreach, and mistreatment at the hands of Government officials."

Unwilling to accept the government's cavalier response to my lawsuit, my attorneys then wrote a letter to Attorney General Eric Holder, stating that the government's conduct violated the letter of the law as well as the high ideals represented by President Obama's "zero tolerance" policy against government leaking and Attorney General Holder's policy. My lawyer continued:

> "The Kelley's were wronged; Mrs. Kelley was subjected to cavalier, sexist treatment that violates the government's own procedures and regulations regarding the treatment of victims; and,… they both deserve an apology and just compensation. In addition, Justice should reaffirm its confidentiality protocols, including with respect to criminal, investigative material shared with other agencies, and tighten adherence to your guidelines for victim and witness assistance. We implore DOJ to live up to the standard set forth in the Attorney General Guidelines for Victim and Witness Assistance which includes seeking justice for "the victims of and witnesses to crime."

I found the government's position that the FBI was not subject to the Privacy Act the kind of imperious claim that has created so much mistrust among the American people. I don't believe that the citizenry is prepared to accept that the government, at its own discretion, can read and then leak private emails — or that we are not entitled to an "expectation of privacy" when reporting a crime. If so, that is chilling! Why would anyone feel safe reporting a crime?

In a column for Bloomberg Business, I wrote about the government's abuse of power, a topic that was already in the news. My point was that until new legislation is passed, our legal protections online are minimal. The Electronic Communications Privacy Act contains a loophole that allows the government to read email over 180 days old without a warrant. In fact, I learned that public email servers are subjected to thousands of government requests every month for private emails. Interestingly, this open-door policy does not apply to snail mail and telephone calls; for these a warrant is required. But our electronic communications are out there, vulnerable to government overreach and exploitation.

The wheels of justice grind slowly. On September 15, 2014, federal Judge Amy Berman Jackson ruled that my lawsuit could proceed on one count of a privacy violation. As of this writing it is still ongoing. I look forward to the day when it is over and I can finally speak about it in greater detail.

My experience had one positive effect: It inspired me to become an advocate for privacy and Internet security, to help publicize this issue and find ways to protect the names and identities of victims of crime. I am determined to fight to deter the government from violating the privacy rights of Americans by exposing the vast overreach of the government's search through private emails. I am more passionate than ever about lobbying to advance the constitutional rights to privacy of every law-abiding citizen, so that what happened to my family will never happen again. I'm hoping that the outcome of my lawsuit will establish that Americans have the constitutional right to privacy in their email communications.

I am precluded from talking specifically about the court case. The concern is that I might reveal new, even more damaging information about the events. But I can tell my story to advocate the need for our government to respect every American's right to privacy. Through journalism, I am able to impart a strong message: If this could happen to me, it could happen to you. I put forth a scary idea for consideration. At a time when the government is currently collecting petabytes of private information on millions of American citizens, it's more than ironic that top law enforcement officials seemingly were unable to detect a security breach — when a stalker was reading the nation's top national security official's emails — and then bypassed it, once it had been discovered.

And here's the rub. Who knows what else might set off governmental invasion of privacy — politics or some other improper motivation might suffice. It's not just about my unique personal situation. We all need to pay attention to this.

And since the disclosure of my name and false description of the content of our emails — at the email address that Scott and I share — I have become the human face of the harms of the government intrusion and unwarranted search of personal communications. This tragedy has motivated me to be a zealous advocate against government snooping into communications of law-abiding citizens.

In addition to my public advocacy, I have met with congressional officials and legislative groups about the harms and abuses of government overreach, and the need to enforce our existing privacy laws and constitutional rights to privacy.

I can't predict the outcome of my lawsuit, but I am determined not to be paralyzed by a lengthy process with an uncertain end. I hope by bringing awareness to my story, it will create a long over-due discussion, so this abuse never happens to another innocent American placing their trust in law enforcement.

I decided to create an opportunity around my situation — to transform a negative into a positive. I felt that all would be for nothing if I couldn't use my platform to help others.

Quietly in 2015, I began to create a foundation whose sole purpose is the defense and advocacy of civil liberties through awareness, education and action. My personal mission is to continue to fight until our privacy laws give us both privacy and protection. I will remain to be a zealous advocate of electronic communications and internet security so other law abiding Americans do not have to go through the challenges my family endured. If we can make a dent in the government's disrespect for the rights of innocent Americans, then speaking up publicly will have been worth it.

As 2015 came to a close, my New Year's gift was a letter from the Internal Revenue Service telling me that the Jill Kelley Foundation, Inc., had been approved as a 501(c)(3) charity. If my personal experience is any judge, I have my work cut out for me.

Appendix A: Declaration of Jill Kelley Regarding General Allen

DECLARATION OF JILL KELLEY

1. I am a citizen of the United States and a resident of Tampa, Florida. My date of birth is June 3, 1975.

2. I met General John Allen and, soon thereafter, his family in or about August 2010. Over time, he and his family and I and my family became friends. We saw each other occasionally at social events, celebrated some holidays together, and participated in life events such as birthdays.

3. I have never had any extramarital affair with General Allen. He and I have never had any sexual relations of any kind. General Allen and I have never been alone together in any private setting.

4. As friends, his family and mine had dinners together and exchanged small Christmas gifts with the kids.

5. Neither I nor my husband participates in any government contracts or has asked General Allen to help us in any business activities or income producing effort. Nor has General Allen asked us to help him or any member of his family in any business activities or income producing effort.

6. General Allen has not provided me with any transportation by military plane to any city to which I was travelling or from which I was coming.

7. I never received anything from General Allen that appeared to be classified or to breach security procedures.

I declare under penalty of perjury pursuant to 28 U.S.C. 1746 that the foregoing is true and correct.

Dated: November 28, 2012   Signed:

                                                Jill Kelley

CPAM: 5078603.22

CPAM: 5078603.2

Appendix B: My advocacy through journalism

In the aftermath of this destructive chapter of my life, I have reinvented myself as an internet privacy and security advocate, journalist and pundit. Here are my journalism pieces.

Washington Post, January 22, 2013:[4]

Jill Kelley on the Petraeus scandal and the loss of privacy

By Jill Kelley and Scott Kelley
Jill Kelley is a resident of Tampa, where Scott Kelley is an oncology surgeon.

We woke up on the morning of Nov. 9 expecting the usual: for one of us, the tending to patients; for the other, the morning rush of packing lunches and getting the kids to school. We were planning a party for our daughter's seventh birthday that weekend.

What ensued over the next 72 hours not only overtook all attempts for a happy family celebration but also made us prisoners in our own home. Our lives were radically upended by the story that emerged after David Petraeus resigned as CIA director. Our names were leaked as that story developed, and we were unable to attend Sunday Mass, see our daughter's Christmas play or otherwise move about without the invasive lenses of paparazzi exposing our private family life for public consumption.

Ours is a story of how the simple act of quietly appealing to legal authorities for advice on how to stop anonymous,

---

[4]http://www.washingtonpost.com/opinions/jill-kelley-on-the-petraeus-scandal-and-the-loss-of-privacy/2013/01/22/676f60c8-64b2-11e2-9e1b-07db1d2ccd5b_story.html

harassing e-mails can result in a victim being re-victimized.
The word "victim" is, we know, better reserved for those who
have suffered far worse than we pray we'll ever experience.
But the reality is that we sought protection, not attention, and
received the inverse.

After our names were linked to the Petraeus story, a horde of
paparazzi stormed our front lawn. Our young daughters were
terrified. We didn't want our silence to validate false
headlines, but we did what most people unaccustomed to such
a blitzkrieg would do: walled it off in the hopes the storm
would fade or pass.

But it didn't go away. And the media filled our silence with
innuendo and falsehoods. We were surprised to read that Jill
had flown on private military jets (never); that she was a
volunteer social planner (wrong); that we were suffering
financially (false); and, most painful of all because of the
innuendo surrounding the allegation, that some 30,000 e-mails
were sent to a general from the e-mail address we share. This
is untrue, and the insinuation that Jill was involved in an
extramarital affair is as preposterous as it is hurtful to our
family. This small sample of junk reporting was emotionally
exhausting and damaging — as it would be to the strongest of
families.

Our family committed no crime and sought no publicity. We
simply appealed for help after receiving anonymous e-mails
with threats of blackmail and extortion. When the harassment
escalated to acts of cyberstalking in the early fall, we were,
naturally, terrified for the safety of our daughters and
ourselves. Consequently, we did what Americans are taught to
do in dangerous situations: sought the help of law
enforcement.

Unfortunately, reaching out to an FBI agent whose
acquaintance we had made resulted in slanderous allegations.
We had never met, nor even knew of, Paula Broadwell when
we sought protection. Our experience of having our privacy

invaded and our lives turned upside down by authorities leaking our names and the existence of private electronic correspondence highlights the need for measures that ensure citizens retain their privacy when they seek assistance and protection from law enforcement and that the names of those who report a crime are not made public.

The breach of civil liberties we experienced never needed to happen. That is why, as Congress considers the Electronic Communications Privacy Act, lawmakers should consider what access to and disclosure of private e-mails of law-abiding citizens will be allowed, and what safeguards should be in place.

Despite our misfortunes, we consider ourselves blessed. Our family has been honored and proud to help patients with cancer and to work with the homeless in the Tampa area. We look forward to resuming our involvement with our community, which includes supporting our nation's military. We appreciate the brave men and women in uniform who sacrifice so much for our country, and we have enjoyed sponsoring events to celebrate their accomplishments.

Our story stands as a cautionary tale. We have experienced how careless handling of our information by law enforcement and irresponsible news headlines endanger citizens' privacy. We know our lives will never be the same, and we want to prevent others from having their privacy invaded merely for reporting abusive, potentially criminal, behavior. That is why we believe Congress must consider how the rights that we carefully safeguard in other forms deserve equal protection in this age of digital communication.

Bloomberg Businessweek, April 13, 2013:[5]

How to Save Privacy

When my name was leaked after I reported a stalking incident last year, leading to numerous false headlines and articles, I learned the scope of the government's authority to view e-mail. Until new legislation is passed, our legal protections online are minimal. For example, the Electronic Communications Privacy Act was written with a loophole that allows government to read e-mail over 180 days old without a warrant. Public e-mail servers receive thousands of government requests a month for e-mail. Your e-mail may be read as you are reading this; the government may be surveilling your business, taxes, and personal conversations. Other forms of communication (U.S. mail and telephone calls) are protected and require a search warrant for surveillance. Another provision in our privacy laws that needs change is the protection of those who report a crime. Otherwise, law-abiding citizens will fear the unexpected consequences of a leak by the authorities. Until our privacy laws give us both privacy and protection, I'll continue to be an advocate for reform, so others don't have to go through the challenges my friends and family endured.

---

[5]http://www.bloomberg.com/news/articles/2013-04-11/how-to-save-privacy-by-petraeus-scandal-casualty-jill-kelley

Wall Street Journal, November 5, 2013:[6]

How The Government Spied On Me

It has been a full year since federal agents snooped through the private emails of my husband and me, setting in motion a series of events that ultimately led to the resignations of Central Intelligence Agency Director David Petraeus and Gen. John Allen, the commander of coalition forces in Afghanistan. The anniversary is a somber reminder of the unintended consequences and harsh realities that can result from unrestrained government probing into Americans' personal communications.

More recent revelations of National Security Agency spying suggest that the government's invasion of citizens' privacy is increasingly common. Millions of innocent Americans should be very concerned about Washington's massive surveillance apparatus, which seems to know no bounds.

My family's ordeal began when my husband, Scott, and I were haunted by multiple, threatening email messages from an apparent Internet stalker. Fearing for the safety of our family, as well as the safety of U.S. officials named in the threatening emails, we took the advice of military leaders and reported the messages to the Federal Bureau of Investigation.

We authorized the FBI to look at one threatening email we received, and only that email, so that the FBI could identify the stalker. However, the FBI ignored our request and violated our trust by unlawfully searching our private emails and turning us into the targets of an intrusive investigation without any just cause—all the while without informing us that they had identified would identify the email stalker as Paula Broadwell, who was having an affair with Mr. Petraeus.(I have never understood why she was stalking me and my

[6]http://www.wsj.com/news/articles/SB10001424052702303482504579179670250714560

family. In any event, she was not charged with a crime.)

Adding insult to injury, the FBI then leaked our identities to the media and distorted the contents of the emails it had illegally obtained, throwing my family into a destructive media vortex.

As a result of the government's breach of our privacy and trust, camera crews showed up at our door and camped outside our home to question us about false and misleading information leaked to the media from "unnamed" government sources. Reckless speculation and innuendo about an inappropriate relationship with Gen. Allen spread throughout the news media, sullying my reputation and honor, to the great distress of my family. To this day the government has not apologized for its indefensible conduct.

I hope that my family's story is a case study about the damage that can be caused by the government's electronic overreach. It appears from the NSA's leaks that the government may be trying to collect everything about everyone and everywhere— including America's closest friends and allies—with or without the knowledge of the White House. Unaccountable individuals given free rein to invade people's privacy—and a government that maintains the tools that permit them to do so—are a prescription for a privacy disaster.

With all the current economic, political, social and diplomatic issues facing the country, it is understandable that many Americans seem relatively unconcerned about intrusions on individual privacy. They shouldn't be. The unauthorized search of my family's emails was triggered when we appealed to law enforcement for protection. But who knows what else might set off governmental invasion of privacy—politics or some other improper motivation might suffice. If this could happen to us, it could happen to you.

As painful as my experience has been, it has motivated me to be an advocate against unwarranted spying on personal communications, and to push for new legislation and better enforcement of existing privacy laws. Congress should strengthen the Privacy Act, update the Electronic Communications Privacy Act. Americans' Fourth Amendment protections against unreasonable search and seizures should be extended to personal communications. My husband and I have filed a lawsuit that seeks to hold the federal government accountable for its flagrant violation of our rights.

The country is not safer after reading my emails. The humiliation of and damage to my family should never have occurred. By raising public awareness and holding the government accountable, my husband and I hope we will help protect other innocent families from intrusive government snooping.

The invasion of privacy that my family endured from the federal government is not unique. Nevertheless, it is un-American.

Politico, November 30, 2014:[7]

I Lost My Privacy. Let's Act to Protect Yours.

Before two years ago, I had never given much thought to how the abuses by Richard Nixon's Watergate scandal and J. Edgar Hoover's FBI surveillance tactics could impact my family's life. Then, when I learned firsthand, it was too late.

I don't want others to have to go through what I've gone through.

And, in fact, with the government deploying ever newer surveillance technologies to collect more and more personal data — even from planes apparently pretending to be authorized cellphone towers — it is even more critical for citizens to demand accountability. I hope my story can warn others of the irreversible damage caused when the government fails to live up to its privacy obligations.

It was just over two years ago that you had never heard of me. I worked hard to keep it that way. In fact, I never used Facebook, nor any social media, and still shared with my husband the same email address that we created years before while doing medical research at the University of Pennsylvania.

To say we are nerds or introverts is an understatement. Our rationale for avoiding any presence on the Internet was the priceless freedom that comes with privacy.

In November 2012, our peaceful life was upended when the government illegally leaked my name from the investigative files of an anonymous cyberstalking crime my husband and I had reported to the FBI. Despite the government's promise to look at only the stalker's threatening email sent to my

---

[7] http://www.politico.com/magazine/story/2014/11/jill-kelley-privacy-act-113219

husband's email address, agents secretly pored through years of my electronic communications in a completely separate account. Then, without regard to our privacy and the 1974 law that protects it, the government publicly leaked and selectively distorted details of my emails to the world.

I learned my emails were read when the entire world found out. There was no "public interest" in rooting through my emails. We were victimized twice — first, by what turned out to be a scorned stalker, then a second time by a government that abused its own limits on personal privacy.

In an instant, I went from being virtually nonexistent on the Web to "trending" with millions of Google hits. There was only a single photo the media was able to capture — me wearing a yellow dress as I went to pick up my children from school.

Within hours, millions around the world learned of my identity, my home address and a multitude of patently false and damaging statements made by malicious (and almost always anonymous) government officials.

A "scandal" was woven from leaks and lies, dubiously packaged as breaking news and designed to distract from a manipulated FBI investigation that turned the innocent victims' lives upside down and deprived the nation of two of its most decorated generals and valuable public servants.

This very tangible experience with the perils of overreaching and disrespectful government demonstrates why Congress needs to rein in excessive electronic surveillance and get serious about holding the administration accountable.

I wish my experience was atypical — but after concerns about millions of phone records of other law-abiding Americans being collected and cell towers being faked, this was not merely an unfortunate blemish on the government's sterling record respecting personal privacy. Not to mention, my experience is hardly the only time government agents have leaked egregiously and damaged innocent parties.

Indeed, in 2001, Sen. Patrick Leahy held an oversight hearing specifically to restore lost confidence in the FBI. He said then that the agency was already back to its old "unaccountable," "unreliable" and "arrogant" ways and cited numerous examples of how the FBI had wrongfully leaked information about ongoing investigations and ended up having to pay damages to the citizens it harmed. In 2008, the government once again had to pay out damages, for illegally leaking the name of the innocent scientist Steven Hatfill.

The genesis of the Privacy Act came out of Watergate. In 1974, after the disturbing disclosures of the FBI's illegal wiretapping of Martin Luther King Jr., along with revelations that the White House conducted secret surveillance to spy on Nixon's enemies and political adversaries, America finally said "Enough!" President Gerald Ford signed the Privacy Act into law following Nixon's resignation.

When Ford signed the law on Dec. 31, 1974, he said it "represent[ed] an initial advance in protecting a right precious to every American — the right of individual privacy" and "codif[ied] fundamental principles to safeguard personal privacy in the collection and handling of recorded personal information by Federal agencies."

This fall, during the dual anniversary of the original Privacy Act and my life being turned upside down by a violation of that very act, my story provides some ammunition for those who would amend the act to bring it back in line with the protections Congress intended after Watergate. Specifically, the government needs to restrain itself — or be restrained — from massive and abusive electronic surveillance, and it must be held accountable for gratuitously and harmfully releasing information from confidential databases.

It seems that the FBI — and, sadly, national security officials more broadly, too — have learned little from their previous abuses. Despite the Privacy Act, the government continues to abuse advanced technology to scrutinize more Americans than under the leadership of Richard Nixon and J. Edgar Hoover combined.

Yet even as evidence mounts that the government is sweeping up ever more of our personal data, instead of empowering citizens to invoke the law Congress passed to control and penalize such abuses, the Supreme Court in 2012 actually weakened the protections Congress intended. In the case of *FAA v. Cooper*, the justices barred the courthouse door to government-embarrassed citizens who could not claim monetary loss from the government's unlawful leaks. They acknowledged, however, that in many cases the primary harm will be "mere" embarrassment and affronts to personal dignity. Yet protecting only against actual monetary damage was never the basis for the Privacy Act.

As Justice Sonia Sotomayor wrote in her eloquent dissent in *Cooper*, "[n]owhere in the Privacy Act does Congress so much as hint that it views a $5 hit to the pocketbook as more worthy of remedy than debilitating mental distress, and the majority's contrary assumption discounts the gravity of emotional harm caused by an invasion of the personal integrity that privacy protects." (Though, to be fair to the Supreme Court, in the justices' 2014 opinion on cellphone privacy, they do seem to get it now.)

After our experience in 2012, my husband and I sued the government over its violation of the Privacy Act. For the past year, we've battled the government to get it to admit that it violated both the letter and the spirit of the 1974 act.

In September of this year, my husband and I were successful in defeating a government motion to dismiss our Privacy Act litigation. By letting our case move forward, at least one federal court is flashing a yellow light to warn those in government against doing the same unwarranted damage to another innocent family. But Congress needs to reaffirm what it said in 1974: that privacy is a "fundamental right," that citizens are entitled to "safeguards ... against an invasion of personal privacy" and to "damages which occur as a result of willful ... violat[ions of] any individual's rights under this Act." If Congress still believes those 40-year-old principles, then it needs to correct the *Cooper* decision and expressly allow injured parties to invoke the act's protections whether or not they have suffered more damage to their reputation than to their pocketbook.

But that alone is not enough.

Congress also needs to add a dedicated privacy watchdog to exercise oversight over the government's sprawling investigative and surveillance apparatus. Congress should establish a Privacy and Data Protection Agency to preserve the sanctity of citizens' private information against the prying eyes and loose lips of a government that can access just about every electronic piece of information possible.

The U.S. is currently isolated among Western democracies in not having a data protection authority dedicated to protecting individual privacy. To remedy that, the mandate of the existing Privacy and Civil Liberties Oversight Board could be extended to enforce all the rights protected by the Privacy Act — and not just those stemming from the massive war on terror surveillance programs. If not that, then the members of Congress and the administration who care about every American's precious right to privacy, as President Ford did, should cross party lines to establish a privacy watchdog to safeguard that right.

Privacy rights, as much as property rights, are the core of American freedom, dignity and personal autonomy. After 40 years, the Privacy Act needs to be refreshed to ensure the right remains "fundamental." Unless Congress and the courts recommit to the protections enshrined in the Privacy Act, history will continue to repeat itself.

Appendix C: So, what is the Privacy Act?

The genesis of the Privacy Act was Watergate. In 1974, after the disturbing disclosures of the FBI's illegal wiretapping of the Rev. Dr. Martin Luther King, Jr., along with revelations that the White House conducted secret surveillances to spy on President Nixon's enemies and political adversaries, America finally said "Enough!" President Gerald Ford signed the Privacy Act into law following Richard Nixon's resignation.

When President Ford signed the law on December 31, 1974, he said it "represent[ed] an initial advance in protecting a right precious to every American — the right of individual privacy" and "codif[ied] fundamental principles to safeguard personal privacy in the collection and handling of recorded personal information by Federal agencies."

The Fourth Amendment of the U.S. Constitution recognizes the privacy interests in electronic communications. Indeed, as the U.S. Court of Appeals wrote in United States v. Warshak in 2010, "An email account ... provides an account of its owner's life. By obtaining access to someone's email, government agents gain the ability to peer deeply into his activities."

The court went on to declare, "If we accept that an email is analogous to a letter or a phone call, it is manifest that agents of the government cannot compel a commercial ISP to turn over the contents of an email without triggering the Fourth Amendment. An ISP is the intermediary that makes email communication possible. Emails must pass through an ISP's servers to reach their intended recipient. Thus, the ISP is the functional equivalent of a post office or a telephone company. As we have discussed above, the police may not storm the post office and intercept a letter, and they are likewise forbidden from using the phone system to make a clandestine recording of a telephone call — unless they get a warrant, that is. ... It only stands to reason that, if government agents compel an ISP to surrender the contents of a subscriber's emails, those agents have thereby conducted a Fourth Amendment search, which necessitates compliance with the warrant requirement absent some exception."

The Privacy Act, 5 U.S.C. § 552a, was enacted in 1974 following the revelation of the illegal surveillance and investigation of individuals by federal agencies during the Watergate scandal. The Privacy Act seeks to protect individuals from unwarranted invasions of privacy by federal agencies that maintain sensitive information about them. In passing the act, Congress recognized that "the opportunities for an individual to secure employment, insurance, and credit, and his right to due process, and other legal protections are endangered by the misuse of certain information systems," and that "the right to privacy is a personal and fundamental right protected by the Constitution of the United States."

In 1985, Congress enacted the Electronic Communications Privacy Act, including the Stored Communications Act, to protect individuals from the "technological advances in surveillance devices and techniques" that "ma[de] it possible for overzealous law enforcement agencies, industrial spies and private parties to intercept the personal or proprietary communications of others." The act sought to remedy what Justice Brandeis had correctly predicted decades before in his famous dissent in Olmstead v. United States, that "the Government, without removing papers from secret drawers, can reproduce them in court, ... by which it will be enabled to expose to a jury the most intimate occurrences of the home," with no protection afforded to the individual's privacy.

These Privacy Act stipulations have been fiercely debate in recent years, especially in the aftermath of 9/11 and the pursuit of the war on terror. But what concerns many privacy advocates is the specter of the government using the cloak of terrorism to excuse a much broader reach into our private correspondence.

Our right to privacy is one of the most sacred tenets of our freedom as Americans. Every breach of privacy instituted by the government should be investigated and brought to public light.

Appendix D: Media Links

http://bigstory.ap.org/article/3dfbd494240d4d21bb3b3db85bdf914a/reporters-face-subpoenas-case-over-cia-chief-resignation

http://www.tbo.com/list/military-news/jill-kelley-says-fbi-first-targeted-her-in-email-leaks-20151023/

http://www.tbo.com/list/military-news/federal-officials-giving-depositions-in-jill-kelley-privacy-suit-20151022/

http://www.tbo.com/list/military-news/judge-lets-jill-kelley-seek-information-feds-want-hidden-20151105/

https://www.washingtonpost.com/world/national-security/how-david-petraeus-avoided-felony-charges-and-possible-prison-time/2016/01/25/d77628dc-bfab-11e5-83d4-42e3bceea902_story.html

http://swampland.time.com/2012/11/15/spyfall/
https://www.washingtonpost.com/world/national-security/fbi-probe-of-petraeus-triggered-by-e-mail-threats-from-biographer-officials-say/2012/11/10/d2fc52de-2b68-11e2-bab2-eda299503684_story.html

http://www.tampabay.com/news/military/inquiry-ends-into-broadwells-affair-with-petraeus-receipt-of-classified/2263813

http://www.tbo.com/list/military-news/feds-wont-revisit-socialite-kelleys-emails-20130703/

http://www.cnn.com/2015/04/19/politics/david-petraeus-paula-broadwell-fbi-case/

http://www.nydailynews.com/news/national/afghanistan-commander-gen-petraeus-massive-ego-bob-woodward-obama-wars-article-1.442960

Media Feeding Frenzy

In case there's any doubt about the firestorm of publicity that erupted in November 2012, here's just a selection of the stories.

Tabassum Zakaria and Mark Hosenball, "FBI probe of Petraeus began with 'suspicious emails,'" Reuters, Nov. 9, 2012, available at http://www.reuters.com/article/2012/11/10/us-usa-petraeus-idUSBRE8A81FP20121110. ("The FBI probe was triggered when Broadwell sent threatening emails to an unidentified woman close to the CIA director.")

"FBI probe of Petraeus' emails purportedly led to discovery of extramarital affair," FoxNews.com, Nov. 10, 2012, http://www.foxnews.com/politics/2012/11/10/fbi-probe-petraeus-emails-purportedly-led-to-discovery-extramarital-affair/. ("The FBI investigation began when someone reported suspicious emails allegedly sent from Broadwell.")

"David Petraeus Affair: FBI Probe Into Inbox of Paula Broadwell Uncovers 'Human Drama,'" ABC News, Nov. 10, 2012, http://abcnews.go.com/Politics/OTUS/david-petraeus-affair-fbi-probe-uncovers-human- drama/story?id=17689348. ("The FBI stumbled across the affair after the unnamed woman, who received the troubling email several months ago, alerted authorities, who began a probe to track the source of the message.")

Sari Horwitz & Greg Miller, "FBI probe of Petraeus triggered by e-mail threats from biographer, officials say," Washington Post, Nov. 10, 2012, available at http://www.washingtonpost.com/world/national-security/fbi-probe-of-petraeus-triggered-by-e-mail-threats-from-biographer-officials-say/2012/11/10/d2fc52de-2b68-11e2-bab2-eda299503684_story.html. ("The woman who received the emails [from Paula Broadwell] was Jill Kelley in Tampa, Fla., according to law enforcement officials. The nature of her relationship with Petraeus is unknown.")

"Report: Emails triggered Petraeus probe," Nov. 11, 2012, available at http://www.politico.com/news/stories/1112/83690.html#ixzz2UbQRzmpz. ("A senior U.S. military official . . . says 37-year-old Jill Kelley in Tampa, Fla., received the emails from Petraeus biographer Paula Broadwell that triggered an FBI investigation.")

Donna Leinwand Leger, "Jill Kelley ID'd as woman who sparked Petraeus inquiry," USA Today, Nov. 12, 2012, available at http://www.usatoday.com/story/news/nation/2012/11/11/petraeus-jill-kelley- scandal/1698203/. ("A senior U.S. military official identified the woman who allegedly received the harassing e-mails from Paula Broadwell as Jill Kelley, 37, of Tampa.")

Henry Blodget & Kim Bhasin, "The 'Other Woman' In the Petraeus Scandal is Tampa Resident Jill Kelley," Business Insider, Nov. 11, 2012, available at http://www.businessinsider.com/jill-kelley-petraeus-2012-11 (characterizing Mrs. Kelley as "the other woman" in the Petraeus scandal and citing an AP source of "an unnamed military official").

Michael Daly, "Exclusive: Paula Broadwell's Emails Revealed," The Daily Beast, Nov. 12, 2012, available at http://www.thedailybeast.com/articles/2012/11/12/exclusive-paula-broadwell-s-emails-revealed.html (citing an anonymous source from "the highest levels of the intelligence community" as describing the emails sent by Paula Broadwell to Jill Kelley as "kind of cat-fight stuff," and speculating that "Kelley likely assisted her 7-year-old daughter. . . in posting an online photo album that includes a picture of the girl and her two sisters with Petraeus").

Emma Brockes, "Petraeus scandal: Jill Kelley and the Tampa society set," The Guardian, Nov. 16, 2012, available at http://www.guardian.co.uk/world/2012/nov/16/petraeus-scandal-jill-kelly-tampa-society.
Christina Ng, Martha Raddatz & Luis Martinez, ABC News, Nov. 13, 2012, http://news.yahoo.com/petraeus-affair-jill-kelley-154817861--abc-news-topstories.html.
("The FBI has now uncovered 'potentially inappropriate' emails

between Gen. Allen and Kelley, according to a senior U.S. defense official who is traveling with Defense Secretary Leon Panetta. The department is reviewing between 20,000 and 30,000 documents connected to this matter, the official said. The email exchanges between Kelley and Allen took place from 2010 to 2012.")

"Gen. Allen's emails to friend of Petraeusfamily were like 'phone sex,' sources say," FoxNews.com, Nov. 14, 2012, http://www.foxnews.com/politics/2012/11/13/top-us-commander- in-afghanistan-gen-john-allen-under-investigation-for-alleged/. ("[T]wo U.S. officials later told Fox News that Allen's contact with Kelley was more than just general flirting. One official described some of the emails as sexually explicit and the 'equivalent of phone sex over email.'")

Craig Whitlock & Rajiv Chandrasekaran, "Petraeus investigation ensnares commander of U.S., NATO troops in Afghanistan," Washington Post, Nov. 13, 2012, available at https://www.washingtonpost.com/world/national-security/scandal-probe-ensnares-commander-of-us-nato-troops-in-afghanistan/2012/11/13/a2a27232-2d7d-11e2-a99d-5c4203af7b7a_story.html. ("According to a senior U.S. defense official, the FBI has uncovered between 20,000 and 30,000 pages of documents — most of them e-mails — that contain "potentially inappropriate" communication between Allen and Jill Kelley.")

Rachel Bletchly, "Sex and the CIA: The woman at the center of the scandal with top US generals," Mirror, Nov. 17, 2012, available at http://www.mirror.co.uk/news/world-news/jill- kelley-woman-at-the-centre-of-the-scandal-1440530.

"The other ... other woman: Florida socialite emerges at center of Petraeus scandal," FoxNews.com, Nov. 13, 2012, http://www.foxnews.com/politics/2012/11/13/florida-housewife-in-petraeus-scandal-reportedly-never-spared-anything-for.html.

Carl Hiaasen, "Jill Kelley, mystery vixen in Petraeus scandal," Miami Herald, Dec. 1, 2012, available at http://www.nationalmemo.com/jill-kelley-mystery-vixen-in-petraeus-scandal/.
Phil Hands, "Four Star General Hospital," Wisconsin State Journal, Nov. 18, 2012, available at http://host.madison.com/hands-cartoon-four-star-general- hospital/image_1f8b1b26-3000-11e2-a64d-001a4bcf887a.html
(depicting Mrs. Kelley as being involved in a soap opera with Generals Petraeus and Allen).

"In the Line of Booty," N.Y. Daily News (cover story), Nov. 18, 2012, available at http://www.tampabay.com/resources/images/blogs/media/61982.jpg.
Benjamin Bell, "Retired General John Allen Recalls Toll of Petraeus-linked Investigation," ABC News, May 26, 2013, available at http://abcnews.go.com/blogs/politics/2013/05/retired-general-john-allen-recalls-toll-of-petraeus- linked-investigation.

Sage Stossel, "Petraeus scandal: History repeats itself," Boston Globe, Nov. 24, 2012, available at https://www.bostonglobe.com/opinion/2012/11/24/petraeus-scandal-history-repeats-itself/I6zGIU63qBEDIicrN0MZgN/story.html
(cartoon depicting Mrs. Kelley as a modern-day Helen of Troy).

Saturday Night Live, "The Situation Room: David Petraeus' Mistress Jill Kelly," available at http://www.nbc.com/saturday-night-live/video/the-situation-room-david-patraeus/n28990/.

Robert Burns, "Gen. John Allen, Top Afghanistan Commander, Investigated For Email Link To Petraeus Scandal," Huffington Post, Nov. 13, 2012, http://www.huffingtonpost.com/2012/11/13/john-allen-petraeus_n_2120609.html.

("A senior defense official traveling with Panetta said Allen's communications were with Jill Kelley... . He would not say whether they involved sexual matters or whether they are thought to include unauthorized disclosures of classified information.")

David S. Cloud, "Gen. John Allen tied to Jill Kelley, Petraeus affair scandal," LA Times, Nov. 13, 2012, available at http://articles.latimes.com/2012/nov/13/news/la-pn-john-allen-petraeus-jill-kelley-20121113. ("One official said that Allen, who is married, had denied having an inappropriate relationship with Kelley.")

"Defense official fires back, denies Afghanistan commander exchanged 'inappropriate' emails," NBCNews.com, Nov. 13, 2012, http://usnews.nbcnews.com/_news/2012/11/13/15130151-defense-official-fires-back-denies-afghanistan-commander-exchanged-inappropriate-emails?lite. ("'There was no affair,' said the official, who spoke on condition of anonymity. The emails in question could be misconstrued, the official said, predicting that the investigation will prove Allen's innocence.")

Max Fisher, "Reports: Gen. John Allen did not send 30,000 e-mails to Jill Kelley," Washington Post, Nov. 13, 2012, available at https://www.washingtonpost.com/news/worldviews/wp/2012/11/13/psa-gen-john-allen-did-not-send-30000-e-mails-to-jill-kelley/. ("He's [Gen. Allen] never been alone with her," the senior official said. "Did he have an affair? No.")

John Cook, "Petraeus' Pal Jill Kelley Loaned $800,000 to Her 'Unstable' Twin Sister," Gawker.com, Nov. 13, 2012, http://gawker.com/5960211/petraeus-pal-jill-kelley-loaned-800000-to-her-unstable-twin-sister. ("[S]he seems to have been a regular on the diplomatic circuit: Rep. Peter King (R-N.Y.) told CNN yesterday that he had met her once or twice at British embassy events.")

Donna Leinwand Leger, "Jill Kelley ID'd as woman who sparked Petraeus inquiry," USA Today, Nov. 12, 2012, available at http://www.usatoday.com/story/news/nation/2012/11/11/petraeus-jill-kelley-scandal/1698203/. ("A senior U.S. military official identified the woman who allegedly received the harassing e-mails from Paula Broadwell as Jill Kelley, 37, of Tampa.")
Fox News, March 9, 2015, "After the Buzz: Media question Petraeus plea," available at http://video.foxnews.com/v/4100632543001/after-the-buzz-media-question-petraeus-plea/?#sp=show-clips.

Associated Press, April 14, 2014, "2 congressmen have questions in Jill Kelley leak," available at http://bigstory.ap.org/article/2-congressmen-have-questions-jill-kelley-leak.

Politico, Sept. 15, 2014, "Court OKs privacy suit over David Petraeus case leaks," available at http://www.politico.com/blogs/under-the-radar/2014/09/court-oks-privacy-suit-over-david-petraeus-case-leaks-195489.

NBC News, Sept. 15, 2014, "Lawsuit by Jill Kelley, Socialite in Petraeus Scandal, Can Proceed," available at http://www.nbcnews.com/news/us-news/lawsuit-jill-kelley-socialite-petraeus-scandal-can-proceed-n203911.

WTSP Channel 10, Tampa's Preston Rudie, March 22, 2013, "Jill Kelley declines invite to CENTCOM Change of Command ceremony."

Victim Assistance Facts

The United States Attorney's Office Middle District of Florida, Victim Witness Assistance, http://www.justice.gov/usao/flm/programs/vw/vwa.html.

FBI Victim Assistance, Rights of Federal Crime Victims, https://www.fbi.gov/stats-services/victim_assistance/victim_rights.

Lawsuit and Privacy Advocacy

New York Times, Jan. 5, 2014, "From Petraeus Scandal, an Apostle for Privacy," available at http://www.nytimes.com/2014/01/06/us/from-petraeus-scandal-an-apostle-for-privacy.html?_r=0.

Aug. 29, 2013, Letter from Kelley Attorney Alan Raul to Attorney General, available at http://i2.cdn.turner.com/cnn/2013/images/08/29/letter.to.ag.holder.8-2-13.pdf.

NBC News, November 22, 2013, "US officials accused by socialite Jill Kelley of leaks as part of 'smear campaign,'" available at http://www.nbcnews.com/news/other/us-officials-accused-socialite-jill-kelley-leaks-part-smear-campaign-f2D11642004.

Fox News' Howard Kurtz, Aug. 20, 2013, "Petraeus mistress secretly followed Tampa socialite," available at http://www.foxnews.com/politics/2013/08/20/petraeus-mistress-secretly-followed-tampa-socialite/.

CNN's The Lead with Jake Tapper, Aug. 16, 2013, "Jill Kelley suing government over Petraeus sex scandal," available at http://thelead.blogs.cnn.com/2013/08/16/jill-kelley-suing-government-over-petraeus-sex-scandal/.

MainJustice, David Stout, Aug. 12, 2013, "Kelley Suit, Alleging Smear, Could Add to Collateral Damage Wrought By Spy Scandal," available at http://thelead.blogs.cnn.com/2013/08/16/jill-kelley-suing-government-over-petraeus-sex-scandal/.

Dr. Scott and Mrs. Jill Kelley Lawsuit Against the Federal Government, available at http://i2.cdn.turner.com/cnn/2013/images/11/22/kelley.v..fbi.amended.11-22-13.pdf.

Yahoo! News, March 5, 2013, "Jill Kelley Calls Gen. John Allen a 'Great Patriot,'" available at https://gma.yahoo.com/jill-kelley-calls-gen-john-allen-great-patriot-163806788--abc-news-politics.html.

Politico, May 23, 2014, "Judge may allow privacy suit over Petraeus case leaks," available at http://www.politico.com/blogs/under-the-radar/2014/05/judge-may-allow-privacy-suit-over-petraeus-case-leaks-189144.

Washington Post, Jan. 22, 2013, "Jill Kelley on the Petraeus scandal and the loss of privacy," available at https://www.washingtonpost.com/opinions/jill-kelley-on-the-petraeus-scandal-and-the-loss-of-privacy/2013/01/22/676f60c8-64b2-11e2-9e1b-07db1d2ccd5b_story.html.

Wall Street Journal, Nov. 25, 2013, "How the Government Spied on Me," available at http://online.wsj.com/news/articles/SB10001424052702303482504579179670250714560.

Bloomberg Business, April 11, 2013, "How to Save Privacy, by Petraeus Scandal Casualty Jill Kelley," available at http://www.bloomberg.com/bw/articles/2013-04-11/how-to-save-privacy-by-petraeus-scandal-figure-jill-kelley.

Additional Information

Page Six, Dec. 24, 2014, "Jill Kelley meets with the Pope and buys orphans' home," http://pagesix.com/2014/12/24/jill-kelley-meets-with-the-pope-and-quietly-buys-orphans-home/.

Tampa Tribune, Nov. 26, 2014, "Kelleys host annual Thanksgiving event for Tampa's homeless," available at http://www.tbo.com/news/kelleys-host-annual-thanksgiving-event-for-tampas-homeless-20141126/.

Politico, December 3, 2013, "Jill Kelley brings spotlight to charity," available at http://www.politico.com/story/2013/12/jill-kelley-charity-event-100577.

Tampa Tribune, June 27, 2014, "Kelley returns to MacDill for retirement ceremony," available at http://tbo.com/list/military-news/kelley-returns-to-macdill-for-retirement-ceremony-20140627/.

Website

For further information about this book and Jill's work as a Privacy Advocate:

www.jillkelleybook.com

Made in the USA
Lexington, KY
30 April 2016